JESUS DRIVEN MINISTRY

JESUS DRIVEN MINISTRY

AJITH FERNANDO

CROSSWAY BOOKS

A DIVISION OF
GOOD NEWS PUBLISHERS
WHEATON, ILLINOIS

Library of Congress Cataloging-in-Publication Data
Fernando, Ajith.
  Jesus driven ministry / Ajith Fernando.
    p. cm.
  Includes bibliographical references and index.
  ISBN 1-58134-445-7
  1. Pastoral theology. I. Title.
BV4011.3 .F47   2002
253—dc21   2002007072

MV		13	12	11	10	09	08	07	06	05	04	03	02
15	14	13	12	11	10	9	8	7	6	5	4	3	2	1

To
MYLVAGANAM BALAKRISHNAN,
JITO SENATHIRAJAH
CHANDRAN WILLIAMS
MARUDU PANDIAN
TIMOTHY GODWIN

With deep gratitude
for their immeasurable contribution to my ministry
through their competence in my areas of incompetence

CONTENTS

ACKNOWLEDGMENTS

I CHOSE TO DEDICATE this book to five men whose help has been invaluable to my ministry over the years. They have helped me not as preachers but through their practical help that has saved me from several mistakes, compensated for my many weaknesses, and relieved me of much labor that they gladly took on for me. Mylvaganam Balakrishnan, Jito Senathirajah, and Chandran Williams are all qualified accountants or administrators, board members of Youth for Christ (YFC), and invaluable friends, confidants, and advisors. Marudu Pandian and Timothy Godwin have served successively as my assistants in YFC. They both became virtual members of our family, and their willing service to me has helped free me to write, study, and teach from the context of a busy ministry.

I must pay tribute here also to two people who influenced me greatly in my teenage years. My pastor, Irish missionary George Good, and our YFC director, Sam Sherrard, exemplified in different ways the glory of the ministry and surely helped set me along a path that ended in vocational ministry. Everything I write about ministry is what I have learned in partnership with my team members in YFC and also in our church. I acknowledge my debt to them. My seminary teacher and mentor, Robert Coleman, has written two books—*The Mind of the Master*[1] and *The Master Plan of Evangelism*,[2] which greatly influenced my life and also showed me what a potent model for ministry the life of Jesus is. Over the years I have read scores of biographies and autobiographies, and these have really helped shape my approach to ministry. So I regard Christians such as St. Augustine, Billy Bray, F. F. Bruce, Amy Carmichael, Samuel Chadwick, G. K. Chesterton, Raymond Edman, J. O. Fraser, Billy Graham, Pastor Ilsi, Stanley Jones, Isobel Kuhn, C. S. Lewis, Henry Martyn, D. L. Moody, Charles Spurgeon, Sadhu Sundar Singh, Hudson Taylor, R. A. Torrey, and John and Charles Wesley as my mentors. I hope that this long list will whet your appetite for biographies—one of God's surest ways to send blessings to his servants.

I am also grateful to the First Presbyterian Church in Hollywood (especially its senior pastor, Dr. Alan Meenan, and its missions leaders, Dr. Jack and Anna Kerr), and to Loran and Merle Grant, Ed and Kay Goodwin, and Philip and Gloria Brooks, who opened their homes for me to "hide" in and write this book. Again I must thank God for my loving wife, Nelun, and children, Nirmali and Asiri, whose love for the Lord and for his ministry has made my work so pleasant. Nelun, my secretary Mrs. Shehana Barbut, and my colleagues Mayukha and Roshan Perera read through all or part of my manuscript and made many corrections. I am very happy to be working on a book again with Crossway Books, and I am particularly grateful to Lila Bishop for enriching this book with her editorial expertise.

INTRODUCTION

I WAS AT THE SINGAPORE airport to take an AirLanka flight back to Sri Lanka and was dismayed to find that the flight had been overbooked. I did not have a seat. I had an important family function the next day and desperately needed to get home. With a few inquiries, I found out that the station manager of AirLanka in Singapore had studied in a school of which my uncle had been the principal and that he also knew a cousin of mine. I told him my predicament, and he arranged for me to sit in the "jump seat" of the cockpit.

It was a wonderful opportunity to observe what goes into the piloting of an aircraft. When the plane was about to take off, one of the officers read out a list of basic things to be checked. It was a fairly long list, and the captain checked each item and expressed his satisfaction about compliance to the standard required. I thought, *Surely they must have read this list a thousand times. Why do they need to read every single item at the start of every flight?* The answer, of course, was obvious. Too much is at stake for the flight to take off with even a small thing not functioning properly. Each and every item had to be checked—no matter how basic it was.

I thought of how this applies to the Christian life. There are some basic things in ministry that we will never outgrow and that will never diminish in importance. My Youth for Christ (YFC) counterpart in Germany, Alfons Hilderbrandt, told me of an older Christian who says that the secret of longevity in the ministry is "Sunday-school faith." He was, of course, referring to the basic things about the Christian life that we learn in Sunday school. When I turned forty, I began to think more about these basics. I had seen some Christian leaders whose lives and ministries seemed to stagnate after they reached forty. So I began a search for secrets of long-term ministry. This book is a major step in recording the results of that search, which will, I think, go on as long as I live.

About ten years ago I was at a retreat with a few other "younger" leaders, led by Dr. Leighton Ford. As part of our personal devotions, we were asked to take a passage that presented Jesus as a leader and jot down what we learned about leadership from that passage. I chose Mark 1, though I do not now remember why. I learned so much that I kept adding material to this study for months to come. The result was a series of Bible studies on "Secrets of Long-Term Ministry" from the life of Christ, which I shared first with the volunteers of YFC and then with numerous groups of Christian leaders and missionaries in different parts of the world. This series has now been developed into this book.

In many biblical books the first chapter often gives a good summary of the major emphases of the whole book. I think this is true of Mark 1. It gives a remarkable description of some of the key features of the life and ministry of Jesus. Having extracted these principles from Mark 1, I have tried to trace them through the rest of the ministry of Jesus and the early church, especially as described in the four Gospels and Acts. It has been exciting for me to see how these themes have been developed and illustrated in Scripture.

You will see that most of the ministry basics discussed here have to do with personal lifestyle. I make no apologies for this. There is a great interest in ministry technique today, and technique is important. In a world that places high value on excellence and quality, our ministries must reflect a professional excellence that will favorably adorn the gospel and commend Christ to this generation. Paul also recommended excellence in ministry to the young minister Timothy (1 Tim. 4:11-15). But I believe the greatest crisis facing Christian leadership today concerns lifestyle—always the burning issue. The well-known evangelist D. L. Moody is reported to have said that he had more trouble with D. L. Moody than with any other person he met!

Christian leaders are failing in the way they live and are bringing great dishonor to Christ. Perhaps the greatest need in the training of leaders today is to provide guidelines to help them live as biblical men and women. But with the preoccupation of our present generation with pragmatic issues, insufficient emphasis has been given to lifestyle training. This book seeks to remedy this situation in a small way.

Over the years I have regularly read devotionally oriented material based on careful exegesis of Scripture. This reading has been a great source of refreshment, nurture, and spiritual renewal in my life. My hope is that the readers would be similarly blessed through this book. I have chosen to quote a lot of Scripture verbatim. While I have labored to write smoothly, the inclusion of Bible verses does affect the smooth flow of the sentences. Yet I believe this is a price worth paying, as the reader will be refreshed and fed through direct exposure to Scripture. The reader should note that when I mention a Greek word from the New Testament, I usually use the lexical form of the word rather than the inflected form.

The context out of which this book has arisen is my work in Sri Lanka at both the parachurch and local church level. I have been director of YFC in Sri Lanka for the past twenty-six years. Because of my conviction that I have a call from God to teach the Bible and write from the context of grassroots ministry, I have always tried to supervise a grassroots work while leading the work nationally. Presently I oversee our drug rehabilitation ministry. In addition, my primary work in YFC has been the pastoral care and teaching of staff.

In 1979 my wife and I transferred to a Sinhala-speaking Methodist congregation whose attendance had dropped to zero. We were joined by a young couple, new Christians converted through the YFC ministry, who were looking for a church. Serving in this congregation has been my primary work outside YFC for over twenty years. About 80 percent of the members there are from Buddhist and Hindu backgrounds, and now we enjoy the privilege of having our own full-time pastor. However, for a year immediately prior to writing this book, our pastor was abroad on study leave, resulting in my having to take on many more responsibilities in the church. I believe that this was providential, as it gave me a more intimate knowledge of church life, which is the context of ministry of many who will read this book.

Just before I started writing the fifth chapter, my friend Dr. Lane Dennis, president of Crossway Books, gave me a copy of the English Standard Version of the Bible that Crossway had released only the week before. I decided to use that Bible for my devotions and was so thrilled with its style that I have used it as the basic Scripture text for this work. The ESV strikes a happy balance by being a quite literal translation of the original that is also easy to read.

I trust the reader will excuse me for writing a lot about my own experiences. Some writers, like the author of Hebrews, say very little about themselves—so little in the case of Hebrews that we do not even know the author's identity. Others, like Paul, often illustrate what they teach from their own experiences. I guess I belong to the latter category!

I must say, however, that while writing this book, I became aware over and over again of how much I have fallen short of the principles I am presenting. Stanley Jones used to say that he was a Christian in the making. I suppose I can say that I am a minister in the making. Actually many of the biblical lessons I have learned in ministry have been burned into my life through the mistakes I have made. It would have been much better if I had followed biblical principles without having to learn through experiencing the folly of not doing so. But I thank God that, because of his mercy, I have learned these principles—by whatever means.

My favorite verse in Scripture is 1 Timothy 1:17: "To the King of ages, immortal, invisible, the only God, be honor and glory forever and ever. Amen." This spontaneous outburst of joyous praise came from Paul after lengthy reflection on the fact that God showed him great mercy in giving him a ministry despite his unworthiness (1 Tim. 1:11-16). Elsewhere he said, "Therefore, having this ministry by the mercy of God, we do not lose heart" (2 Cor. 4:1). Our greatest qualification for the ministry is the mercy of God. Such reflection on mercy does not cause discouragement; rather it causes great joy. However great our weaknesses may be, the grace of the God who called us to ministry "super-abounds" (lit. for *huperpleonazō,* 1 Tim. 1:14) so that we can continue to serve him. I have faced much discouragement and pain in ministry, but I can never get over the fact that God in his mercy called me to this amazing work of being an ambassador of the King of kings and the Lord of lords. This work is a source of great, great joy.

I pray that this book will help many men and women to commit themselves afresh to those vital basics of ministry that make for long-term ministry that is both fruitful and joyful.

1

IDENTIFYING WITH PEOPLE

I WAS RELUCTANT TO begin this book with a chapter on the need to identify with the people to whom we minister. It seemed too negative. But that is how the passage we have chosen starts, and we will have to follow that order. Yet as I worked on this chapter, I realized that this is indeed an appropriate place to begin, for it is a basic feature of the Christian ministerial lifestyle. I believe that, though there is some talk of identification and incarnational ministry today, there is still a need for a fresh understanding of its implications if we are to be both effective and joyful in our Lord's service.

THE BIBLICAL EVIDENCE

John begins his Gospel by presenting the mystery of the Incarnation with a profound theological meditation. Mark also begins by presenting the Incarnation, though he does so in the "vivid and fast-paced"[1] style that characterizes his Gospel. He first records the anticipation of John the Baptist, who would prepare the way for the Messiah (1:2-3). Then he describes the ministry of John who "appeared, baptizing in the wilderness and proclaiming a baptism of repentance for the forgiveness of sins" (1:4). Mark says, "And all the country of Judea and all Jerusalem were going out to him" (1:5). Jerusalem was the great city of the religious elite. Among those who came, says Matthew, were "many of the Pharisees and Sadducees" (Matt. 3:7).

Then in verse 9 Mark presents a vivid contrast by saying, "In those days Jesus came from Nazareth of Galilee and was baptized by John in the Jordan." Nazareth in Galilee was the place about which a fellow Galilean, Nathaniel,[2] asked, "Can anything good come out of Nazareth?" (John 1:46). Even the natives of Galilee seemed to have looked down on Jesus' hometown.

But that is not all. Jesus goes and gets "baptized by John in the Jordan"

(Mark 1:9b). Why does the sinless Savior need to submit himself to "a baptism of repentance for the forgiveness of sins" (1:4)? Matthew records that "John would have prevented him, saying, 'I need to be baptized by you, and do you come to me?'" (Matt. 3:14). Jesus' answer gives us a key to the reason why he submitted to baptism: "Let it be so now, for thus it is fitting for us to fulfill all righteousness" (Matt. 3:15). Craig Blomberg explains that the phrase "to fulfill all righteousness" means "to complete everything that forms part of a relationship of obedience to God."[3] Jesus did not personally need to be baptized because he was not sinful. But for all other people this was part of fulfilling all righteousness. As their minister he went through this experience with them. Donald English says, "In baptism he shares the circumstances in which people become aware of their needs precisely in order to meet those needs."[4]

In order to identify with those to whom he was going to minister, he became like them, submitting himself to this rite even though it was unnecessary for him to do so. Such identification was a feature of the whole of Jesus' life on earth. Here it did not entail suffering for Jesus. But much of his life is an illustration of the great price he paid in order to identify with us and be our Savior.

The great American theologian Jonathan Edwards has shown that the sacrifice Christ made actually started at the Incarnation—when he emptied himself and took upon himself the form of a servant—and went on to the point of taking upon himself the sin of the world.[5] Edwards's point is that when the Lord of heaven left his eternal throne in glory and became a helpless babe, an infinite gap was bridged. This is why the sacrifice of this one man can suffice to pay for the sins of the whole world. It was an infinitely great sacrifice.[6]

Jesus was born in a stable because there was no room in the inn. As a child he had to flee to Egypt as a refugee because it was not safe for him to live in his homeland. After his return he grew up in a somewhat obscure town from which many people did not expect "anything good" to emerge (John 1:46). Though he was Lord of creation, we are told that he was obedient to his parents (Luke 2:51). As a youth he probably had to take on his dead father's business and thus be deprived of a higher education. This was considered a disqualification for him when he launched into his ministry (John 7:15). Yet all of these deprivations are very common to a large segment of the world's population.

He took on emotional pain the way all of us do. His parents did not understand him when as a boy he spent time in the Jerusalem temple talking to the leaders there (Luke 2:50). His family initially thought he was insane and did not believe in him (Mark 3:21). Though he was going to raise Lazarus from the dead, he allowed himself to be so moved by the tears of Lazarus's sister that he himself wept (John 11:35). His closest friends did not understand the heart of his mission. One of these friends stole from their common purse (John 12:6) and later betrayed him. Another friend vehemently denied knowing him. On the night before his death, shortly after he had demonstrated servanthood by washing the feet of these friends, they argued among themselves about who was the greatest (Luke 22:24). Then they forsook him and fled when he was arrested (Matt. 26:56). His opponents constantly accused him falsely, even attributing his acts of kindness to Beelzebul, the prince of demons (Matt. 12:24). Through their false accusations, they finally succeeded in getting him crucified.

Certain incidents during his ministry vividly present the paradox of the self-sufficient Lord of all creation being in need:

• The Creator of everything went for forty days without food so that "he was hungry" (Matt. 4:2) and vulnerable to temptation to satisfy his hunger in the wrong way.

• The one who owns the whole universe did not even have a place to lay his head (Matt. 8:20).

• Later we find him ministering to so many that he had no time to eat. So he told his disciples, "Come away by yourselves to a desolate place and rest a while." But he was unable to have the rest he wanted because the crowds followed him. So, instead of resting, he taught the people. But after a long teaching session, he was able to feed five thousand with five loaves and two fish (Mark 6:31-42). So the Creator of food and time had no time to eat or rest, but he was able to multiply the meal of one person so that it fed five thousand people.

• When Jesus found out that his friend Lazarus was ill, he did not simply command the sickness to leave, as he did on another occasion (Luke 7:6-10). He walked at least twenty miles (some scholars think it was about ninety miles) to Bethany in Judea (John 11). This journey is particularly significant because he had recently left the hostile Judean region after eluding an attempt to capture him, and he had come to a place east of the Jordan where he was having an effective ministry (John 10:39-42). The disciples expressed reservations about this trip: "Rabbi, the Jews were just now seeking to stone you, and are you going there again?" (John 11:8).

• Then at the Last Supper the Lord of all, whom the disciples called "Master," stunned them by donning a towel and doing the work of a servant in washing their feet (John 13).

• The climax of Jesus' choice to deprive himself of his rights in order to save humanity comes at his death. His agony in the garden shows that this was a very difficult thing for him to endure. He did not breeze through his death with consummate ease. His attitude contrasted with that of the Christian martyrs throughout history who went to their deaths joyfully. But his death was different, for the spotless Son of God "who knew no sin" was "made . . . to be sin [for us]" (2 Cor. 5:21). The tie of the Trinity, the depth and unity of which our human minds cannot even begin to fathom adequately, was going to be broken to such an extent that Jesus cried out, "My God, my God, why have you forsaken me?" (Mark 15:34). Martin Luther, while meditating on this verse, reportedly got up in despair after a long time and exclaimed, "God forsaken by God! Who can understand it?" Yet twice in the midst of our Lord's passion, he said that he could call on God's angels or his servants to prevent those things from happening (Matt. 26:53; John 18:36).

Paul vividly describes the immensity of Christ's self-emptying in a memorable passage:

> Christ Jesus, who, though he was in the form of God, did not count equality with God a thing to be grasped, but made himself nothing, taking the form of a servant, being born in the likeness of men. And being found in human form, he humbled himself by becoming obedient to the point of death, even death on a cross (Phil. 2:6-8).

The one who was equal with God has become nothing. The Lord of all creation has become a slave. The Creator of life has died. The King who is sovereign over history has become obedient to death. The sinless one has had to pay the wages of sin (death).

The whole life of Christ was a paradox propelled by the need to redeem sinful humanity. He took on burdens that he did not have to take on, and he gave up things that were his legitimate right. And shortly before he left the world, he told his disciples: "As the Father has sent me, even so I am sending you" (John 20:21). So his mission becomes our mission. At the Last Supper he told the disciples that they too must give their lives for others as he did (John 15:12-13). Then he went on to say that their willingness to give their lives for others showed that they were his friends (John 15:14).

Paul eminently followed his Master in this practice of incarnation and identification with the people he served. He expresses this well in 1 Corinthians 9 where he mentions several legitimate rights that he foregoes in order to be more effective in his ministry (1 Cor. 9:1-18). Then he says, "For though I am free from all, I have made myself a servant to all [lit. I enslaved myself to all men], that I might win more of them" (1 Cor. 9:19). Next he tells how he became "as a Jew," "as one under the law," and "as one outside the law" in order to win the people belonging to those categories (vv. 20-21).

In the next verse he drops the word that the ESV translates "as" (*hōs*; NIV "like") and says "To the weak I became weak, that I might win the weak" (v. 22a). He did not become *like* (NIV) a weak person; he actually became weak. I think all of us like to operate in our ministries from a position of strength. It is too much of a blow to our egos to be weak. But that is what servants are: weak. Paul closes the paragraph by saying, "I have become all things to all people, that by all means I might save some" (1 Cor. 9:22).

The word *doulos*, which is used in the New Testament to describe our servanthood, is usually translated "servant" in most English translations (ESV often has a footnote indicating that the Greek is "bondservant"). But a more accurate translation would be "slave."[7] Biblical identification and incarnation entail taking on weakness for the sake of others. Of course, we cannot do this without the strength that comes from our identity in Christ, and we will discuss that in chapter 3, "Affirmed by God."

So our lives are also a paradox. We are children of the King and servants of the people. We pay a price so that we can identify with people and serve them effectively.

CHALLENGES FROM THE POSTMODERN MOOD

The lifestyle of servanthood, where we give up our rights and plans for the sake of something outside ourselves, is getting harder and harder to practice in this postmodern society. Postmodernism, which is said to have come into full flower in the third quarter of the last century, is, among other things, a reaction to the strict rationalism of the modern era. Postmodern thinkers claim that people were depersonalized in the modern era because of its bondage to rational, objective, and scientific principles. They claim that the subjective instincts of our human nature were overpowered by the desire for productivity and the constraints brought about by various dogmas.

In reaction the postmodern approach emphasizes the more subjective aspects of life—"my" feelings, "my" preferences, and "my" instincts. The postmodern generation has been called "an instinctually stimulated generation" where "people prefer to feel than to think."[8] Postmodern people are uncomfortable with principles outside themselves governing their decisions and behavior.

Some welcome results have come from the postmodern emphasis on sub-jective experience. For example, spirituality has become much more promi-nent, and people are no longer satisfied with a dry religious orthodoxy devoid of spiritual warmth. But the reluctance to have our lives governed by princi-ples can be hazardous to our spiritual health. Biblical leaders should be so devoted to their people that in order to help them, the leaders abstain from doing some things that they want to do and perform some tasks that they do not like to do. Because of their commitment to a group of people, they will persevere in working with them even though inconvenient and seemingly fruitless. The leaders' feelings may say, "Drop this work and do something more productive and satisfying. These people do not deserve your commit-ment." But because of the leaders' commitment to these people, they refuse to give up on them.

I was once in the West when I was preparing a talk on the stresses and strains of ministry. Alert to any conversation that related to this topic, I was surprised when a significant number of Christians told me that they or their loved ones had been liberated from bothersome commitments that had been causing them stress and strain. One had given up a difficult assignment, another had left a difficult church, and another had separated from a diffi-cult spouse. They testified that God had freed them from pain. The question I had was whether God was asking them to embrace the pain because of com-mitment to these people or causes.

While reading the journals of John Wesley during the past two years, I have been surprised at the rather matter-of-fact way he notes some of the frus-trations, hardships, and sufferings in his ministry. Things that I would vehe-mently grumble about and would consider a "big deal" if I were to experience them are reported in a casual way, as if they were not serious problems at all. I realized how much my understanding about fulfillment in ministry is dif-ferent from Wesley's. We are not used to experiencing frustration and pain. So when we face such, we tend to shrink from it. But frustration and pain are essential features of incarnational ministry.

So if we are to truly identify with our people, we must expect frustration and pain. If we don't, we may be taken by surprise when we encounter it and be tempted to leave this work for an easier path or be so disillusioned that we lose the joy of ministry. I think many people are suffering unnecessary pain in ministry today because they did not fully anticipate the suffering that min-istry inevitably involves. This pain has caused them to be discontented when actually they should be rejoicing in tribulation.

The path of commitment to principles and causes outside of us is not as costly as it may seem at first. In the Christian understanding of fulfillment, truth is an objective reality that is embraced, and that truth makes people free (John 8:32), opening the door to a truly fulfilling life (John 10:10). Sacrificing for principles yields deeply satisfying consequences. Jesus said, "For whoever would save his life will lose it, but whoever loses his life for my sake and the gospel's will save it" (Mark 8:35). I have found eighteen passages in the New Testament that link suffering and joy.[9] Paul expresses this well when he says, "Now I rejoice in my sufferings for your sake, and in my flesh I am filling up what is lacking in Christ's afflictions for the sake of his body, that is, the church, of which I became a minister according to the stewardship from God that was given to me for you, to make the word of God fully known" (Col. 1:24-25). He rejoices in the sufferings he endures as a servant of the people. He even thinks that his sufferings are essential for completing his union with the crucified Christ.[10]

Because of the postmodern challenge today, I believe we need to do much more reflection on the reality expressed in the words of George Matheson's hymn, "Make me a captive, Lord, and then I shall be free."

I have a fear that the church in the West will disqualify itself from being a missionary sending region by portraying to its membership a Christianity that is a nice religion but that lacks a radical edge. In my visits to the West, the most common response I hear to sermons I have preached is something to the effect: "I enjoyed that sermon." Sermons should disturb, convict, and motivate to radical and costly obedience. I have wondered whether people's desired result from sermons is to enjoy themselves rather than to be changed into radical disciples who will turn the world upside down. If this is so, the church has assimilated the postmodern mood that considers inner feelings more important than commitment to principles. A minor feature of worship—bringing enjoyment—has become a primary feature. Such a church may grow numerically, but it would not be able to produce the type of missionaries that the world needs—men and women who will pay the price of identification with the people they serve and endure the frustrations that involves.

In missionary training today there is a welcome emphasis on cultural anthropology and contextualization. This can be a real aid to missionary identification. But this training will be useless if the willingness and ability to pay the price of commitment do not accompany it. And the key to paying that price is the ability to identify and persevere with a group to which one is committed even when it is frustrating to do so.

When young Westerners tell me that they are sensing a call to missions and ask me what they should do to prepare, usually the first thing I tell them is to stick to the group to which they belong. That will give them a good training in incarnational identification, which is a key to effective missionary service. Today Christians are often too quick to abandon their church, organization, small group, friend, or spouse when the going gets tough. People would rather split than go through the frustrations of working through the problems. This tendency results in shallow relationships, which in turn result in minimal depth to the fruit of their labors. In fact, learning to pay the price of commitment is a key to developing deep fruit in ministry anywhere in the world.

SOME EXAMPLES OF FRUSTRATION-PRODUCING IDENTIFICATION

Let me give some examples from the various spheres of life where I have had to practice identification. I asked my wife for some examples from home-life, which is perhaps our most important arena for identification. She gave me two. When I am working on a book or involved in a big program or problem, it is easy for me to be so preoccupied that I do not participate fully in the conversation at mealtime. I would be physically there but not there emotionally. If I am to be a good husband and father, I need to discipline myself to fully concentrate on my family when we're together, even though many urgent issues may occupy my mind.

My wife also told me about the need for me to help her with the dishes at night when she is tired (we do not have a dishwasher). Sri Lankans usually have their evening meal after 8:00 P.M. I come alive at night and usually do much of my writing after dinner. I am often raring to go to my desk and get to work, but I have to control my enthusiasm in order to identify with my wife's needs.

Some years ago I was leaving for home from one of our Youth for Christ centers when a staff worker asked me to convey a message to a home in a village I was to pass by. When I went to the home, the family asked me to stay on to have a cup of tea. I told them that I was rushing to be on time for a meeting, and I left immediately. But in our villages it is impolite to leave like that without giving our hosts an opportunity to show us hospitality. The word went out that the YFC director had come to the village but was too proud to stay and have a cup of tea. I later realized that if I was not willing to stay for a cup of tea, I should not have gone there at all.

When I was doing postgraduate studies in the United States, I became part of a church that had a young adult group. The leader of this group was a theologically untrained first-year seminary student whose teaching and programming left much to be desired. This was a source of frustration to me. But this was the young adult group of "my church." So, though I often did not feel like going to the group, my theology of the body informed me that absenting myself was not an option. Participation was part of my commitment to the local church to which I belonged. With time I developed some wonderful friendships in that church, and my involvement in that group is one of the happiest memories I have of my young adult days.

Over the past twenty years or so we have had a civil war in Sri Lanka over issues involving two ethnic groups. I belong to the majority Sinhala-speaking ethnic group. Some from the Tamil-speaking ethnic group are asking to separate from Sri Lanka and have an independent country in the north and east. As part of their strategy militants often come to the south where I live and plant bombs in strategic places. Because of this, young people from the Tamil ethnic group living in the south are often arrested as terrorist suspects—that is, as those belonging to the group called the Tamil Tigers, which is fighting the government. As I am an older person from the majority group, I am often able to go to the police station the moment they are arrested, guarantee that they are not members of the Tigers, and get them released. If this is not done within about thirty-six hours, they are usually kept in custody for a long time. One of my colleagues was in prison for fifteen months (and the Lord gave him a glorious ministry in the prison!). So the moment I hear that someone I can fully vouch for has been arrested, I go to the police station. I may be very busy at the time, and I may have to spend as much as six hours on this project.

So these interruptions are quite costly. But they are part of identifying with the pain of our people. A famous Christian leader is reported to have said that he used to complain to God about the interruptions he had from his work when God reminded him that these interruptions *were* his work! Dennis Kinlaw has some wise advice here: "All of us have been irritated by occurrences that seem to be demonically designed to disturb our peace of mind and upset our program of life. But we must remember that God is sovereign; nothing happens in our lives without his consent. Therefore we should look carefully at annoyances to see if we can discern God's hand at work."[11] John Wesley was walking with one of his preachers when they encountered two women quarreling. The preacher suggested that they walk on, but Wesley checked him: "Stay, Sammy, stay, and learn to preach!"[12] Certainly a quarrel tells one much about human nature.

Frustration is a daily experience for us who live in a land submerged in the crises of war, corruption, and a crumbling economy. I sense this acutely when I return to Sri Lanka from a trip to the West. It takes so long to get things done. Sometimes because we don't pay a bribe, things never get done! Programs we plan are suddenly cancelled because a curfew is clamped down to cover the time of the program. Last month I spent about forty hours preparing a talk to be given at a conference in England, but I could not get to England in time for the talk because our airport was attacked. Yet I have to keep reminding myself that these experiences of frustration are part of identifying with my people for whom disappointment is a daily experience. I have to believe that these frustrations will help me minister more effectively to these people. Anyone who works with people will face frustration. How much of this Jesus faced with his disciples! We preachers should not try to avoid frustration by handing over unpleasant things to others so that we can concentrate on our preaching ministry. Facing frustration is part of our preparation for penetrative preaching.

In some of the spheres of ministry that I am involved in, we have people whose weaknesses bring much pain to my life. They misunderstand what we do and express their anger about our actions to others. It usually takes several hours to explain the facts to these people. And we are always struggling with time. There are two temptations we face when working with such people. The first is to ignore their problems and go ahead with our work as if nothing happened. This would save us some time and also the unpleasantness and pain that would come from talking with an angry person. But Jesus said that if we find that someone has something against us, we must immediately go and meet that person. This is so urgent that we are to leave the gift we brought at the altar and go to the person concerned (Matt. 5:23-24). Jesus did not say that the anger of weak people is exempt from this directive. We must go, and we must endure the pain and frustration of the conversation. To identify with a community is to identify with its weak and with its strong.

The second temptation we have is to give these incessant complainers a signal that they are not welcome in the church. Often today Christian leaders give some of their members the message: "If you do not agree with the direction we are taking, perhaps you should find another group." But we cannot do that if we are the family we claim to be. Can you tell family members that they are not welcome because they regularly get upset with what is happening in the family? I suppose this happens today, but that is not the Christian understanding of family. Despite our claims that our organizations and churches are families, most of them are run like corporations.

We stick to such people and willingly take on the frustration of talking with them because we believe that we will not ultimately lose through such costly commitment. It will be necessary for our theology to override our feelings on this. We must believe that we will be blessed if we pursue the implications of the biblical understanding of the body of Christ. To do this, of course, we must develop an approach to life where our theology is more important than our natural inclinations and instincts—a difficult task in this postmodern era!

Some reject the approach advocated here, stating that it takes too much time and distracts from the mission they are called to. Our pragmatic generation finds the frustration of identification a waste of time and energy. But on the long run this approach results in a deeper ministry with more lasting fruit. Once after our Central Bank (the equivalent of the Federal Reserve in United States) was bombed, two of our volunteers were arrested on suspicion of being terrorists. I was able to vouch for them and secure their release. But I spent about six hours in the police station.

I was preparing some studies on Galatians at the time, so I took some paper and a commentary on Galatians. I studied and wrote notes, sometimes standing in a line and sometimes seated. At one point there was a person next to me with blood all over his clothes. He had been in the building that was bombed and had come to report the loss of his identity card. Also next to me was a woman who was bruised by assaults by her husband. I realized that this might be a better place to prepare my Bible lessons than my study at home, for here before me were some of the problems that the gospel addresses. It was a great context for theologizing.

Frustration and identification also produce people who, seeing our commitment to them, will reciprocate with a deeper commitment on their part to the church or organization that we lead. We will discuss that in chapter 11.

When one is committed enough to pay the price of identifying with people, he or she *is* adopting a pragmatic approach to ministry. Commitment does pay, for it begets commitment in others and makes our ministry more effective!

2

EMPOWERED BY THE SPIRIT

THE FIRST ACT OF Jesus' ministry recorded by Mark shows him identifying with the people. The second shows him receiving an anointing by the Spirit for his work. Incarnation and anointing are both vital aspects of Christian service. One shows how we must be committed to people, while the other shows how we must derive our strength from God. Sometimes people recognized as "Spirit-filled" are insensitive to culture and to human need, and their ministries suffer as a result. But a more serious problem is when people who wisely identify with people and adopt the right methods are nevertheless not spiritually powerful because they rely more on their methods than on the Spirit's power.

POWER FOR JESUS' MINISTRY

Mark says that after Jesus' baptism, "when he came up out of the water, immediately he saw the heavens opening and the Spirit descending on him like a dove" (Mark 1:10). The verb translated "opening" (schizō) means to "split, tear, separate or divide."[1] Mark may have been alluding here to Isaiah 64:1: "Oh that you would rend the heavens and come down." That chapter in Isaiah is an urgent plea to God to save Israel. If Mark has this passage in mind, then he would be implying that God is acting to save his people by sending the Messiah. Now God is anointing this Messiah by the descent of the Holy Spirit.

The Spirit is said to descend "like a dove." We cannot be sure whether Mark is thinking about the shape of the descending Spirit or the manner in which the Spirit descended. Neither can we be sure of what Mark intends to convey by the dove metaphor, though many proposals are made today. There is some evidence, however, that the dove was associated with the Spirit of God in first-century Judaism.[2]

This incident also reminds us of Isaiah 61:1: "The Spirit of the Lord GOD is upon me, because the LORD has anointed me to bring good news to the poor." This is the passage that Jesus quotes a few days later as he inaugurates his ministry in Nazareth (Luke 4:18-19). After quoting a longer portion of this text, Jesus commented, "Today this Scripture has been fulfilled in your hearing" (Luke 4:21).

Shortly after recording the descent of the Spirit, Luke is careful to point out twice that Jesus was proceeding in the Spirit's anointing. Luke writes that soon after his baptism "Jesus, full of the Holy Spirit, returned from the Jordan and was led by the Spirit in the wilderness" (Luke 4:1). Then after describing the temptation, he records that "Jesus returned in the power of the Spirit to Galilee" (Luke 4:14). Matthew also uses a passage from Isaiah to make a connection between the ministry of Jesus and anointing by the Spirit: "I will put my Spirit upon [my servant], and he will proclaim justice to the Gentiles" (Matt. 12:18, quoting Isa. 42:1). And Matthew records Jesus saying, " . . . it is by the Spirit of God that I cast out demons" (Matt. 12:28). Clearly then the Gospels present this anointing by the Spirit as the key to Christ's life and ministry.

BAPTISM WITH THE HOLY SPIRIT

Luke extends this principle of filling with the Spirit, which stood at the heart of Christ's ministry, to our ministries also. He records Jesus saying that the power of the Spirit is an indispensable requirement for ministry. In Luke's Gospel, just after giving the Great Commission, Jesus says, "And behold, I am sending the promise of my Father upon you. But stay in the city until you are clothed with power from on high" (Luke 24:49). A parallel statement in Acts indicates that the power spoken of here comes from the Spirit: "And while staying with them he ordered them not to depart from Jerusalem, but to wait for the promise of the Father, which, he said, 'you heard from me; for John baptized with water, but you will be baptized with the Holy Spirit not many days from now'" (Acts 1:4-5). A little later Jesus says that the coming of the Spirit results in power for witness: "But you will receive power when the Holy Spirit has come upon you, and you will be my witnesses . . ." (Acts 1:8).

It is unfortunate that there has been so much controversy over these passages. Is the baptism with the Spirit something that happens at conversion, thus initiatory, or is it a second experience of filling that takes place subsequent to conversion? The verb *baptizō* can take both meanings, depending on the context. A popular lexicon says that in Greek literature the word generally has the idea of "to put or go under water" in a variety of senses. Figuratively it could also carry the idea of soaking.[3] *Baptizō* could take the idea of cleansing as in washing and thus refer to what accompanies repentance. Thus this word could be used for the initiation that followed repentance and purifying. The word could also take the meaning of immersion as in a flood, which gives it the idea of fullness. Here the word could be used for an experience of fullness subsequent to initiation. The context helps us decide on the meaning in the particular text in which it is used.

Unfortunately the context in the places where the baptism with the Spirit occurs does not enable us to be fully sure which of the two options is meant. The passages from Luke and Acts that we looked at seem to suggest that a subsequent filling is intended because the apostles have already repented and trusted in Christ. The ways the baptism is described suggests that the focus is on filling rather than initiation. Luke 24:49 and Acts 1:8 talk of power. John the Baptist says of Jesus, "He will baptize you with the Holy Spirit and with fire" (Luke 3:16). All these verses suggest that an experience of filling is intended. The events recorded in Acts 2 on the day of Pentecost when the baptism first took place bear this out.

Are the instances in Acts examples of a second experience subsequent to conversion? If so, are they normative for all believers? Should all who are baptized with the Spirit speak in tongues? Some say these things are normative, and others say that these instances in Acts were special events in the history of salvation and thus should not be regarded as normative. Today many Christians testify to new power as a result of infilling subsequent to conversion, and they identify these experiences with the baptism with the Holy Spirit. However 1 Corinthians 12:13 says, "For in one Spirit we were all baptized into one body—Jews or Greeks, slaves or free—and all were made to drink of one Spirit." Here the context shows that the whole church is intended. Then the baptism here is initiatory, taking place when believers were initiated into the church. As we look at the evidence presented above, we should not be surprised that there is controversy on this topic!

My personal opinion is that this issue does not need to be a huge problem. Whether the baptism is initiatory or subsequent, it is clear that the way the figure of baptism is used implies fullness. For a Christian filling is the norm. It is commanded of us in Ephesians 5:18 where Paul says, "Be filled with the Spirit." If the baptism is initiatory, then filling is implied in that baptism, and the door is opened to pursue that filling through entrance into God's salvation. What is clear is that God intends all Christians to be filled with the Holy Spirit. So without battling over the time and way in which this happens, I believe our focus should be on ensuring that we are filled. Our lives must be lived and our service accomplished by the power of the Spirit.

Robert Coleman says:

> The promise [of the fullness of the Spirit] is not a dogma to be argued, but a reality to be experienced. Nor is it a fringe benefit of a few Christian zealots, or the peculiar teaching of some evangelical churches. True, it may be called by different names and variously interpreted according to one's doctrinal viewpoint, but the reality of the all-encompassing, Christ-possessing holiness of the Spirit is basic New Testament Christianity.[4]

FULLNESS AS A QUALITY OF LIFE

The filling with the Holy Spirit has two aspects in the book of Acts. One is a quality of life that should characterize all Christians. The other is an anointing for special challenges.

First, then, the fullness of the Spirit is a quality that characterizes people. When the church in Jerusalem looked for people to take over some of the administrative tasks of the church, the requirement was that they should be "men of good repute, full of the Spirit and of wisdom" (Acts 6:3). Both Stephen and Barnabas are described as filled with the Spirit (Acts 6:5; 11:24). That this is something required of all Christians is evidenced by Paul's command to "be filled with the Spirit" (Eph. 5:18). But the fullness of the Spirit appears in Acts as a requirement for appointment to service or as a description of people. This shows that some in the church may not have been filled. These are anomalous Christians.

So this first reference to the fullness of the Spirit reminds us that this is something we must seek in our lives and expect from all Christians. This qualification must be taken into account especially when we appoint people to offices in the church. In the first church fullness of the Spirit was a requirement not only for people who preach and teach but also for those doing administrative tasks.

While the book of Acts does not have many references to the fullness of the Spirit as a condition, this subject is a major aspect of Paul's teaching about the Spirit. Paul lays great stress on the Spirit's work in the formation of Christian character. The most familiar passage is the one listing the fruit of the Spirit (Gal. 5:22-23). The wording relating to fullness is not found, but there it is clearly implied. Fullness is specially implied two verses later when

Paul says, "Since we live by the Spirit, let us keep in step with the Spirit" (Gal. 5:25 NIV). These are different ways of describing a condition of being filled with the Spirit. His discussion on the gifts of the Spirit in 1 Corinthians is abruptly interrupted so that he could insert a piece on the primacy of love (1 Cor. 13). He uses fullness language when he says, "God's love has been poured into our hearts through the Holy Spirit who has been given to us" (Rom. 5:5). The word translated "poured" here (*ekcheö*) has the idea of extravagance and abundance.

In a statistical study of the occurrence of certain themes in Paul's Epistles, I was able to find fifty-nine references covering eighty-one verses that connect the ministry of the Holy Spirit with the fruit of the Spirit and other holiness-related issues in the lives of believers.[5] Romans 8 is the classic statement of the Spirit's ability to help us live holy lives according to the Spirit rather than according to the flesh.

We conclude then that when the Bible speaks of the fullness of the Spirit as a condition, it is speaking of a state where the Spirit governs people's lives so that his work is evident in both their behavior and ministry. There is an urgent need to recover this emphasis today. The aspect of the Spirit giving power for service has become very prominent in the church, and the display of this power has been effective in attracting outsiders to the church. This is good and to be desired. But, perhaps because of the current marketing orientation of the church, this feature that attracts outsiders has been emphasized almost to the exclusion of the other role of the Spirit as the one who helps form character.

The result of neglecting the latter aspect of the Spirit's work is that we are seeing a high incidence of moral and spiritual failure among people with powerful ministries that demonstrate some of the miraculous gifts of the Spirit. It has been a cause for amazement to me to find that some people who seem to be powerfully exercising these gifts are living immoral lives or are quite prominently failing to exhibit some of the fruit of the Spirit. This situation continues to puzzle me. But one thing is certain, when the unholiness of these prominent and "gifted" ministers becomes known, the dishonor to Christ is going to be immense. We all, including those of us whose primary gifts are preaching and teaching, have to guard against Satan's trap that lulls us into neglecting the battle against unholiness. He may convince us that we are doing all right because of the apparent power that accompanies our ministries.

The power that we exercise is certainly not going to stay with us for very long. If we persist in ungodliness, one day we will suddenly find that our gifts have left us, and we are unable to carry on our ministry. Our life will catch up with our ministry, as it did with Samson, who suddenly found out (too late) that the power had left his life (Judg. 16:20). The result is dishonor to God and usually shame to us. So we should be constantly alert to these issues.

First Corinthians 13:1-3 mentions great gifts that we usually regard as very valuable to the church. But they are accompanied by some stinging phrases warning of emptiness if these gifts are not accompanied by love. Paul's admonition to Timothy is pertinent here: "Keep a close watch on yourself and on the teaching. Persist in this, for by so doing you will save both yourself and your hearers" (1 Tim. 4:16). This instruction follows an admonition to excellence in ministry (vv. 14-15). Excellence is important, but if it is not backed by a godly life, it is useless.

I find that I sometimes allow little acts of compromise and carelessness to nibble away at my commitment. If I do not take care, these could end up ruining my life. I think such behavior is one way that we could "grieve the Holy Spirit of God" (Eph. 4:30). This verse in Ephesians is surrounded by things that we could do to grieve the Spirit, such as "corrupting talk" (4:29), "bitterness and wrath and anger and clamor and slander . . . [and] malice" (4:31). Interestingly, the other similar Pauline text that says, "Do not quench the Spirit," goes on to speak about stifling the use of a certain gift: "Do not despise prophecies" (1 Thess. 5:19-20). So we can hinder the Spirit both through ungodly lives and through not giving the freedom for the proper use of spiritual gifts.

A key to maintaining the fullness of the Spirit and a godly life is having a heart receptive to the Holy Spirit. If we are looking to the Spirit, he will show us when we are moving in dangerous directions. One of his ministries to us is to be our teacher (John 14:26), and the Bible tells us that God will guide us in paths of righteousness (Ps. 23:3). Surely, then, he will show us when we are veering away from God's path for us. Another of the Spirit's ministries is to "convict the world concerning sin and righteousness and judgment" (John 16:8). What he does with the world he will certainly do with those who belong to him.

How can we have a heart that is receptive to the Spirit's prompting? Paul says we should examine ourselves before going to the Lord's Supper (1 Cor. 11:28). If so, how much more should we examine ourselves before leading God's people in worship or witness. Again Paul says, "Examine yourselves, to see whether you are in the faith. Test yourselves" (2 Cor. 13:5). The psalmist prayed, "Search me, O God, and know my heart! Try me and know my thoughts! And see if there be any grievous way in me, and lead me in the way everlasting!" (Ps. 139:23-24).

An ideal time for such examining is before we go to represent God in ministry. I have found that before I preach, I often get hit by a sense of desperation about making sure that nothing is going to hinder God working through me. Perhaps I had been careless about something in my life, and the prospect of preaching brings this into focus. At such times I am in a receptive mood, and the Spirit often reminds me of things that need to be straightened out. Sometimes I realize that I need to talk to someone or write a letter. If I cannot do it before preaching, I will promise the Lord to do that later and then proceed with my preparation for preaching.

A great American preacher, when interviewed about preaching, said that often on Sunday morning he would park his car in the church parking lot and, before getting out, plead with his wife to forgive him for something he had done. He knew he needed to get that cleared up before representing God in the pulpit. Once while D. L. Moody was preaching, he saw someone with whom he was not in harmony in the audience. He promptly asked the audience to stand, announced a hymn, and went and made peace with this person while the people were singing. Then he came back to the pulpit, had the people to sit down, and proceeded with his preaching![6]

After retiring from running his orphanages, George Mueller (1805-1898) launched into an itinerant evangelistic ministry at the age of seventy and continued until he was eighty-seven years old. During those seventeen years he traveled 200,000 miles, ministered in forty-two countries, and preached to about three million people. These figures are amazing, considering that this was before the time of airplanes and sound systems.

Someone asked Mueller the secret of his long life. He gave three reasons. The second was the joy he felt in God and his work. The third was the refreshment he received from the Scriptures and the constant recuperative power they exercised upon his being. The first reason is pertinent to this discussion—"the exercising of himself to have always a conscience void of offence both toward God and toward men."[7] He was alluding to Paul's statement to Felix (Acts 24:16). The word (*askeō*) translated "exercise" (KJV) or "take pains" (ESV) means "to apply oneself with commitment to some activity."[8] This practice is something we do with great dedication. It is a huge burden to go through life with unsettled spiritual business. The burden of guilt drains us of our energies and leaves us debilitated and devoid of the fullness of the Spirit.

I fear that the behavior of the present generation of Christian leaders is such that we are going to give the next generation a very poor example of godliness. If we do not arrest this trend, we could be responsible for an outbreak of cynicism in the younger generation, where doctrines are not honored anymore because the leaders of the earlier generation did not adorn the doctrine with holy lives (Tit. 2:10). This situation in turn could give rise to another Dark Age, when rampant nominalism and powerlessness will plague the church.

The words of a simple chorus express the cry that should be in the heart of every minister of the gospel:

> *Let the beauty of Jesus be seen in me:*
> *All his wondrous compassion and purity.*
> *O thou Spirit divine, all my nature refine,*
> *Till the beauty of Jesus is seen in me.*

Of course, long-term effectiveness in ministry is a result of a life characterized by the fullness of the Spirit. Jesus said, "If anyone thirsts, let him come to me and drink. Whoever believes in me, as the Scripture has said, 'Out of his heart will flow rivers of living water.'" John explains: "Now this he said about the Spirit, whom those who believed in him were to receive" (John 7:37-39). A major reason for the high incidence of burnout in the ministry today could be that we are ministering in our own strength rather than in the Spirit's inexhaustible resources. Susan Pearlman, a leader in the Jews for Jesus ministry, once said, "Burnout takes place when the wick and not the oil is burning."

I think the biggest fear I have for myself is that I will lose this fullness of the Spirit out of which authentic ministry flows. People will not at first notice that I am ministering in the flesh. I think I have enough knowledge, experience, and abilities that I would be able to fool people for a considerable amount of time. Even if they noticed, they probably would not mention it. But in terms of effectiveness in the agenda of the kingdom, I would be a castaway, disqualified from the service that meets God's approval. It is a comfort to know that Paul also lived with that fear. He said, "But I discipline my body and keep it under control, lest after preaching to others I myself should be disqualified" (1 Cor. 9:27).

THE IMMEDIACY OF THE SPIRIT

I should add one more point to this discussion on the quality of life of those who are filled with the Spirit. Jesus said that it would be better for the disciples if he went away, for then the Counselor would come (John 16:7). The verses that follow describe the Spirit's work of convicting the world. But I think we could infer that one of the blessings Jesus implied of the Spirit's coming was the immediacy of his presence. He will be with us not just sometimes (as was the case with the disciples when Jesus was on earth) but constantly. God's presence seems to be one of the features of the New Covenant that Jeremiah and others anticipated—when all of God's people will have the law written in their hearts and know the Lord intimately (Jer. 31:31-34; see Ezek. 11:18-20). In the Old Testament era the immediacy of the Spirit was the experience only of a privileged few.

The New Testament describes a new level in the intimacy of our relationship with God through the Spirit (Rom. 8:9, 11; 1 Cor. 3:16; 6:19; 2 Cor. 13:14; Phil. 2:1). He witnesses with our spirit, giving us the assurance that we are children of God (Rom. 8:15-16). God is not a distant being with whom we have a relationship entirely on an intellectual plane. We really do experience him. We experience his power in our day-to-day life (Luke 24:49; Acts 1:8). In fact, in the book of Acts the reception of the Spirit was not only believed intellectually but was also something personally experienced (Acts 8:17-19; 19:6). There were times in Acts when believers clearly knew that the Spirit had spoken to them with a word of guidance (Acts 13:2-4; 16:6-7). Sometimes this guidance came through the exercise of a spiritual gift, as the ministry of the prophet Agabus showed (Acts 11:27-28; 21:10-11; see 1 Cor. 12 and 14).

Throughout the centuries Christians from various theological traditions in the church have experienced this sense of the immediacy of God through the Holy Spirit. But often a dry orthodoxy (or sometimes heterodoxy) invaded the church and acted as a wet blanket to squelch such experience. Over the years revivals have resulted from Christians experiencing this immediacy of the Spirit afresh so that it came back into the forefront of the Christian life. In the past three centuries this happened through the Wesleyan and the Charismatic revivals.

Indeed the belief in the blessings of the Spirit's immediacy has been abused. Some Christians have claimed that God has told them certain things that were more probably creations of their own imaginations. And sometimes this practice has been very harmful. But the misuse of a gift should not result in its disuse. Problems should cause us to develop guidelines for its proper use, which is what Paul did in 1 Corinthians 12—14.

One of the results of experiencing the immediacy of the Spirit is a new vibrancy in worship. The first Christians demonstrated this in the way they praised God on the day of Pentecost (Acts 2:1-12). Just after Paul admonished the Ephesians to be filled with the Spirit (Eph. 5:18), he said, "addressing one another in psalms and hymns and spiritual songs, singing and making melody to the Lord with all your heart, giving thanks always and for everything to God the Father in the name of our Lord Jesus Christ" (5:19-20). It was said that the early Methodist homes could be recognized by the sound of singing.[9] Today the whole church has been stimulated to think afresh of the primacy and vibrancy of worship as a result of the Charismatic revival. It has furnished the worldwide church with a lot of new music (some good and some not so good!).

THE FULLNESS AS ANOINTING FOR SERVICE

The second way that the idea of the fullness of the Spirit is used is as an anointing for special challenges. We see this use several times in Acts. Luke begins his description of Peter's first ever response before the Jewish leaders to charges against the church: "Then Peter, filled with the Holy Spirit, said to them . . ." (Acts 4:8). The Spirit filled him in order to respond adequately, for Jesus promised, "And when they bring you to trial and deliver you over, do not be anxious beforehand what you are to say, but say whatever is given you in that hour, for it is not you who speak, but the Holy Spirit" (Mark 13:11). Here is an anointing to face opposition.

On this occasion the Jewish leaders "charged them not to speak or teach at all in the name of Jesus" (Acts 4:18). The disciples responded saying, "We cannot but speak of what we have seen and heard" (v. 20), and then they came to the rest of the believers and shared what happened. It was the first huge crisis for the church. Their supreme task had been declared illegal. When the believers "heard it, they lifted their voices together to God" in prayer (v. 24). In this prayer they said, "And now, Lord, look upon their threats and grant to your servants to continue to speak your word with all boldness" (v. 29). God answered that prayer immediately: "And when they had prayed, the place in which they were gathered together was shaken, and they were all filled with the Holy Spirit and continued to speak the word of God with boldness" (v. 31). This too is an anointing to be faithful amidst opposition.

We often react in the wrong way when we face opposition and crisis. We can become overcautious, as the following responses show: "I will never witness in hostile surroundings again." "I will never suggest a radical departure from the norm again. This church is not ready for or interested in change." "I am not cut out for this work. Maybe I should resign." Sometimes we are overly aggressive in our responses. After the elders make an unreasonable decision not to allow a somewhat controversial youth meeting, the pastor responds: "Is that what the elders say? Well, I am the pastor. I will show them that I have the authority to approve this program." Or a harsh letter comes from a member accusing us of something wrong. We respond with a harsher letter and send copies of it to several others.

When we are under attack, we really need the wisdom and boldness that comes from the Spirit. This is why in such situations it is vitally important to wait upon the Lord for his direction and strength. Usually our first reaction when we face a problem is to get busy trying to solve it. Often we go to prayer only after all the other things we tried did not work.

The biggest crisis I have faced in ministry came a few years ago when some of the staff were upset with certain decisions. They felt that I, as their leader, had betrayed them. I experienced some deep hurts as I listened to their anger. During this time God taught me a principle that I found extremely helpful: In a time of crisis, before we meet hostile people, we must first meet God. Our ministry is primarily not a reaction to the anger and rejection of people. It springs from God's acceptance of us as his valued servants and from the filling by the Spirit to meet the challenges that we face.

Sometimes during this crisis, I would just stay in my room alone for hours—thinking, praying, and reading his Word—conscious that I was in the presence of God. I would then go to meet the people in the strength of that time with God. I believe it helped me respond to their anger in the Spirit rather than in the flesh. In this way I trust that, without contributing to the problem, I became an agent of healing. Jacob's all-night encounter with God, when he heard that his brother Esau was coming to meet him with a large army, is a good example of this principle (Gen. 32:22-32). We note that he went to that mountain as a fearful man, but he left the following morning with a rich blessing from God to face the challenge before him.

The third instance in Acts of the fullness as an anointing comes just before the death of Stephen. He brings his great speech to a conclusion by accusing the people of disobeying the law and crucifying their Messiah (Acts 7:51-53). The next verse says, "Now when they heard these things they were enraged, and they ground their teeth at him." Then we are told, "But he, full of the Holy Spirit, gazed into heaven and saw the glory of God, and Jesus standing at the right hand of God. And he said, 'Behold, I see the heavens opened, and the Son of Man standing at the right hand of God'" (vv. 55-56). What follows is a description of Stephen's death by stoning by the furious mob.

Here Stephen does not perform a ministerial function such as preaching

after receiving the fullness of the Spirit. The challenge before him is the experience of dying a painful death. This is, then, an anointing to face death. And
the particular form the anointing takes is that of a fresh vision of the glory of
Jesus. There are many instances in history of God's people experiencing a
fresh vision of God and his nature at a time of deep crisis. In the year that the
righteous King Uzziah died and was replaced by a wicked king, Isaiah "saw
the Lord sitting upon a throne, high and lifted up" (Isa. 6:1).

The great Indian preacher Sadhu Sundar Singh was disowned and poi-
soned by his Sikh family when he became a Christian. Some time later he was
preaching close to his family home, and he decided to visit his father. Sundar
Singh reports what happened: "At first my father refused to see me, or to let
me in, because by becoming a Christian, I had dishonored the family. But after
a little while he came out and said, 'Very well, you can stay here tonight; but
you must get out early in the morning. Don't show me your face again.'"
Singh says, "I remained silent, and that night he made me sit at a distance
that I might not pollute them or their vessels, and then he brought me food,
and gave me water to drink by pouring it into my hands from a vessel held
high above, as one does who gives drink to an outcaste."

He related, "My father, who used to love me so much, now hated me as if
I was an untouchable." It was very hard to bear. "When I saw this treatment,
I could not restrain the tears flowing from my eyes." At that time he experi-
enced what I believe was the fullness of the Spirit. He says, "In spite of all this,
my heart was filled with inexpressible peace. I thanked him for this treatment
also . . . and respectfully I said, 'goodbye,' and went away. In the fields I thanked
God and then slept under a tree, and in the morning continued on my way."[10]
Many years later Sundar Singh's father also became a Christian.

A Christian martyr was smiling as a person lit the fire that would kill him.
The person lighting the fire was very upset to see him smile and asked him
why he was smiling. The martyr replied, "I saw the glory of God and was
glad."

Times of literal and emotional death when we are suffering for righteousness are very difficult to endure. Anger is a natural response because we
have not done wrong, whereas those who seem to have the upper hand are
clearly in the wrong. These situations are going to try our Christian character
to the fullest. We need the support of God's sufficient grace to face them. We
need a special touch from God—an anointing with the fullness of the Spirit.

The fourth occurrence of the fullness as an anointing for a task is when
Barnabas and Saul were witnessing to the Roman proconsul Sergius Paulus,
who was eager to hear the word of God. The sorcerer Elymas "opposed them,

seeking to turn the proconsul away from the faith" (Acts 13:8). Then Paul, "filled with the Holy Spirit, looked intently at him" and rebuked him and proclaimed that he would be blind. And he did become blind (vv. 9-11). Here is an instance of the fullness for rebuking.

We need the boldness of the Spirit to rebuke people, as sometimes we prefer to ignore the issue because confrontation can be difficult and unpleasant. We need the control of the Spirit too, for we can be impatient and make the rebuke so bitter that it does more harm than good. When I need to rebuke someone, I try to steep the encounter in prayer before and during the event so that I may speak under the control of the Spirit.

The situations out of which special anointings arose in Acts are somewhat restricted. But this list is helpful, for we find the anointing associated with dying and rebuking, situations with which we would not usually associate it. We tend to restrict the possibility of anointing to public ministries such as preaching and healing. In Acts we also see anointing for facing crisis.

The passage from Isaiah (61:1-2) that Jesus quoted in Nazareth about his own anointing mentions many aspects of ministry. "The Spirit of the Lord is upon me, because he has anointed me to proclaim good news to the poor. He has sent me to proclaim liberty to the captives and recovering of sight to the blind, to set at liberty those who are oppressed, to proclaim the year of the Lord's favor" (Luke 4:18-19). The variety of ministries mentioned here shows that we need God's anointing for everything we do for him. It may be speaking at a meeting or facing a need to discipline someone. It may be facing opposition or discouragement. It may be teaching children in Sunday school or in regular school. It may be visiting a sick person or singing a song or explaining something to one's daughter or father. It may be working for social justice or doing social work. It may be working in an impure and corrupt work environment. All these challenges require the anointing of the Spirit.

Sometimes this anointing comes in a way that is clearly visible to others, as in some of the instances in Acts. I think we can assume that at other times, though the anointing may not be obviously displayed, it is there. Sometimes I am surprised to find that people have been ministered to clearly through a message I regarded as a real flop. I thought the Spirit had abandoned me, but he was working through the message in spite of me.

PRAYER AND ANOINTING

We must then make sure that we minister with God's anointing. Is there anything we can do to ensure this blessing? Certainly the sovereign Lord will bless us with supernatural power according to his will, and sometimes we will find that he uses us most when we seem to be least prepared. But on our part we can seek to be in tune with God so that we can be vessels fit for his use. In the passage where Paul uses the vessel metaphor, he goes on to tell Timothy, "Therefore, if anyone cleanses himself from what is dishonorable, he will be a vessel for honorable use, set apart as holy, useful to the master of the house, ready for every good work" (2 Tim. 2:21). We have looked already at the need for holiness in the lives of God's servants.

In the New Testament, especially in the writings of Luke, there is also a close link between prayer and experiencing the Spirit. After his baptism Jesus was in prayer when the heavens opened and the Holy Spirit descended on him (Luke 3:21-22). Jesus said that our "heavenly Father [will] give the Holy Spirit to those who ask him" (Luke 11:13). Before the great day of Pentecost, "All [the disciples] with one accord were devoting themselves to prayer, together with the women and Mary the mother of Jesus, and his brothers" (Acts 1:14). The church prayed after Peter and John were told that they must not preach the gospel, and immediately after the prayer they were filled with the Spirit (Acts 4:31).

In some acts of ministry, such as praying for the sick, prayer directly unleashes the power of God. In the context of praying for healing, James said, "The prayer of a righteous person has great power as it is working" (James 5:16). In our ministries we often lead people in prayer and pray for specific needs of people in public and private. But in addition to this, we must remember that prayer is a key to opening up our lives to the Spirit so that he can fill us. Jesus explicitly stated that prayer is the key to power in ministry. When the disciples asked Jesus why they were unable to drive out an evil spirit from a young boy, he said, "This kind cannot be driven out by anything but prayer" (Mark 9:29). On this occasion there is no record of Jesus praying before he raised up the boy. Mark says, "Jesus took him by the hand and lifted him up, and he arose" (9:27). But just before this incident Jesus had been praying on the Mount of Transfiguration (Luke 9:29).

So when Jesus told the disciples in Mark 9:29 of the need for prayer for power in ministry, he was talking about a life of prayer as a vital aspect of preparation for ministry. Isaiah 40:31 promises, "Those who wait for the LORD will gain new strength; they will mount up with wings like eagles, they will run and not get tired, they will walk and not become weary" (Isa. 40:31 NASB).

Prayer helps us to be in tune with the heart of God. Jude says, " . . . praying in the Holy Spirit, keep yourselves in the love of God" (Jude 20-21 NASB). "Praying" is a participle in the Greek, and "keep yourselves" is an imperative verb, and that is borne out in the NASB rendering. How do we keep ourselves in the love of God—that is, ensure that we are fully in tune with the Holy Spirit? By praying in the Holy Spirit. When we pray, we set our sails in the direction that will catch the wind of the Spirit so that we can be carried along in his stream. When we linger in his presence, we deepen our intimacy with him, and this means that we can represent him better when we minister.

W. E. Sangster uses an old word *unction* to describe what we have called anointing here. He describes unction as "that mystic plus in preaching which no one can define and no one (with any spiritual sensitivity at all) can mistake."[11] He says, "Unction comes only of praying. Other things precious to a preacher come by prayer *and* something else. Unction comes only of praying. If nothing else revealed the poverty of our secret prayers, the absence of unction would. Able preaching can often reveal the cleverness of a man. . . . Unction reveals the presence of God."[12]

E. Stanley Jones demonstrated amazing vitality in his ministry until he was almost ninety years old. My homiletics teacher Donald Demaray tells of the time when, as a young preacher, he had the privilege of giving a ride to Dr. Jones after a meeting. Demaray asked him what made him such an effective communicator of the gospel. Apparently Dr. Jones was rather embarrassed by the question and was at a loss for words. But just before he got out of the car he said, "Prayer." Jones once wrote: "Someone asked me how I maintained my spiritual life—certain hours do not belong to the day—they're out. They belong to getting strength for the day. If I let down these hours, the day lets down with them. I am better or worse as I pray more or less. The day sags if the prayer hour sags."[13]

Sometimes when we are in the middle of preparing for an assignment, such as writing a sermon, God may prompt us to stop the preparation so as to prepare ourselves. When we sense this need, it would be wise to stop immediately and go to prayer.

Sometimes our preparation can hinder our prayer. The church I attend meets in the afternoon, and it is my usual practice to pray for the members before going to the service on Sunday. This means that I have to plan to stop whatever I am doing about half an hour early so that I can give this time to prayer. One day I was having a great time at the computer working on a Bible study that would eventually develop into this book. Then I realized that it was time for me to stop and go to my prayer time. But I just kept putting off stopping. Suddenly it was time to go. So I quickly directed the word processor to save what I had been writing so that I could close the computer. And just at that moment the computer jammed. I lost about half an hour's work! It was a good lesson to me to get my priorities straightened out.

As we pray before an event, we must plead with God for his fullness as we minister. Paul asked the readers of his letters to pray for different aspects of his ministry. He told the Ephesians: "Pray also for me, that whenever I open my mouth, words may be given me so that I will fearlessly make known the mystery of the gospel. . . . Pray that I may declare it fearlessly, as I should" (Eph. 6:19-20 NIV). If he asked others to pray this prayer for him, then he must surely have prayed that prayer himself. I often sing a hymn relating to Christian service or the anointing of the Spirit as part of my prayer time before an assignment because sometimes hymns express my desires better than I can. And as I walk to the pulpit or podium to begin my message, usually I am pleading with God silently for his anointing.

However, I don't think we need to spend all our prayer time before an event only asking God to fill us. Other types of prayer such as intercession also help us get in tune with God. When we are praying, we are in direct touch with God. If I am having my regular prayer time before I preach, then I usually just go ahead with praying for the people on my regular prayer list. Recently I gave a morning message at the Amsterdam Conference for Evangelists. Speaking to ten thousand evangelists is a challenging and spiritually draining task. I got up early in the morning to pray. But after I had prayed for some time for God's anointing, I realized that there was no point in saying the same thing over and over again. So I took my prayer list and prayed for my family and colleagues as I try to do every day. Later I realized that this intercession was also preparing me for the talk. For I was spending time with God, and thus I was getting in tune with the heart of God.

Usually the day before the event, I try to ensure that adequate time has been set apart in my schedule for prayer. But there have been several times when, owing to unavoidable circumstances, I could not spend this time as planned. Then I had to depend on God's grace that is sufficient for every need and go in faith believing that he would bless my ministry.

Last year I was speaking daily at a conference of missionaries in England, and on one day I was going to discuss the need for Christian workers to have a regular time with God. The night before, I set four alarms one minute apart on my wristwatch so that I could be sure to get up in time to have a time of prayer before going to speak. I slept through all four alarms, and I got up really alarmed! After rushing, I barely got to the meeting on time. But God's grace was sufficient for that challenge!

I have also had times when just before I went to speak, a new idea related to my topic suddenly emerged, and I knew I needed to work on that point. Because of this, sometimes my prayer time has been shortened. On such occasions I need to ask God to look after me and go to the speaking engagement, promising God to "catch up" on my intercessions some other time that day. This happened to me the day I was first typing this. I got some good new points for a message I was giving that morning. Writing these points down ate into my prayer time. So I promised God to give time to prayer in the evening. But by evening I had forgotten this promise and started back on my typing without completing my intercessions. After typing this paragraph, I stopped the typing and went to praying!

All this shows that we cannot be legalistic about the connection between the exact time of praying and anointing for the tasks of ministry. What is important is that we maintain our closeness to God. And I know of no better way to maintain that connection than by praying.

So let us make sure that we are ministering in the Spirit. Ultimately we go in faith, trusting in God to see us through, well aware of our unworthiness for such a great work. But if there is any hindrance to God's working that we can see, we deal with it with utmost urgency. That is our part—just an attempt to remove a hindrance to God's working. It is God who ultimately does the work.

Our prayer is not the only prayer key to anointing. Paul's Epistles show us that he depended on the prayers of others for power in his ministry. I found eleven instances in eight Epistles where he asked his readers to pray for him. Two requests occur in Hebrews too. Paul requested prayer for a variety of things, as the following list shows:

- One is a general request: "Brothers, pray for us" (1 Thess. 5:25). Hebrews 13:18 has a similar request.
- Five times he asks for prayer for his deliverance from prison or from enemies (Rom. 15:31; 2 Cor. 11:1; Phil. 1:19; 2 Thess. 3:2; Philem. 22).
- He asks for prayer that words may be given to him to fearlessly make known the gospel of Christ (Eph. 6:19).
- Again he asks prayer to be fearless in proclamation (Eph. 6:20).
- He asks for clarity in proclaiming the message (Col. 4:4).
- He asks for open doors for evangelism (Col. 4:3) and ~~~~~~~~~ message may spread rapidly and be honored (2 Thess. 3:1).
- The author of Hebrews has a request for praye~ restored to his readers soon (Heb. 13:19).

The list above shows that there are a variety of thir people to pray for regarding our lives and ministries. I k ple are reluctant to do this. Some wonder whether they are imposing on others by adding to their burdens. Some wonder whether those who receive the requests are really interested. Some feel that they are unnecessarily making themselves vulnerable by talking about their needs. Some think that it is below their standing as ministers to ask for prayer for their problems and needs. I believe that the large number of references given in the Epistles, most of which were addressed to whole churches, would answer these objections and reasons for hesitance.

My practice is to send letters by mail and e-mail to a fairly wide list of people when I have a special need. Often in these letters I tell the recipients not to feel obligated to read the letters, to reply, or even to pray for the needs mentioned. We should not be upset if some throw away our letters without reading them. Considering the large number of letters many people get, they may have to prioritize their responses. But I know that some of those who get the letters will pray, and I believe that their prayers are a key ingredient to the effectiveness of my ministry.

As for the matter of becoming vulnerable by exposing to people our weaknesses and needs, I do not think this should be a problem. After all, none of us are qualified for our ministries. We are jars of clay, the weak things of the world to whom God has given a ministry by his mercy (2 Cor. 4:1-7). Without God's anointing we are nothing. So we will use whatever legitimate means we can find to mediate that anointing to our lives and ministries.

AFFIRMED BY GOD

IN THE FIRST CHAPTER we looked at a feature of ministry that is primarily our work—the need for incarnation/identification. In the second chapter we looked at a feature of ministry that is primarily God's work—empowering with the Spirit. Now we look at another key to ministry, affirmation, which is also something God does. The ministry is so challenging that when we think of it, the primary focus always needs to be on what God does for us. Otherwise when problems come and we are faced with our own inadequacy, we could react in harmful ways. We could become discouraged or fearful because of tough situations. We could become timid, cynical, or bitter because of difficult people. We could become dictatorial or driven because of a threat to our sense of control over situations and people.

GOD'S ACTS OF AFFIRMATION

At the Start of Jesus' Ministry

After the Spirit descended on Jesus, "a voice came from heaven, 'You are my beloved Son; with you I am well pleased'" (Mark 1:11). The voice is obviously God's. His proclamation here probably alludes to two Old Testament passages. The first is Psalm 2:7: "The LORD said to me, 'You are my Son; today I have begotten you.'" Psalm 2 is a "royal psalm," which has to do with "the anointing and coronation of a Davidic king."[1] The other passage is Isaiah 42:1: "Behold my servant, whom I uphold, my chosen, in whom my soul delights; I have put my Spirit upon him; he will bring forth justice to the nations." Matthew quotes this passage explaining that the ministry of Jesus was a fulfillment of this prophecy of Isaiah (Matt. 12:18). Both the Old Testament passages alluded to were used by some in those days as foreshadowing the Messiah. What we see in God's proclamation is "a combination of the lowly suffering servant of whom Isaiah spoke and the royal prince of the Psalms."[2]

If such a message were accepted, it would satisfy three of the most basic human needs. First, by calling Jesus his beloved Son, God satisfied the human need for identity. Second, by saying that he is pleased with Jesus, God satisfied the need for security. If God is pleased with us, there is nothing to fear. Paul said, "If God is for us, who can be against us?" (Rom. 8:31). Third, by affirming that Jesus is the Messiah, God satisfied the human need for significance. Jesus had an important work to do.

Did Jesus need such affirmation? Whether he needed it or not, he received it. And we can assume that, as he was fully human, he needed the things that other humans need. We certainly need affirmation regarding our identity, security, and significance.

This word of affirmation was given to Jesus just as he was starting out on his ministry. All of us could do with a word of affirmation when we start a new ministry or a new task. We wonder whether we can adequately face the challenges before us, and often the Lord feeds our faith in his ability to see us through by sending us a word of affirmation.

I believe that when God shook the place where the first church in Jerusalem was assembled in Acts 4, he was intending to affirm them. Peter and John had just reported that the Jewish leaders had outlawed their supreme task—evangelism. They prayed to God to give them boldness to proclaim the word and to stretch out his hand to heal and perform miraculous signs (Acts 4:29-30). "And when they had prayed, the place in which they were gathered together was shaken, and they were all filled with the Holy Spirit and continued to speak the word of God with boldness" (v. 31). It was God's way of telling them that their prayer had been heard and that he would enable them to do the work they had to do.

I remember well what happened when I first heard that two Christian leaders whom I admired and respected much had fallen into sexual sin. The news of the first fall came to me while I was at a conference and had just given my morning Bible exposition. I went to my room utterly shaken. *If this great man has fallen, what hope is there for me?* I thought. At that conference I was doing my personal devotional Bible reading after my Bible exposition. I opened my Bible to Exodus, which I was reading at that time. My reading for the day was loaded with promises that God would look after and lead the people of Israel. It was just the message I needed.

The news of the second fall came when a friend phoned me while I was at home having my devotions. I was even more shocked this time, as I was closer to this person. I went to the piano, randomly opened to familiar hymns, and began to sing them. The first or second hymn was "Leaning on the Everlasting Arms." Here I was, asking the question, "Will I make it?" And God was reminding me that he is faithful and that we are secure in his care. I was challenged to believe that he would see me through!

When Faced with Loneliness and Discouragement

There are two other times recorded when Jesus heard a voice from heaven to affirm him. The next time came a few days after Jesus at Caesarea Philippi had disclosed to the disciples the nature of his mission. The incident is recorded in all three Synoptic Gospels (Matt. 16:13ff.; Mark 8:27ff.; Luke 9:18ff.). This could be the first time Jesus told them clearly that a violent death was a primary aspect of his mission. Peter had just presented his great confession that Jesus is "the Christ, the Son of the living God," which prompted Jesus' encouraging commendation of Peter (Matt. 16:16-19). But when Jesus talks about his death, Peter speaks up so vehemently against it that Jesus has to exclaim, "Get behind me, Satan! You are a hindrance to me. For you are not setting your mind on the things of God, but on the things of man" (Matt. 16:23). After this Jesus goes on to teach them about the cost of discipleship.

We will follow Luke's narrative from this point. Luke 9 is one of the loneliest chapters in the Bible. A few days later Jesus takes Peter, James, and John up a mountain to pray. Jesus is transfigured, and he talks with Moses and Elijah "of his departure" (that is, probably his death, resurrection, and ascension). But the disciples "were heavy with sleep," and even though they wake up, Peter talks inappropriately about building shelters. Luke comments that he spoke, "not knowing what he said" (Luke 9:28-33). It is at this point that a cloud envelops them, and God speaks from heaven: "This is my Son, my Chosen One; listen to him!" (vv. 34-35).

The loneliness of Jesus does not end after the Transfiguration. When he returns to society, he finds that his disciples have been unable to drive out a spirit from a boy (Luke 9:37-40). After the boy's father explains the situation, "Jesus answered, 'O faithless and twisted generation, how long am I to be with you and bear with you?'" (v. 41). I wonder how many times you have silently said something like that to yourself. I have often.

Jesus heals the boy, and the people are amazed at the greatness of God (vv. 42-43a). Then Luke says, "But while they were all marveling at everything he was doing, Jesus said to his disciples, 'Let these words sink into your

ears: The Son of Man is about to be delivered into the hands of men'" (vv.
43b-44). Jesus wants them to listen carefully when he tells them the deepest
burden of his heart. But "they did not understand this saying, and it was con-
cealed from them, so that they might not perceive it. And they were afraid to
ask him about this saying" (v. 45). Jesus is once again hit by loneliness.

Jesus' loneliness would have grown when "An argument arose among
them as to which of them was the greatest" (v. 46). Then comes John's statement that they tried to stop someone who was not one of them from driving
out demons in Jesus' name, and Jesus' rebuttal (vv. 49-50). This is followed
by a description of hesitancy from a Samaritan village to welcome Jesus and
the question of James and John about whether to "call fire down from heaven
to destroy them." Jesus has to rebuke them again for this (vv. 51-55). The
chapter ends with the description of three would-be followers who receive
unexpected responses from Jesus, probably resulting in all three deciding not
to follow him (vv. 57-62).

What loneliness! What strong reasons to be discouraged! Yet sandwiched
in between these lonely experiences is the Transfiguration with the conversation with Moses and Elijah and the voice from heaven. God not only spoke
audibly but also provided two people who talked to Jesus about his "departure." The failure of his closest companions on earth to understand the meaning of this "departure" must surely have been a major reason for Jesus to
experience loneliness.

It is most interesting that both Moses and Elijah also experienced great
loneliness during their years of service, and they too experienced God's miraculous affirmation. I believe the most serious of the many complaints Moses
made to God about the burden of having to lead such a troublesome people
was the one recorded in Numbers 11:11-15. On that occasion God answered
powerfully by anointing seventy elders with the Spirit that was in Moses
(Num. 11:16-30). Elijah's greatest experience of loneliness on record followed
the great conflict at Mount Carmel when he ended up severely depressed.
Here too God spoke to him in the middle of his depression and told him of
others who had been faithful to God like him and gave him a new commission to service (1 Kings 19). It is interesting that in both these instances one
of the means God used to remedy the loneliness was to direct the lonely servants of God to other colleagues. But going into that is beyond the scope of
the present study!

Paul had a similar experience in Corinth (Acts 23:11) during his first visit
to Europe. He had received the Macedonian call and traveled there, but he had
to escape under threat from every Macedonian city he visited. In Philippi he

was assaulted and imprisoned, but when the embarrassed officials released him, they also requested him to leave the city (Acts 16:22-40). In Thessalonica there was a riot, and the believers sent him away as soon as it was night (17:5-10). From there Paul went to Berea where he initially met with a positive response. But Jews came from Thessalonica and stirred up the crowd, and Paul was hurriedly sent off to the coast (17:11-14). He then went to Athens and met with an indifferent response, which included some intellectuals sneering at his belief in the Resurrection (17:16-34). We are not surprised, then, that he came to the next city on his itinerary, Corinth, "in weakness and in fear and much trembling" (1 Cor. 2:3). There he had an initial positive response, but soon the Jews abused him, and he had to leave the synagogue (Acts 18:6).

Paul must have been emotionally very low at that time, but the Lord spoke to him in a vision: "Do not be afraid, but go on speaking and do not be silent, for I am with you, and no one will attack you to harm you, for I have many in this city who are my people" (Acts 18:9-10). Buoyed by this message, Paul "stayed a year and six months, teaching the word of God among them" (18:11). Despite the early problems in the Corinthian church, a church has existed there throughout the past two millennia right up to the present day.

Paul received a similar vision after he was arrested on his last visit to Jerusalem. He was arrested not for preaching the gospel but for desecrating the temple. Paul was a patriot, and he had gone to the temple at the request of the Jerusalem church in order to demonstrate his devotion to the Jewish law (Acts 21:20-26). So this arrest must have been very difficult to stomach. But one "night the Lord stood by him and said, 'Take courage, for as you have testified to the facts about me in Jerusalem, so you must testify also in Rome'" (23:11). The encounter with the angel in a ship on his journey to Rome during the terrible storm (27:23-24) could also come under this category of words from God to encourage workers facing loneliness and discouragement.

When Contemplating the Sacrifice He Had to Make

The third time a word from heaven comes to Jesus is in John 12 when he is considering the costly sacrifice he is to make. John had previously presented "the hour" or "time" of his great act of sacrifice as something that was in the future (2:4; 4:21, 23; 7:30; 8:20). Now for the first time Jesus says, "The hour has come for the Son of Man to be glorified" (12:23). From this point on John presents the hour as something that has come (12:27; 13:1; 17:1).

Our passage has Jesus' mind in turmoil as he faces the prospect of his death. He says, "Now is my soul troubled. And what shall I say? 'Father, save me from this hour'?" Jesus rejects the thought of avoiding the cross by restating his mission: "But for this purpose I have come to this hour. Father, glorify your name!" (John 12:27b-28a). This is John's equivalent to the prayer in Gethsemane.

None of us takes to the cross naturally. Sacrifice hurts, and the hurt is real. But there is a deeper desire in us than that of simply avoiding pain. We want to do the will of God. So in the prayer in the Synoptic Gospels, Jesus prays " . . . not what I will, but what you will" (Mark 14:36). In the equivalent prayer in John he prays, "Father, glorify your name!" (John 12:28a). Of course, in John's thinking, the cross and Resurrection represent the greatest expressions of glory in the life of Christ.

God's response to Christ's words is most pertinent: "I have glorified it, and I will glorify it again" (John 12:28b). God had already glorified his name through the miracles of Jesus (2:11). Now he says he will glorify it again through Jesus' death, resurrection, and exaltation. God is essentially saying that he can be trusted. He has helped Jesus in the past, and he will help him now too as he faces his death. The death will result in glory. Then Jesus says, "This voice has come for your sake, not mine" (12:30). Jesus does not mean to say that the voice did not encourage him. While the message was primarily for the benefit of his disciples, it was God's response to the request that Jesus made to God to glorify his name. So it was intended for Christ too.

This word from God teaches us that when we come face to face with the immensity of the sacrifice we must make because of our call, God reminds us that he will turn this event to bring glory to him, just as he made previous events glorious. This truth helps us brace ourselves to face the cross before us.

Many people do not think about suffering when they think of Christian service. This is a big mistake. All through the New Testament we are told that if we are faithful to God, we will suffer. When we do Christian ministry, we take on the mantle of Jesus, the suffering servant. The long lists of his sufferings for Christ that Paul gives in his Epistles are very vivid. In fact, he describes his personal sufferings as Christ's own sufferings (Phil. 3:10; Col. 1:24-25), indicating that suffering was an aspect of his union with Christ. If we do not anticipate suffering, we could be disillusioned when it comes or try to avoid it through disobedience.

But suffering is not easy. Those who make love their goal in life are going to hurt deeply when they are rejected, unappreciated, exploited, or opposed by the very people they seek to love. But that is the lot of God's servants.

However, as we face the prospect of suffering, God will remind us that, just as Christ's sufferings produced great glory, our sufferings will also bring great glory to God. The guarantee we have of this is that he has already glorified his name through us. Surely then he can do it again through this difficult challenge that we face.

THE WITNESS OF THE SPIRIT

So the three affirmations that Jesus received had to do with his identity, security, and significance. They affirmed his relationship with God and God's acceptance of him and his work. Having a conviction of these facts is very important if we are to be contented in Christian service. In fact, without these convictions we could be living unhappy lives and become vulnerable to some major errors in ministry, as we shall see. With these convictions we are secure in God and can pursue our life in the freedom of the Spirit. Paul describes this freedom as follows: "For you did not receive the spirit of slavery to fall back into fear, but you have received the Spirit of adoption as sons, by whom we cry, 'Abba! Father!'" (Rom. 8:15). We too need this freedom as we minister.

Unfortunately most of us do not experience this freedom automatically even after we become Christians. We have all received blows from people who failed or rejected or hurt us. This has impacted us right from the time we were children. Being in the ministry has not exempted us from such experiences. The message given to us that we do not measure up clings to us so closely that we suspect deep down that it is true. Then we hear the message that we are children of God who are accepted by him and have been given an eternally significant work to do. We believe this in our minds, but we find it difficult to behave like people who enjoy such identity, security, and significance. The truth, which we believe intellectually, has not really traveled down to our hearts. Often that journey from the mind to the heart is blocked by the memory of hurts we have encountered.

How do we truly possess this possession that is our right as children of God? Many things will be used by God to help us. The most important key is belief in what the Bible says about us. The time-tested method of teaching people about assurance of salvation is still the basic method: The Bible says it; therefore, we believe it. Yet we are more than intellects; our full humanity includes our feelings and emotions. And hurt emotions could hinder the truth, which we intellectually believe, from influencing our emotions and producing security, joy, and freedom. God works by other means too in testifying to the truth that the Bible proclaims about us. I think a skillful and godly counselor can help to heal us so that we are freed to fully believe the truth about ourselves. So does an affirming group of believers who are committed to us.

Romans 8 gives another important way in which God works to help us accept what the Bible says about our status in Christ. Paul follows his description of our freedom as children, in verse 15, by describing how God acts to convince us about our adoption. He says, "The Spirit himself bears witness with our spirit that we are children of God" (v. 16). I believe that what this verse describes could have an affirmative effect similar to that caused by the audible divine voice Jesus and Paul heard. We will call it the witness of the Holy Spirit to the human spirit. This is a sense that comes to us that God has spoken to us individually and affirmed that we belong to him and are accepted by him.

How do we get this sense? How does the Spirit testify to our spirit? Let me give some examples:

• It happens when what we are reading from the Bible at a given time ministers specifically to a personal need of ours. We are delightfully surprised when we realize that God knew our situation and arranged for us to read this passage at this particular time.

• It could be a strong impression in the mind. Sometimes this impression is a scriptural truth, but what is special is that it surfaces at the right time to minister to our particular need.

• It could be a word of prophecy or some such specific ministry to us by a gifted servant of God.

• It could be an audible voice, a vision, or a dream, which is what Jesus and Paul received.

• It could be a sermon we hear or a letter we receive or something we read that specifically ministers to our need.

• It could be a circumstance that meets a need, like a check that comes in the mail when we are badly in need of funds.

Through such means God speaks to us and tells us that he is with us, that we are his, and that he is committed to us. The result is a deep peace and joy and an assurance that God will look after us. When we experience this affirmation over and over again, the messages we got from the world that we are useless, inferior, and insignificant lose their power. We learn to believe that we belong to God, that God is with us and will look after us and use us. We not only believe the truth that we are God's precious children with our intellect, but we also accept it in our heart, and this markedly influences our behavior.

Of course we must tread cautiously in this area because many today have misused this idea that God speaks to them. Sometimes what we regard as God's voice is actually our own imagination. Sometimes, using some questionable methods to discern God's voice, we can convince ourselves that God has told us something that we want very much to hear. In some circles reliance on "a special word from God" is taking the place of diligent study of the Word. Some who should be figuring out solutions to their problems through research and study are expecting God to speak to them directly.

Because of these abuses we need to be discerning when considering messages said to be words from God. If such "messages" are "received," they should be checked to see whether they are in accord with what the Scriptures teach, for God will never give us a message that contradicts his Word. Such messages should also be discussed with members of the church body to which we belong, with a view to receiving some confirmation. Still we can never attribute to these messages the 100-percent reliability and authority that we assign to the Scriptures. There is a very real possibility of being mistaken about supposed messages from God.

In the New Testament instances we saw above, Jesus and Paul were encouraged to pursue the costly way of obedience as a result of God's affirmation. That should be the result of hearing God's voice. We are strengthened to pay the price of obedience. We become secure in our trust in God, and when we face rejection or other obstacles, we can remain faithful without giving up.

Yet I must also say that it will take more than a lifetime for us to comprehend the full extent of the truth of our adoption. Our phobias and complexes and weaknesses can be greatly reduced by applying the implications of this truth. But we will never be absolutely perfect on earth. We will sometimes have anxieties and fears that have to do with our weaknesses. How good to know that the Scriptures tell us that "the Spirit helps us in our weaknesses" (Rom. 8:26).

So in the final analysis, we are not used because we are perfectly mature and rounded individuals but because it delights God to use jars of clay. Then all the glory will go to him!

WHAT WE CAN DO

There are a few things that we can do to ensure that we go through life with this sense of God's affirmation. All through our ministries we will encounter situations that could take away our peace and joy and the general sense of God's smile upon us. People will harm us and misunderstand us. We will face difficult circumstances. I believe that at such times we should grapple for the sense of God's joy without giving in to despair or bitterness or rage. When I turned fifty years old, I decided to make a list of the really big battles in my life. My third point (following the battles to keep the mind pure and to give adequate time for prayer) was the battle to overcome anger over the way people have treated me. This is a crucial battle, and I know that if I do not win here, my life and ministry could be ruined.

In the Old Testament, especially in the Psalms, we are told to seek the Lord and wait for him when things are not going well. David expresses his determination to do this in Psalm 27, which was written amidst much turmoil. In verse 4 he says he seeks to "dwell in the house of the LORD all the days of my life, to gaze upon the beauty of the LORD and to inquire in his temple." Verse 8 expresses David's decision to seek God's face. The psalm ends with the admonition, "Wait for the LORD; be strong, and let your heart take courage; wait for the LORD!" (v. 14). Willem Van Gemeren says that when the psalmist says that he wishes to seek the Lord ("inquire" in ESV), "it is probable that he was looking for a divine word or action that would satisfy the longing in his heart."[3] I think that what is meant here is grappling with the problem in the presence of God as Jacob did at Peniel. There Jacob wrestled with God with determination saying, "I will not let you go unless you bless me" (Gen. 32:26).

One of the first serious struggles for joy in my Christian life came when I was a university student. My heart was in the ministry, but I was studying botany, zoology, and chemistry for my degree. One-third of our grades depended on practical work done in the laboratory. But I was, and am, terribly clumsy with my hands! The result was that I never did well in my studies, even though I worked hard at them. I would often struggle with deep discouragement. During this time I got into the habit of going for long walks. I would not turn back to where I was staying until I had a sense that the joy of the Lord was restored. Sometimes this did not happen for a long time, but I would persevere in grappling with the Lord until I sensed his joy. Then during the walk back, I would give myself to intercession. At the heart of the joy that was restored on these occasions was the assurance that God was with me and was looking after me. When I accepted that in my heart, I had no reason to be depressed.

Since beginning "full-time" ministry, life has become a little more complex. My hurt and anger come now from people I am ministering among, and the wounds are deeper. But the same principle of grappling with the Lord till the joy returns has served me well. Sometimes it takes longer now. Often an issue I thought I had settled with the Lord resurfaces to torment me with bitterness. This means that I now have to be even more conscientious in my battle for the joy of the Lord. But most often the victory will not come until I can heartily affirm, without any reservation, that because God is with me and is going to turn this thing that I resent into something good, I do not need to be angry or anxious.

These days I often spend time with my hymnbook when I am discouraged and upset. Too unsettled to use my own words to worship God, I rely on the words of the hymn writers. The music, of course, aids in getting the truths in the songs to travel down to the heart because music is the language of the heart. Sometimes when I start, I am so downhearted that I do not sing the words out loud. I just play the music on the piano and read the words silently. But with time, the eternal truths enshrined in the hymns begin to impact me, and I am freed to sing lustily and with much joy.

I believe this assurance that comes to me after grappling with God is a parallel experience to the affirmation that Jesus and Paul got in their times of crisis. God ministers with a word to our troubled souls so that we emerge confident in him despite the difficulties that surround us.

Sometimes our crises can become opportunities for a fresh experience of the glory of God's affirmation. Human rejection can become an opportunity to experience the depth of divine acceptance. Then the thrill of being ministered to by God more than compensates for the pain that people inflict on us. David was able to say, "For my father and my mother have forsaken me, but the LORD will take me in" (Ps. 27:10).

SERVING WITHOUT THE SENSE OF GOD'S ACCEPTANCE

Ministering without this sense of identity, security, and significance that comes from God's acceptance of us can be very dangerous. History has shown that often people who work hard and climb to the top have deep-seated insecurities. Their sense of inadequacy drove them to compensate for the insecurity by working hard to be successful. Many Christian leaders may be people who struggle with problems of inferiority and insecurity. That they have become leaders can be a great testimony to the grace of God. But they must replace the deep-seated insecurity with a deep-seated trust in God and with joy over the fact that he has adopted them and called them to his service.

If we minister without this security in Christ, our insecurity could express itself in various ways. Often such Christian workers look to other people and to the ministry as the primary source of their identity and affirmation.

- Some become too possessive of the people they minister to and cling too tightly to them. The time comes when some people need to be released to go elsewhere if they are to really blossom, but the leaders refuse to allow them.

- Insecure leaders are reluctant to expose their people to the ministries of other gifted preachers and teachers, fearing that they might lose their hold on these people if they are impressed by the other ministers.

- Some become too possessive of the work itself. They will not hand over a job to another person who can do it better. Sometimes board members and colleagues face the difficult and embarrassing task of telling leaders that it is time for them to retire or to hand over leadership to another person.

- Insecure leaders find it difficult to handle the criticism and obstacles in their way. Anyone will get hurt and discouraged when such things happen. But those who derive their primary satisfaction from God can snap back after a time. Those who get their primary satisfaction from their work often lose control and react excessively in a way that harms people and the work. Among these harmful responses are bitterness, rage, revenge, depression, and disillusionment. Some decide to play safe and never again try a risky new venture.

- Some are obsessed by a burning desire to show people that they are capable. In the back of their mind are statements made to them in their formative years that they would never amount to anything. Now they want to demonstrate through success that those people were wrong. Such individuals will never be happy, for people are fickle and unreliable when it comes to expressing appreciation for our work.

- Some seem to be very humble, examples of a servant spirit. They work hard and carefully follow instructions. They are ever ready to help others, but deep down they are bitter. They feel that others are exploiting them. They may say that they do not work for recognition, but they are angry that they have been taken for granted. We may not see this anger at first, but sometimes it comes out, usually in an outburst of pent-up rage that leaves the recipient stunned. Nothing can make these people happy, for if they are happy with something that another does for them, they would be indebted. But they can't risk being indebted; that would take away an essential part of their identity. They cling, as part of their identity, to the idea that they have been wronged after all their hard work. It is an excuse for their lack of joy. "I am unhappy because others have been bad to me." Such people need to become children of the King before they become servants of the people.

I think most of us suffer to some extent with the tendencies we have just outlined. It is when these attitudes control us that the problems become serious. When we find such reactions welling up inside of us, we should take it as an occasion to seek God afresh so that our identity, security, and significance come primarily from him.

SERVANTHOOD RESULTS FROM ACCEPTANCE

People who get their identity, security, and significance from God have the strength to be servants. Servants do many things that may seem to be demeaning. Their schedules are at the mercy of those they serve, and often things requiring attention crop up at the most inconvenient times. One has to be strong to remain joyous while doing such things.

It is significant that two of the most familiar passages given to illustrate Jesus' servanthood first talk about his exalted status. The first passage is his washing of the feet of the disciples. John prefaces his description of this incident with the statement: "Jesus, knowing that the Father had given all things into his hands, and that he had come from God and was going back to God . . ." (John 13:3). This is a strong statement of his identity, authority, destiny, and significance. "Knowing" here is a participle, and the verbs are in the next verse, which says that Jesus " . . . rose from supper. He laid aside his outer garments, and taking a towel, tied it around his waist." The verbs "rose," "laid aside," and "tied" are possible because Jesus knew that the Father had put all things in his hands; Jesus knew where he came from and where he was going. Jesus' exalted identity gave him the strength to be a servant.

The other statement is Philippians 2:7-8, which says that Christ "made himself nothing, taking the form of a servant, being born in the likeness of men. And being found in human form, he humbled himself by becoming obedient to the point of death, even death on a cross." But the verse before that description of servanthood says that Christ, "though he was in the form of God, did not count equality with God a thing to be grasped" (v. 6). The verses after this describe his exaltation: "Therefore God has highly exalted him and bestowed on him the name that is above every name, so that at the name of Jesus every knee should bow, in heaven and on earth and under the earth, and every tongue confess that Jesus Christ is Lord, to the glory of God the Father" (vv. 9-11).

Those who have a firm grasp of their exalted identity in Christ do not need to put on airs or act superior or look down on others. They are thrilled with the amazing status that has been conferred on them even though they do not deserve it. They are madly in love with the Christ who gave them this status. Now they want to spend the rest of their lives trying to lift up others, and they do so in the strength of what God has done to them. People are not a threat to them because the eternal God has given them eternal significance. They are freed to be servants!

Let us then go into our ministries out of the strength of the identity, security, and significance that come from the fact that we are children of God, accepted by him, and given a role to play in his eternal kingdom.

4

RETREATING FROM
ACTIVITY

JESUS IDENTIFIED WITH THE people through baptism; he was anointed for service through the descent of the Spirit; God affirmed him in his identity, security, and significance, but his preparation for public ministry was still not complete. His next step was to go on what I am calling a retreat.

LEAVING BUSY ACTIVITY TO BE ALONE

Mark 1:12-13a says, "The Spirit immediately drove him out into the wilderness. And he was in the wilderness forty days, being tempted by Satan." Matthew tells us that he fasted "forty days and forty nights" (Matt. 4:2). Matthew, Mark, and Luke all mention the forty days, a time span that echoes some Old Testament traditions. Moses spent forty days on Mount Sinai waiting to receive the Law from God (Exod. 24:18). Later he went to the mountain to receive the law once more after the apostasy involving the golden calf. On this occasion also he stayed for "forty days and forty nights," and this time "he neither ate bread nor drank water" (Exod. 34:28). In Exodus forty-day events are times of revelation and salvation. The ministry of Jesus inaugurated an era of revelation and salvation in an even more radical way than the inauguration of the law through Moses. Elijah also spent forty days walking in the wilderness after being fed by ravens. He ended up in Horeb, the mountain of God (1 Kings 19:8). There God spoke to him and gave him a fresh commissioning.

Matthew gives a reason for the retreat: "Then Jesus was led up by the Spirit into the wilderness to be tempted by the devil" (Matt. 4:1). This does not mean that temptation was the only purpose for the retreat. The fact that Jesus spent the time fasting suggests that this was a time of seeking God. Craig Blomberg explains, "Jews commonly practiced fasting in order to spend more time in prayer and to develop greater spiritual receptivity."[1]

The pattern of leaving busy activity in order to be alone with God is found often in the life of Jesus. Once after a very busy Sabbath day during which he did extensive ministry (preaching and healing), "rising very early in the morning, while it was still dark, he departed and went out to a desolate place, and there he prayed" (Mark 1:35). He did this also after the feeding of the five thousand (Mark 6:46). The whole night before choosing the twelve disciples was spent in prayer on the mountainside (Luke 6:12). Later it was when he had gone to a mountain to pray that he was transfigured (Luke 9:28). Between the Last Supper and his arrest he went to Gethsemane to be alone in prayer (Mark 14:32-35). Luke reports that "Jesus often withdrew to lonely places and prayed" (Luke 5:16 NIV). What is special about all of these instances is that he went away from the busy world, with its many needy people, to be alone with God.

I think the most basic expression of the retreat idea for us would be our quiet time, which will be discussed in the last chapter of this book. Jesus would have followed the usual Jewish pattern of daily prayer. But at least some of the instances we have presented above seem to be special times in addition to the regular quiet time.

Matthew, Mark, and Luke all mention that the Spirit sent Jesus to the desert. God sent him to be alone before he started his great work. This is certainly a good pattern to follow before starting points in our lives—like the start of the year, a new season of the church calendar, a new career, or a new responsibility. Just as the Spirit directed Jesus, he may sometimes prompt us to take time off to be alone with God. We must be sensitive to this prompting and try to arrange our schedule so that we can obey.

BENEFITS OF RETREATS

Let me present five benefits of retreats here.

Retreats Affirm the Priority of the Spiritual

Retreats give us an opportunity for unhindered concentration on God and his Word. This helps change our perspectives in several ways. It helps burn off the dross of worldliness in us by showing us that the things that consume people's desires and energies are not as important as they think. A retreat also acts as an antidote to activism where our fulfillment comes from our busy activity rather than from God. Activism is one of the great pitfalls we face in ministry, and being away from our busy schedules helps orient our minds in a spiritual direction.

Indeed we must always affirm the priority of the spiritual. But in the economy of God, he has given us special experiences to burn that priority into our hearts and minds. This principle lies behind the biblical festivals. We believe that God is the supplier of all our needs, but God ordained the festivals during the different harvests in Israel's calendar to especially affirm that fact. Every day belongs to the Lord, but God ordained the Sabbath, the day of the Lord, to especially affirm that truth. In the same way, everything we do is done in the Spirit. Daily we spend time with God in prayer and the Word. But to especially affirm the priority of the spiritual, we have retreats— extended times given totally to spiritual exercises.

Retreats Slow Us Down

On a retreat it becomes easier for us to spend time lingering in the presence of God. Sometimes we get so rushed through our busyness that we find it difficult to quiet our minds so that we can wait in God's presence. The ability to do this is a key to a healthy Christian life. God instructs us saying, "Be still, and know that I am God" (Ps. 46:10).

A few years ago I got a painful attack of chicken pox. Knowing that I would be confined for a long time, I put a mattress in my study at home so that I could stay there and get some work done while I was ill. But I was so sick that I could not do much reading after about two days into the attack. I even found it difficult to pray. However, after recovering from the chicken pox, I found that I could get into concentration in prayer really soon and have wonderful times of intercession. Usually it takes me at least fifteen minutes to get into the real mood of prayer. I realized that my rushed personality had slowed down during my illness so that it was easier for me to linger in the presence of God. I thanked God for this unplanned and painful "retreat."

Sometimes our busyness results from our insecurity. We know that things are not right between God and us. We have lost the security of walking close to God. We cannot face the trauma of frankly coming to grips with who we really are. So we keep ourselves busy in order to avoid honest self-examination. I once heard the Singaporean Methodist bishop Robert Solomon say, "We are uncomfortable with silence because silence forces us to face God."

Even when we have free time, we let the entertainment industry help us to use up this time, entering the unreal world provided by television. Such pursuits further keep us from facing reality. How sad this is! God wants to heal us and restore us, but Satan and self stop us from facing up to our need. The answer is to retreat into the presence of God with the attitude of David when he prayed, "Search me, O God, and know my heart! Try me and know my thoughts! And see if there be any grievous way in me, and lead me in the way everlasting!" (Ps. 139:23-24).

Retreats Help Make Us Receptive to God's Voice

In Scripture there are several instances of God speaking to his servants and guiding them when they had gone aside to pray. We have already mentioned the times Moses and Elijah spent forty days alone. After his Damascus experience, Paul was fasting and praying when Ananias came to him and gave him directions from God. During this time God had made known to Paul in a vision that a man named Ananias would come to him (Acts 9:9-12). God spoke to Peter about the historic step of going to the home of Cornelius when Peter had gone to the roof to pray (Acts 10:9-16). The Holy Spirit gave the historic missionary call to the church in Antioch "while they were worshiping the Lord and fasting" (Acts 13:2). Being away from busy activity and in touch with God makes us especially receptive to his voice.

Psalm 139:23-24 says that one way God ministers to us is by testing us: "Search me, O God, and know my heart! Try me and know my thoughts! And see if there be any grievous way in me, and lead me in the way everlasting!" Retreats open the door for God to guide us in evaluating our priorities and taking a hard and critical look at our schedules. We can see whether we are living daily in a way that is in keeping with God's call to us. We will see in the next chapter that the primary purpose of the temptations of Christ, which formed the major agenda of his retreat, was to affirm the priorities that would govern his life.

I try to go on a daylong retreat with my wife either at the end or at the beginning of each year. Usually one of the things we do is talk about the year that lies ahead. One year when we were discussing my foreign assignments, I suddenly realized that I had slipped in too many assignments at the back or front of other trips. This had caused me to go over the annual limit of 20 percent of my time away from Sri Lanka, which my family, board, and I had agreed to. One of the results of this conversation was the canceling of two overseas commitments—ones that I could back out of without causing difficulty for the other parties. How important it is to regularly subject our schedules to spiritual scrutiny, and that requires time set apart for quiet reflection.

Retreats Help People Escape the Tyranny of Busyness

Sometimes we are so rushed that we do not think straight because we do not have time to think reflectively. The pressure and the rush could cause us to have a short temper and blow up unnecessarily, especially at home or at work. We need to slow down! Retreats help us to do this.

Adequate time given to solitude affects our life so much that it will influence our approach to ministry. Many of us minister to people who are under the tyranny of busyness. The idea of listening to God in silence is strange to them. When they come under our influence, they should see the beauty of spirituality and desire to be freed from the trap of busyness ruling their lives and ruining their emotional, spiritual, and family lives.

Unfortunately many supposedly successful Christian workers are also under this tyranny. They will not be able to help others get free. But they will be able, through their hard work and capable leadership, to develop large ministries or grow large churches. They can organize activities that are able to attract many people, even though they themselves are in great spiritual need. On the other hand, a person of prayer helps breed people of prayer.

Henri Nouwen says in his book *The Way of the Heart*: "In a society in which entertainment and distraction are such important preoccupations, ministers are also tempted to join the ranks of those who consider it their primary task to keep other people busy." He says that we can perceive the youth as people who need to be kept *off* the streets by giving them worthwhile activities. And we can perceive the elderly as people who need to be kept *on* the streets. Thus "ministers frequently find themselves in fierce competition with people and institutions who offer something more exciting to do than they do." Nouwen says, "Our task is the opposite of distraction." He says, "The question that must guide all organizing activity in a parish is not how to keep people busy, but how to keep them from being so busy that they can no longer hear the voice of God who speaks in silence."[2]

As a leader of a youth organization, I want young people to see our staff and volunteers first and foremost as people in touch with God. We can capture their attention through our brilliant programs. (And I am convinced that brilliant programs are effective and necessary in attracting youth today. In a world where our youth are so used to top-quality programming through the media, we must work hard at excellence.) But our primary task is not just to give young people programs to keep them busy during the tumultuous years of their lives. I think that is what a lot of parents wish youth ministries would do. They want us to keep youths out of trouble. They think that it is better for them to have fun with Christians than with people who can influence them along evil paths. And *this is* an important function that Christian youth programs fulfill. One of my desires for our work is that we will provide such hilariously attractive fun that youths realize that they do not need the sinful fun of the world.

But attracting young people to our programs is just a small aspect of youth work. We want to help make our youths saints who walk close to God and acknowledge him in all their decisions and all they do. Sometimes parents are not too happy about this, as they fear it might hinder their children's progress in society! If youth workers are to nurture youths who walk close to God, the workers need to be people who walk close to God and enjoy deep communion with him. They must know what it is to seek God in silence, and they must know how to teach young people to seek God in this way.

Retreats Affirm God's Help Amid Life's Challenges

Every Christian who serves God with a burning desire to please him and to truly minister in depth to people will regularly face serious crises. Sometimes we would like to flee from these situations. During a time when I faced a serious crisis in our ministry, a thought would often flash through my mind: *It would be nice if I were knocked down by a vehicle and taken immediately into the presence of God!* We like to escape. This is why, in my twenty-six years as director of Youth for Christ in Sri Lanka, there have been many, many times when I have wished to resign from my job. A few times I even wrote a draft of a letter of resignation. But we know that we cannot escape from our challenges so easily!

Jeremiah often had such desires to escape from the heat of the battle. Once he said, "Oh that I had in the desert a travelers' lodging place, that I might leave my people and go away from them! For they are all adulterers, a company of treacherous men" (Jer. 9:2). But God did not grant this wish. Once when the prophet complained that his lot was very difficult, God answered him by saying that things were going to get much worse. How would he survive at that time if he was already complaining (Jer. 12:5)? Jeremiah couldn't run away from his call when he was overwhelmed, but he could run to God for strength and comfort. The answer for Jeremiah was not to *migrate* to the desert away from people as he had wished, but to *retreat* to the desert to meet God so that he could be strengthened in order to live amid the conflicts that come when we are serving people.

The writer of Psalm 73 learned the lesson of retreating to God when he grappled with the fact that he was facing apparent failure while the wicked were prospering. Verses 2 to 15 contain a sustained dirge about the futility of the righteous life in comparison to the success of the wicked. Then come two verses that represent a turning point in the psalmist's thinking: "But when I thought how to understand this, it seemed to me a wearisome task, until I went into the sanctuary of God; then I discerned their end" (vv. 16-17). After that, his perspective changed so much that the rest of the verses of the psalm contain a joyous song of praise to God (vv. 17-28). The change took place when he went to the temple of the Lord and, we assume, lingered in the presence of God.

Turmoil is the background of Psalm 46, and this psalm speaks of God being "our refuge and strength, a very present help in trouble" (v. 1). The psalmist invites his readers to "Come, behold the works of the LORD" (v. 8). But how can one see such things when overwhelmed by problems? God himself speaks in this psalm and gives the answer to that question: "Be still, and know that I am God" (v. 10). When we come into the presence of God, rather than feverishly trying to solve our problems, we begin to look at things from God's perspective, and our perspective changes. Then we can joyfully proclaim, as the psalmist does, that God is our refuge and strength.

During the worst crisis I faced in my many years in ministry, God taught me the value of spending nights alone with him. For me this was the equivalent of a retreat. There were days when I came home overwhelmed with worry. I did not know what to do about the problems. So I would go to my room at night and just sit quietly for hours. Some of the time would be spent praying, and some of it reading the Bible. But a lot of the time was spent in reflection. I was not praying anything in particular, but I knew that I was in the presence of God. Toward morning, I would go to bed. Usually when I completed these times of retreat, I did not have a concrete solution to the problems, but I knew that I had been with God and that my strength comes from him.

One night I had been up till about 4.00 A.M. I slept a short time and then went to conduct a training session with some of our volunteers. Shortly before I was to speak, a beloved staff worker came to me and poured out his anger over what was happening. It was extremely painful to listen to what he said. But I listened, and I went into the teaching right after the conversation. My heart was heavy as I taught. But I had been with my Refuge and Strength, and through his strength I derived strength to minister and, I hope, to act Christianly at that time. I think I was facing the problem with "the peace of God, which surpasses all understanding," which Paul says comes after we "let [our] requests be made known to God" (Phil. 4:6-7). It was during this crisis that the Lord taught me the principle that I described in another chapter: In a time of conflict, before we meet hostile people, we must first meet God. Our ministry is not a reaction to people's rejection of us but a response to God's acceptance of us.

So in times of crisis, we should develop the discipline of retreating to God's presence in order to get our strength from him. Then we can return to act as his representatives who have been called and strengthened by him.

BRIEF RETREATS

Sometimes we see Jesus going on short retreats during his busy schedule. After feeding the five thousand, "Perceiving . . . that they were about to come and take him by force to make him king, Jesus withdrew again to the mountain by himself" (John 6:15). In the evening the disciples got in a boat and set out for Capernaum. They encountered a storm, and while they were struggling to row the boat, Jesus met them (6:16-21). Jesus had had a short retreat of possibly a few hours on the mountain. We do not know how long he spent in Gethsemane, but it was not more than a few hours during which he gave himself to prayer before the final challenge of his arrest, trial, and crucifixion. Peter's time on the roof in Joppa could also be considered a short retreat (Acts 10:9).

Immediately after Hudson Taylor's first wife, Maria, died, he went upstairs to his room to be alone. Strengthened by that brief time, he came down to attend to the various matters relating to the burial. Just before the coffin was closed, he took one last look at his wife and then went again to his room. He got his strength from God and came back for the burial.[3]

About twenty years ago I was appointed to an international board on which I was the youngest member. I felt quite out of place with the other experienced Western Christian leaders and did not have much confidence to speak on the issues being discussed. During this meeting members considered how to use a promised gift of at least $1 million for ministry in China. As the impressive plans developed, I plucked up the courage to ask and to keep on asking whether the Chinese Christians would be happy with our plans and whether they would agree with what the board had decided their church needed. To put it mildly, some of the people involved in securing this donation were not happy with me, especially because the donor was at the meeting as an observer. I felt so out of place! Sometimes during our coffee breaks, I would run up to my hotel room, kneel down, and pour out my heart to God. *At least God understands what I'm trying to say*, I thought. This was a mini-retreat with God at a very stressful time.

These days I take short breaks often when I have a lot of pressure or face a major problem in my work. Sometimes I slip out of the office and go for a short walk. Sometimes I drive to the beach, which is about fifteen minutes from my office, and walk there. Sometimes I go to a church that is open for people to come and pray. If I am at home, I may take my hymnbook and go to the piano and sing a few hymns. These are mini-retreats that help me get in tune with God so that I will behave in a spiritual way rather than in a fleshly one.

Let me urge you to make concrete plans for including both mini-retreats and regular retreats in your life. Life usually moves so fast for a Christian leader that if a regular retreat is not planned ahead of time, and if concrete convictions are not formulated for when one should take mini-retreats, we may never get around to taking the needed break.

FASTING

We noted that Jesus fasted during the forty days that he spent in the wilderness (Matt. 4:2). Fasting was a common feature of the life of the Israelites, both during Old Testament and New Testament times. But once Jesus started his ministry, he and his disciples did not fast as often as other religious people. In response to a query about why his disciples did not fast like those of John the Baptist and of the Pharisees, Jesus said, "Can the wedding guests fast while the bridegroom is with them? As long as they have the bridegroom with them, they cannot fast. The days will come when the bridegroom is taken away from them, and then they will fast in that day" (Mark 2:19-20). This reduction in fasting was to be temporary for the disciples, who would go back to normal practices after Jesus left this world. In the book of Acts we find that the church was once more holding regular fasts (Acts 13:2-3; 14:23).

In the Old Testament national leaders often called the people to fasting by "proclaiming a fast." Usually the fast was for noble reasons such as repentance and petitioning God (2 Chron. 20:3; Ezra 8:21; Jonah 3:5). But sometimes it was for ignoble reasons, which was the case when Jezebel proclaimed a fast in connection with Naboth's refusal to sell his vineyard to Ahab (1 Kings 21:9, 12). The prophets often warned about the abuse of fasting—

when this practice was not accompanied by a righteous life (Isa. 58:3-7; Jer. 14:10-12; Zech. 7—8). In the Sermon on the Mount Jesus warned against making fasting an occasion for a parade of piety. But he started his two statements with the words, "And when you fast," assuming that the faithful fast regularly (Matt. 6:16-17). He then went on to say that God will reward those who fast with the proper attitude: "And your Father who sees in secret will reward you" (6:18).

In Old Testament times the Jews had national fasts in connection with special days and special needs. "As a whole, however," Eugene H. Merrill points out, "fasting appears to be a private matter in the Bible, an expression of personal devotion linked to three major kinds of crisis in life: lamentation/penitence, mourning, and petition."[4] Paul fasted after the crisis of his vision on the Damascus road and before Ananias met him (Acts 9:9). Some people seemed to be specially called to the ministry of fasting, such as the prophetess Anna who "did not depart from the temple, worshiping with fasting and prayer night and day" (Luke 2:37). Many pious Jews fasted two days of the week during the time of Christ. This practice was recommended in the early Christian writing *The Didache* (8:1), which suggests fasting on Wednesdays and Fridays so as not to be like the hypocrites who fasted on Mondays and Thursdays![5] John Wesley speaks of "the half-fasts" of the ancient Christians on Wednesdays and Fridays "on which they took no sustenance till three in the afternoon, the time when they returned from the public service."[6]

I could not improve on Eugene Merrill's description of the significance of fasts:

> The purpose of fasting is never explicitly stated in Scripture, but its connection to penitence, mourning and supplication suggests a self-denial that opens one to God and to the immaterial aspects of life. Inasmuch as food and drink typify life in the flesh and all its demands and satisfactions, their absence or rejection speaks to the reality of a higher dimension, one in which the things of the spirit predominate. The theology of fasting, then, is a theology of priorities in which believers are given the opportunity to express themselves in an undivided and intensive devotion to the Lord and to the concerns of the spiritual life.[7]

Do Christians need to fast today? As there is no command in the Bible about it, I do not think that we can insist on any form or pattern of fasting that should apply to all. Each of us, as individuals or as part of a church community, should decide on this issue. John Wesley recommended that Methodists follow the practice of the ancient Christians of fasting on Wednesdays and Fridays, unless they were sick. He bemoaned the fact that many Methodists were not fasting.[8] Wesley recommended that those who could not carry out regular fasts for health reasons should abstain from some substances on a "fast" day—tea or coffee or chocolate in the morning or meat during the day.[9]

For many years I did not do much fasting because I have suffered from acid indigestion and gastric reflux. I thought that fasting would not be good for my health. But I came to realize that I should trust God to look after my stomach and make moderate use of this spiritual discipline that could aid my walk with God. Fasting has afforded me an opportunity to express the earnestness of my quest for God's best at key times. Here are some examples of such times: before an important event in Youth for Christ or in my family and when we face a serious need or a difficult situation. I must be honest, however, and say that I have a long way to go in this area.

Churches and organizations can also decide on special days when the whole community could give themselves to fasting and prayer. Our staff team spends the first working day of each year in fasting and prayer. Times of crisis in the group could also be times when the leaders "proclaim a fast." Fasting could be a great way to prepare for an important event, such as a building project, an evangelistic mission, or revival services. The church in Antioch was fasting when the Spirit asked that Paul and Barnabas be set aside for missions and also when they sent them off, shortly afterwards, on their first missionary journey (Acts 13:2-3).

Considering how easy it is for us to become lax in our spiritual lives, we should use every means we can find to help us remain "fervent in spirit" (Rom. 12:11). Fasting is one of those means.

AFFIRMING THE WILL OF GOD

IN THE LAST CHAPTER WE looked at Jesus' retreat into the wilderness (Mark 1:13) and discussed the importance of spiritual retreats for our own ministries. It is rather surprising to find that the gospel writers say that temptation was the purpose of Jesus' retreat. This stated purpose is clear in Matthew's description of the event, which we will follow here because it is more comprehensive than Mark's. Matthew says, "Then Jesus was led up by the Spirit into the wilderness to be tempted by the devil" (Matt. 4:1). There was clearly a divine plan for this temptation. Of course, this is not to say that God caused the tempting. James says that "God cannot be tempted by evil, nor does he tempt anyone" (James 1:13). Leon Morris explains, "It means rather that God can use the efforts of evil people and even of Satan himself to set forward his purposes."[1]

THE VALUE OF TESTING

It is interesting that the temptation followed immediately after the baptism, anointing, and affirmation of Jesus. Often temptation hits us very strongly after a great event or a great victory in our lives. But God can use our times of temptation as a means of internalizing the results of the victory. Perhaps what is more significant is that the temptation comes at the start of Jesus' ministry. Craig Keener points out that many Old Testament heroes, such as Abraham, Joseph, Moses, David, and Job, went through a period of testing before beginning their primary work.[2] At his baptism Jesus received a strong affirmation as Messiah and Son of God. Now through testing he is going to learn some important aspects of these roles.

In this case the temptations helped clarify the priorities for Jesus' life and ministry. In our lives too, at the beginning of some journey, God permits us to be tested so that we will affirm the priorities that should characterize that journey. Dealing with these issues early helps us for the rest of the journey.

Oneness of heart and mind is a key to a healthy marriage. An important way to achieve that is to talk about things that cause us to be angry or upset with our spouses until oneness is restored. Paul's advice, "Do not let the sun go down on your anger" (Eph. 4:26), is very appropriate here. Early in a marriage situations will come where anger is expressed. And if the couple disciplines themselves to talk about these until the anger is gone, they are laying a great foundation for a happy marriage. Those who do not talk about such things discover, often too late, that they have grown dangerously distant. My wife and I usually give the advice of Ephesians 4:26 as an indispensable ingredient to marital success to those we help prepare for marriage. We urge couples to begin practicing this Scripture truth from the first day of their lives together, for neglect at the start could cause them to get into a pattern of avoiding key issues that need to be discussed.

This happens often in the marriages of Christian workers. Early in the marriage the wife might express displeasure about a ministry-related activity of her husband. He responds by saying that she should not hinder his God-given ministry. Being a devoted Christian, and thus fearful that she might oppose God's work, she decides to bear up with the thing she does not like. A pattern develops where she continues to keep her displeasure to herself. After ten or fifteen years of marriage, this pattern has produced an unhappy home and deep discontentment in her. She decides that she must do something to change it. Often it is too late by then, and the result of confronting the issue is a huge conflict and more unhappiness. While even these situations are redeemable, how much better it would have been if they had learned to come to be "of the same mind" (Phil. 2:2) on important issues at the start their marriage.

Early in our ministries we may be called upon to work with a difficult person who demands a lot of time and drains us of energy. But working with this person helps us develop the discipline of persevering with people, which is a key to effective service. Later, as we become more and more busy, especially with public ministries, it is very easy to neglect personal work such as discipling others, witnessing, and home visitation. But doing so would ruin our ministries. Early in our ministries the Lord will give tests to help burn into our hearts the priority of personal work.

Keener has pointed out that "Jewish teachers instructed by example as well as by word."[3] Similarly Christ's triumph over temptation is an example for all believers. The disciples weren't with Jesus in the wilderness, and so Jesus himself must have told them about the temptations. Similarly our struggles and how we faced them can become examples to younger Christians. We can tell about these experiences just as Christ did.

GOD'S WILL OVER OUR RIGHTS

The first temptation was to turn stones into bread. Matthew reports, "And the tempter came and said to him, 'If you are the Son of God, command these stones to become loaves of bread'" (Matt. 4:3). When Satan said, "If you are the Son of God," he probably did not doubt Jesus' identity. The previous verse said, "And after fasting forty days and forty nights, he was hungry." Satan seemed to be saying that the Son of God did not need to be hungry. He was reminding Jesus of his privileges.

Satan often brings such temptations our way. He tries to get us to shun the way of the cross by reminding us of our privileges. "With all your qualifications, you deserve more than this. Go to a job that gives you greater satisfaction, that gives you more fulfillment—a job that is more in keeping with your qualifications." Unfortunately much of the thinking about rewards and fulfillment in ministry today are more secular than biblical. They do not take into account the indispensability of the cross for the fruitful Christian life. So such temptation could come to us with great force.

Jesus knew that he could use his powers to provide food. He would do that later on two occasions and feed five thousand and then four thousand hungry people. But he refused to use this ability for his own gratification, listening to Satan and missing God's call. We too are called to a cross. Like Jesus, we also give up our rights for a greater ultimate good (Phil. 2:5-11). How many lose their spiritual credibility and authority by using the ministry and its privileges for temporary personal gain!

Consider the example of gifts we take from people. There is obviously no rule against receiving gifts. Jesus benefited from the gifts of women who ministered to him (Luke 8:2-3). Often personal gifts from people meet great needs that we have and are evidences of God's miraculous provision and care. Paul also received gifts for his ministry, such as from the Philippians (Phil. 4:10-19). But when he was in Corinth, he did not receive gifts from the people there. Instead he worked to cover his expenses until a gift came from the Macedonian church (Acts 18:3-5). Later he was able to use that decision to forego financial help to defend his credibility when under attack by the Corinthians (1 Cor. 8:3-15).

Paul says that he is willing to give up his rights for the cause of the gospel. "If others share this rightful claim on you, do not we even more? Nevertheless, we have not made use of this right, but we endure anything rather than put an obstacle in the way of the gospel of Christ" (1 Cor. 9:12). Then he says, "But I have made no use of any of these rights, nor am I writing these things to secure any such provision" (v. 15a). Today Christian workers often speak of their deprivations in the hope that their hearers will provide for them! For Paul his credibility as a preacher of the gospel was so important that he would rather die than lose it. He said, "For I would rather die than have anyone deprive me of my ground for boasting" (v. 15b). The overriding motive was the freedom to minister unshackled by obligations to others.

So we must be careful about getting under unhealthy obligation to those we minister to. This is even more crucial when it comes to taking loans from these people. I have seen many Christian workers in Sri Lanka who are not free to minister as they should because they have taken such loans. Of course, I'm not laying down absolute rules. What is important is our freedom to minister as we should.

Nehemiah gives another reason why ministers sometimes may not take what is their legitimate right. He refused his rightful allowance because the poor had been exploited in order to raise funds for the treasury that paid his allowance (Neh. 5:14-19). He even refused to claim his expenses because he didn't want to burden the people. Those working with the poor know that if they adopt a much higher lifestyle than that of the people among whom they minister, they will not be able to really identify with the people. The effectiveness of their ministry will be greatly reduced.

Of course God is no one's debtor. He will meet our needs in his best time, and he certainly would have met Christ's need for food. Many commentators think that provision of food was part of the ministry performed by the angels who visited him a short while later (Matt. 4:11). If God is going to provide for us, we do not need to risk losing our spiritual freedom and fruitfulness by meeting our needs through questionable means. Now, in the wisdom of God, he may choose to take us through a "fasting period" when his provision may seem to have dried up. For example, individuals and groups may have times of financial shortage. At such times we must resist the temptation to compromise, knowing that God will provide in his time. We will soon discover that the value of the lessons learned in the period of deprivation far outweigh its pain.

Jesus' answer to Satan gives the key to how Jesus avoided the pitfall of using questionable methods to meet his needs. He said, "It is written, 'Man shall not live by bread alone, but by every word that comes from the mouth of God'" (Matt. 4:4). For a long time I had thought that what Jesus was saying here was that spiritual food is more important than physical food. While that may be implied, an older classic commentary on Matthew by J. A. Broadus helped me to realize that this was not what Jesus was primarily talking about.[4] Jesus was quoting something that Moses told Israel. Moses said, "And he humbled you and let you hunger and fed you with manna, which you did not know, nor did your fathers know, that he might make you know that man does not live by bread alone, but man lives by every word that comes from the mouth of the LORD" (Deut. 8:3). God did feed them in this case. But the point Moses was making is that God will determine the best way to feed us. Our task is to depend on the words that come from his mouth.

In other words, our passion should not be focused on how to provide for our needs. It should be to know and do God's will. If we concentrate on that, God will provide what is necessary for us. Later in his ministry, Jesus would say, "My food is to do the will of him who sent me and to accomplish his work" (John 4:34). So the way to avoid violating God's will when going about the business of living is to make the pursuit of God's will our great goal in life. God will look after us and provide what is best for us. The only way we can forfeit God's provision is by being disobedient. We will, therefore, concentrate on obedience and leave the provision to God. Jesus put this principle another way when he said, "But seek first the kingdom of God and his righteousness, and all these things will be added to you" (Matt. 6:33).

So we will not disobey the teachings of Scripture in order to provide for ourselves in a time of need.

• I must not neglect personal appointments with those I supervise at a time when I am very busy, especially busy with public ministries. Public ministry must spring from personal ministry, and therefore personal ministry must always have priority.

• When our church is having a financial crisis, we must not cut back our missionary giving. Those commitments are a priority and must come even before our own needs.

• I must not withhold my tithes at a time when I would dearly wish to use that money to meet some personal need.

• We may be called to a frustrating ministry where our gifts don't seem to be used properly or where only a small number benefits from the use of our gifts. When a job is offered to us that seems to be more in keeping with our giftedness, we must not immediately take it without seriously asking whether this is God's will for us. Actually I think that the biblical doctrine of gifts is being greatly abused today because it is not being considered alongside the biblical doctrine of the cross.

• In the book of Acts and in the history of the church, some of the most brilliant people gave themselves to minister to the unreached. One thinks of Paul, Henry Martyn, and Stephen Neill. Is this same thing happening today? Some of the most brilliant minds in the church should be working among AIDS patients, the desperately poor, the extremely rich, Muslims, New Agers, and in nations where the percentage of Christians is negligible. There is so much in our ministerial structures that prevents this from happening. It seems very unusual for a brilliant preacher, who could be senior pastor in a huge church, to be preaching each Sunday to a congregation consisting only of his family and three Muslim converts!

When Christians seek to know the will of God, they do not only ask about their qualifications and rights. They want to know what the will of God is. And when they face something attractive but are not sure whether it is God's will, they would rather be safe than sorry. That is, they prefer to remain in what they know is God's will for them rather than go into something new without being sure about it.

After about twenty years of war, Sri Lanka is in a dreadful state in terms of economic stability, security, and morality. Capable and motivated people find it very frustrating to remain here. Many have migrated to other countries. Now this is not a sin, for we have a good tradition of migration in the Bible too. However, I have met many capable ministers who once had wonderful ministries in Sri Lanka but who are now languishing in foreign lands, quite prosperous economically but painfully aware that they are missing the satisfaction of using their gifts where these are most needed.

GOD'S WILL OVER UNCRUCIFIED DESIRES

For his second temptation (third in Luke), Satan challenges Jesus to jump from the highest point of the temple in Jerusalem. The idea is that God would intervene in keeping with the promise of Psalm 91:11-12 where he commands his angels to look after his servant so that his follower will not strike his foot against a stone (Matt. 4:5-6). Satan uses a wrong method here, one that we also often use, of utilizing a biblical text to buttress something that is not God's will. Jesus answers by using another Scripture, again from Deuteronomy, that shows that Satan's application of this text is wrong: "Again it is written, 'You shall not put the Lord your God to the test'" (Matt. 4:7). Jesus' point is that though God does protect his children, they do not have the license to test him.

Jesus' answer shows that this temptation was not primarily to demonstrate to the people that he was the Messiah. Rather it had to do with putting the Lord to the test. What does it mean to test God? The full verse in Deuteronomy (6:16) says, "You shall not put the LORD your God to the test, as you tested him at Massah." In Massah "the people quarreled with Moses and said, 'Give us water to drink.' And Moses said to them, 'Why do you quarrel with me? Why do you test the LORD?'" (Exod. 17:2). The people responded by scolding Moses for bringing them out of Egypt to die of thirst in the wilderness (17:3). "So Moses cried to the LORD, 'What shall I do with this people? They are almost ready to stone me'" (17:4). In answer God provided them with water.

Moses renamed the place Massah, meaning "testing," because "they tested the LORD by saying, 'Is the LORD among us or not?'" (17:7). Moses was displeased with the way the people had demanded water from God without trusting the Lord to give what they needed in his own time and way. It was a case of uncrucified desire. Describing this era in Israel's history, Psalm 78:18 says, "They tested God in their heart by demanding the food they craved." The word *craved* suggests the idea of desire out of control.

Can the Lord be manipulated in this way? This is indeed a mystery! But we see from this story that God may let us have some things that we demand from him in the wrong way. The granting of the request is a minor matter. The important factor is, did our demand dishonor God? Sometimes I wonder whether it is God or Satan who gives us some of the things we ask for! When I see some of our choice Christian leaders leaving Sri Lanka, testifying to "God's marvelous provision of a visa and a job," I really wonder if these could merely be cases God permitted, similar to his letting the Israelites have the water they demanded in Massah?

The key to our prayer requests should be asking in faith. Some people define faith as believing that God will give them everything they ask. I have heard people rebuke those who added, "if it is your will," to a prayer for the healing of a sick person. On the contrary, faith is wholeheartedly submitting to God's will with the firm assurance that God knows what is best for us. When we demand something from God without at the same time asking whether our request is right or wrong, we are not asking in faith. Those who demand things from God in this way may get what they want, but they could harm themselves, for they have defied the sovereignty of God. Those who ask in faith may not get what they ask for, but that does not distress them. They know that the sovereign God knows what is best, and he will answer their prayers in the best way possible. Even if they cannot understand why something is best, faith rests on the assurance that God knows what is best.

One who prays, "I want this person to be my husband whatever happens," may have her wish granted. But her attitude may have become a barrier between her and God. Though her wish is granted, she may have missed God's best for her life. That best may have been singleness. Of course with God there is always the availability of mercy. People who make wrong decisions may find that God turns the situation around to produce something beautiful out of the mess, if they go to him in humble repentance.

But to launch into something believing that God will have mercy would be a very dangerous way to trifle with God's goodness. I once remember trying to persuade a friend in Sri Lanka to change his mind about the way he was attempting to go to a Western country. He was trying to get a visa by telling a lie. He told me that he *had* to go and that God would have to have mercy on him! What a dangerous attitude to adopt with the God to whom we are asked to "offer . . . acceptable worship, with reverence and awe" because he "is a consuming fire" (Heb. 12:28-29).

In his *Journal* John Wesley presents an interesting illustration of the principle we are talking about:

> To-day I received from Prudence Nixon herself the strange account of her late husband:—In November last, on a Sunday evening, he was uncommonly fervent in prayer, and found such a desire as he never had before, "to depart, and to be with Christ." In the night she awakened, and found him quite still, and without either sense or motion. Supposing him to be either dying or dead, she broke out into a vehement agony of prayer, and cried for half an hour together, "Lord Jesus! Give me George! Take him not away." Soon after he opened his eyes, and said earnestly, "You had better have let me go." Presently he was raving mad, and began to curse and blaspheme in a most horrid manner. This he continued to do for several days, appearing to be under the full power of an unclean spirit. At the latter end of the week she cried out, "Lord, I am willing! I am willing he should go to thee." Quickly his understanding returned, and he again rejoiced with joy unspeakable. He tenderly thanked her for giving him up to God, kissed her, lay down and died.[5]

Often God leads us to a step of surrendering something we love before blessing us with his marvelous provision. God asked Abraham to sacrifice his precious son. While I was abroad as a student for four and a half years, my future wife, Nelun, had been praying to God to bring us together if it were his will. Because of cultural factors we did not communicate with each other during this period. In fact, though I was very interested in her, I did not even know that she had similar feelings toward me! She was getting on in years, and her loved ones were becoming concerned. Shortly before I returned to Sri Lanka, the Lord brought her to an important point of surrender. She was led to lay this relationship on the altar and to pray for grace to be happy even if she were to be single. Of course, when the Lord brought us together, there was immense joy on all sides!

I believe that the principle of surrender has helped us to remain happily married for the past twenty-five years. Often she has had to surrender me to God, especially after I started traveling. On my part I have surrendered my plans by deciding that I will never take on a traveling assignment about which she is not completely happy. And I have not been angry when she has requested that I do not take a certain trip because I knew that it was a surrendered person, not a selfish person, who was making the request. With the surrender we are able to be content even when we are separated and lonely (as I am right now, writing away from home), knowing that God will look after us. This is why surrender is not a big sacrifice. Whether we get what we desire or not, we are happy and contented—and that is what people want most.

There is a very dangerous attitude of self-assertiveness that takes a religious form and finds expression in prayer. Some people demand everything they desire and are able to get what they want through hard work and the force of their personalities. Such people can develop an attitude that is not submissive to God. They may be Christian leaders, but their self is not crucified. Soon they find it difficult to discern the difference between their will and God's will. Unfortunately, because they are leaders, others can think that these leaders' will is God's will. These leaders seem to be very disciplined because they work hard, but their will is not under God's control.

Many of us leaders are insecure people who have worked hard to overcome our insecurity, and through that hard work have reached our positions of leadership. This is a wonderful testimony to God's grace. But along the way we should have graduated from getting our identity from success to getting it from the wonderful truth that God has accepted us and given us an eternally significant work to do. Unfortunately this has not happened with some leaders. Though they are leaders, they remain spiritual infants, getting their satisfaction from conquests that boost their ego or from receiving what they want.

A lot of these conquests take "Christian" forms. Others admire these leaders for their discipline, determination, and hard work in reaching their goals. But behind that Christian garb is a child seeking affirmation through personal conquests. Suddenly they have a sinful desire, such as the temptation to sexual sin. This desire becomes a new conquest to attempt, a prize to win, and the results are tragic. A respected leader, whom others regard as being highly disciplined, has committed a sexual indiscretion, and the resulting scandal is very damaging to the cause of Christ. I believe that one reason why so many leaders are falling in this area is that they are insecure people needing such conquests to boost their egos.

If we are to avoid falling into this trap, we must become skilled in crucifying ungodly desires. Sometimes God sees to it that we do not have some things that we want. At such times we should gladly accept the discipline from God without exerting a huge effort of the will to fulfill this desire. For example, because of a spouse's illness you may need to cancel plans to attend a prestigious conference that would enable you to meet and interact with some famous people. You could go to the conference and miss the joy of ministering to the one you love and the opportunity of becoming skilled in crucifying fleshly desires.

George Mueller, when asked for the secret of his service for God, said, "There was a day when I died, utterly died: died to George Mueller, his opinions, preferences, tastes and will—died to the world, its approval or censure, died to the approval or blame even of my brethren and friends—and since then I have studied only to show myself approved unto God."[6]

I think I need to add that what we are talking about is not a life without passion and ambition. It is a life with a transformed passion—a passion to please God. It is a life with a new ambition—godly ambition. We reason that God has put us on this earth for a purpose. We yearn to fulfill that purpose for his glory. And God is great; so we also strive for excellence in what we do. This is not so that people may say that we are great, but that they will recognize that we represent a great God.

Jesus had a burning sense of mission as he marched toward Jerusalem and to the cross. No one could stop him, though some of those who were close to him tried. After his resurrection he instilled this sense of passion in the disciples as he challenged them again and again with the Great Commission. I have found seven separate statements of the Great Commission attributed to Jesus in the New Testament (Matt. 28:18-20; Mark 16:15; Luke 24:46-49; John 17:18; 20:21; Acts 1:8; 10:42).

Paul caught this passion from his Master. We clearly see Paul's passion for the gospel as he says: "For necessity is laid upon me. Woe to me if I do not preach the gospel!" (1 Cor. 9:16). This passion caused him to pay a price in order to reach people with the gospel. So a little later he describes how he gave up his legitimate rights and even changed his lifestyle in order to win different types of people for Christ (vv. 19-23). These verses climax with the words: "I have become all things to all people, that by all means I might save some. I do it all for the sake of the gospel, that I may share with them in its blessings" (vv. 22-23). But he ends this discussion with a statement that shows that he was not only a passionate person; he was also a crucified person. He says, "I beat my body and make it my slave so that after I have preached to others, I myself will not be disqualified for the prize" (v. 27 NIV).

In addition to this general passion for the gospel, Paul also had some specific ambitions relating to it. One of these ambitions was to bring the good news to Spain. The gospel had made inroads in Asia Minor, Greece, and Italy. Now he wanted to take it farther westward. He dreamed about this for a long time and wrote to the Roman church, hoping that he could make Rome the base of his operations (see Rom. 15:24, 28).

Paul shows in Romans 15 that this desire was not just an attempt to add a feather to his own cap. His commitment was to the kingdom of God, not to his record as a missionary. Therefore, he says, "I make it my ambition to preach the gospel, not where Christ has already been named, lest I build on someone else's foundation" (Rom. 15:20). I always grow uneasy when I hear people say things like, "We must have our ministry in every city of our nation," or "I want to preach the gospel in every country in Asia." The one with godly ambition would say, "There needs to be a ministry *like ours* in every city in the nation." If someone else does what we were hoping to do, we will be satisfied.

Paul had no desire to start ministries in places already evangelized by others. His dream of visiting Spain lay behind his great desire to go to Rome, mentioned in Romans 1:8-14 and 15:22-32 and often in the book of Acts. His desire is expressed in statements such as, "I long to see you" (Rom. 1:11); "I am eager to preach the gospel to you" (Rom. 1:15); "I have longed for many years to come to you" (Rom. 15:23). But in both Romans 1 and 15 Paul says that he will come only if it is God's will (Rom. 1:10; 15:32).

Here then is transformed passion and godly ambition. It voluntarily limits itself (1) to do only what is the will of God; (2) to refrain from doing what other people should be doing; and (3), in personal life, to "beat [the] body and make it [one's] slave." Today too these would be good standards to use in judging whether our ambitions are truly godly.

Sometimes our ambition to please God takes us along paths that go against our own ambitions and preferences. John Calvin's friend in Geneva, Guillaume Farel, sent him a plea to come back to minister there a few years after Calvin had been banished from that same city. Calvin did not want to go, but he discerned that it was God's will. He wrote to Farel, "If I had any choice I would rather do anything than give in to you in this matter, but since I remember that I no longer belong to myself, I offer my heart to God as a sacrifice."[7] He stayed in Geneva and performed the ministry he is best known for until he died—about twenty-four years later. Today, when deciding on a place of service, many use criteria that in an earlier era would have been called "selfish." How different this attitude is from Calvin's. But his is the stuff out of which greatness emerges.

GOD'S WILL OVER WRONG PATHS TO SUCCESS

For his third temptation, "the devil took [Jesus] to a very high mountain and showed him all the kingdoms of the world and their glory" (Matt. 4:8). "'All these I will give you,' he said, 'if you will fall down and worship me'" (v. 9). Satan was offering a quick path to power and influence. By showing the splendor of the kingdoms, he was underscoring the potential of what could be achieved in the world under the rule of Christ. Considering the mess the world was in and the great potential for justice and welfare in a world ruled by Jesus, this must really have been a powerful temptation. Just one compromise and the needy world would be his to change for the better. It was a temptation to receive a crown without the cross.

How real this temptation is to us today! We reason, "If we get to the top, how much good we could do for so many people. Aren't a few compromises a small price to pay for a position of such influence?" In our world success is measured by size, influence, and other trappings of power, such as how many people we have working for us. Therefore, the lure of success is all the more real and a common temptation in the world of business and government. A person will bend the rules a bit to grant the wish of a powerful person, who in turn will sponsor his promotion in his job. It is common to hear of people giving sexual favors to top people so that their chances of upward mobility may be enhanced.

Parents can take wrong paths to successful family life. A mother may tell a lie to her little son to get him to do something good, such as threatening that the boogie man will take him away if he doesn't eat his food. When a father is going out, and his small daughter is crying, he may tell her that he will come back soon, though he is actually going on a long trip. The parents may succeed in achieving their end in both these cases, but through their bad example, the children will come to believe that it is acceptable to tell lies.

The wrong path to success is a temptation in the ministry too. Take the case of a preacher or a musician who is gifted to draw big crowds for events. But something is seriously wrong with this individual's personal life; it would be best for him to stay away from public ministry until that is cleared up or until he completes a period stipulated by a discipline process. But that would ruin the program, and success is usually measured by our ability to attract large numbers of people to our programs. So we will use this person in our ministry. By doing so, we hinder the person's chances of recovering fully from the problem, and even though the program will be considered a success by human standards, we forfeit God's blessings because we broke his principles. If the problem is not dealt with adequately, it often increases with time, and there is a public scandal. Great shame comes to the group that used this person, and great dishonor comes to the name of God.

As ministers we are vulnerable to many other similar traps.

• As we strive for success in ministry, we can neglect our families.

• In order to expand our ministries, we could put into leadership those who are not yet fit for it.

• We could come into a leadership position by slandering a rival for that slot.

• As we have to "go on with our programs," we could drop or ignore a person who once worked very hard and was very useful to us but is now having some personal problems. The push for growth leaves us with no time to care for those wounded in the battle.

• We could eliminate from positions of influence people we do not like or who question our plans for growth.

• By offering a bigger salary, we could lure a person who is invaluable to another group to come join us. We forget that when we hurt another group, we hurt the body of Christ to which we belong.

• We could avoid preaching on unpleasant topics because the people do not like it and because "you cannot make a church grow by preaching sermons people do not like."

Many evangelical groups and churches are in big trouble today because they have broken Christian principles in their pursuit of growth and success. A passion for Christ and the lost (which should have caused people to be obedient to Christ in all things) seems to have been replaced by a passion for growth that tempts them to use questionable means to achieve it.

If this process goes unchecked, we could have a huge crisis in the church. Because evangelical leaders have been unprincipled in their behavior, other people could reject Christianity as an impractical and false religion. This situation could also cause an epidemic of nominal Christianity, where the disobedience of leaders encourages the rank and file to believe that it is possible to take responsibilities in the church without practicing Christianity. We may see a new Dark Age in the church. We must urgently take steps to prevent this calamity by rejecting the use of questionable means to achieve our ends. God's work must be done in God's way. Hudson Taylor said, "Depend on it, God's work done in God's way, will never lack God's supplies."[8]

When we use Satan's methods to achieve our goals in life, we are really bowing down to Satan. Jesus' answer to this temptation was, "Be gone, Satan! For it is written, 'You shall worship the Lord your God and him only shall you serve'" (Matt. 4:10). As with the other two temptations, Jesus' response was drawn from Deuteronomy (6:13). Jesus was saying here that the way to overcome the temptation to use wrong means to success is to concentrate on worshiping and serving God. This would help us overcome our selfish desires and the lure of questionable methods. God is too exalted and almighty to need our sinful methods to do his work. But considering the power of the temptation to use lowly methods in our quest for success, it will be necessary to keep our eyes fixed on God so that our values are acquired from him and not from the world.

Paul's advice in Colossians 3 is very pertinent here. He says that because we have been raised with Christ, our ambitions are to be about heavenly things: "If then you have been raised with Christ, seek the things that are above, where Christ is, seated at the right hand of God" (Col. 3:1). This perspective must influence the things we passionately pursue: "Set your minds on things that are above, not on things that are on earth" (Col. 3:2). As a result we "put to death . . . what is earthly in [us]" (Col. 3:5).

We have seen the glory of God, and our hearts are focused on heaven. It is God alone that we worship and serve. This truth has shaped our identity: We are princes and princesses in the glorious kingdom of God. Therefore, earthly methods are below our dignity. He showers his grace on us, and so we are gracious in our dealings with people. He is glorious, and so we are honorable in all we do. He is holy, and so we will not resort to methods that compromise our integrity. He is faithful, and so we will not tell lies. Revenge, politicized behavior, dishonesty, slander, and ingratitude are below our dignity. They will dishonor God and remove his glory from the church.

I am convinced that the answer to the serious lack of integrity and holiness throughout the church is for Christians to understand and have their identities shaped by the glory of the God they worship. The culture of many Third World nations has not been shaped by the idea of a supreme God who is absolutely holy and to whom we will have to give an account someday. When people come to Christ from other faiths, they bring with them an understanding of God as a magician who grants favors to people who fulfill certain conditions. They transfer this idea to their understanding of the Christian God.

Many in the affluent West also seem to have jettisoned the biblical idea of God in favor of a pantheistic God, a divine force that indwells everything in the universe. Others dismiss the concepts of judgment and hell and see God as a benevolent being who unconditionally embraces all people no matter how they behave. This view eliminates the fear of the Lord that acts as a great deterrent to sin. So people in both the East and the West need a vision of God as the glorious, gracious, holy, and truthful one who will one day judge all humanity.

When we have a biblical vision of God, we will measure success not by earthly standards but by the extent to which we conformed to the principles and the will of God. This standard will deter us from trying to achieve ambitions with the wrong methods, but it will not discourage godly ambition. When we see that God is glorious, we are fired by an ambition to do great things that reflect his glory. So we too will dream big. But in achieving those ambitions, we will not do things that will diminish his glory. The vision of glory will give us the courage to pay the price on the path to victory. This price is the way of the cross, which Christ embraced at his temptation by refusing the crown Satan offered him. "Therefore . . . let us also lay aside every weight, and sin which clings so closely, and let us run with endurance the race that is set before us, looking to Jesus, the founder and perfecter of our faith, who for the joy that was set before him endured the cross, despising the shame, and is seated at the right hand of the throne of God" (Heb. 12:1-2).

It is significant that all three of Jesus' temptations had to do with choosing the will of God over alternate paths. With the first temptation it was the will of God over his rights and privileges. The second dealt with God's will over uncrucified desires, and the third with God's will over wrong paths to success. The will of God is ultimately the most important thing in our lives. As John said, "And the world is passing away along with its desires, but whoever does the will of God abides forever" (1 John 2:17).

SATURATED IN THE WORD

IT IS VERY SIGNIFICANT THAT when Jesus answered Satan's temptations, all his answers came directly from the Old Testament. Here we see the high priority that the Scriptures had in the life and ministry of Jesus.

THE WORD AS OUR AUTHORITY FOR LIFE AND MINISTRY

It is common to find New Testament Christians spontaneously quoting or alluding to Scripture in response to various situations they faced. Mary's song of praise, the Magnificat (Luke 1:26-55), "is an outbreak of praise largely in Old Testament language."[1] Zechariah's prophecy, the Benedictus (Luke 1:68-79), "paraphrases or alludes to a number of Old Testament passages."[2] The Gospels have Jesus referring to the Old Testament at least ninety times, through quotation, allusion to an event, or language similar to biblical expressions. This number expands to 160 when one counts duplication in parallel accounts.[3]

The book of Acts shows a church clearly living in the sphere and under the authority of Scripture. There are nearly two hundred references to the Old Testament in Acts, either by direct quotation, synopsis of a passage, or allusion to some event. In some of the speeches to Jewish audiences, such as Peter's Pentecost sermon and Stephen's defense, over half of the recorded sermon consists of Old Testament Scripture.[4] Paul's philosophical message to the intellectuals at Athens does not contain any direct quotations from the Old Testament, but it was a thoroughly biblical message. F. F. Bruce says, "his argument is firmly based on biblical revelation; it echoes throughout the thought, and at times the very language, of the Old Testament."[5] The Jerusalem church spontaneously prayed a prayer saturated with Scripture when they heard for the first time that evangelism had been outlawed (Acts 4:24-30).

The example of Christ and the early church shows the need to have the Word of God hidden in our hearts (Ps. 119:11) so that we can use it to respond to challenges we face. Paul summed up why the Scriptures are so important to us when he said, "All Scripture is breathed out by God and profitable for teaching, for reproof, for correction, and for training in righteousness, that the man of God may be competent, equipped for every good work" (2 Tim. 3:16-17). We usually use this text to define the inspiration of Scripture, but that was something Timothy would have had no doubts about. Paul's purpose here is to tell Timothy that, because Scripture is inspired, it is *profitable* for teaching and training on the one hand and for correcting wrong on the other. So the Bible is our supreme authority for faith and practice.

If we are to live holy lives, we need to be saturated with the Word. Jesus prayed, "Sanctify them in the truth; your word is truth" (John 17:17). The Word is one of our primary weapons against the darts of Satan. Jesus' use of the Word to avoid sin illustrates Psalm 119:11: "I have stored up your word in my heart that I might not sin against you," and Psalm 119:9: "How can a young man keep his way pure? By guarding it according to your word," and Ephesians 6:17 where Paul listed the whole armor of God and said, ". . . take . . . the sword of the Spirit, which is the word of God." The Word is a weapon to strike a blow on Satan when he attacks us. Susannah Wesley is reputed to have told her son John, "This book will keep you from sin, or sin will keep you from this book."

I remember a time when someone in whose life I had invested much hurt me deeply. I was emotionally and spiritually numb for days. After my encounter with this person, I kept my regular quiet time with God, but I found it very difficult to read the Bible or pray. However, I clearly sensed that the Word of God hidden in my heart was ministering during this time. I would remember what the Scriptures said about loving and forgiving those who hurt us, and all thoughts of revenge were defeated. This ministry of the "hidden" Word sustained me during those three or four days as an emotional and spiritual cripple. The Word prevented me from entertaining ideas of revenge and helped me not only to come back, but also to understand and love the person who had caused me pain.

Most of the verses quoted above imply that the Word is our primary authority for ministry also. When I was a young volunteer in Youth for Christ, one of my YFC friends told me something that I have tried to follow ever since. He advised me that I should never make a major affirmation in my preaching without basing it on Scripture. His point was that everything I teach must be derived from the Scriptures. That should be the source of authority in my entire ministry.

In those early years I was taught the important place that the great Christian leaders in church history gave to the Bible. It is well known that knowledge of the Scriptures sparked the great Protestant Reformation of the sixteenth century. Martin Luther discovered truths in the Scriptures that were not being emphasized by the church, and he began to teach those truths. He won a following, but he also earned the rage of the church authorities. He went to the famous Diet of Worms in 1521 to defend his position before the authorities. They were not convinced. Then Luther's opponent, the Catholic scholar Johann Eck, asked him for a simple response: Did he or did he not wish to retract? This question elicited Luther's famous words:

> Since then your serene majesty and your lordships seek a simple answer, I will give it in this manner, neither horned nor toothed: unless I am convinced by the testimony of the Scriptures or by clear reason . . . , I am bound by the Scriptures I have quoted, and my conscience is captive to the Word of God. I cannot and will not retract anything, since it is neither safe nor right to go against conscience. May God help me. Amen.

Let Skevington Wood describe what followed: "There was an uproar as Luther left. Outside, he raised his arms like a knight who had unhorsed his opponent, and shouted: 'I've come through!' And so he had, with the sword of the Spirit, which is the Word of God."[6]

John Wesley was very vocal about his dependence on the Bible. He liked to describe the early Methodists as "Bible Christians" and himself as a man of one book. In the preface to his book of sermons, he said:

> To candid, reasonable men, I am not afraid to lay open what have been the inmost thoughts of my heart. I have thought, I am a creature of a day, passing through life as an arrow through the air. I am a spirit come from God, and returning to God: just hovering over the great gulf; till, a few moments hence, I am no more seen; I drop into an unchangeable eternity! I want to know one thing—the way to heaven; how to land safe on that happy shore. God himself has condescended to teach the way; for this very end he came from heaven. He hath written it down in a book. O give me that book! At any price, give me the book of God! I have it: here is knowledge enough for me. Let me be *homo unius libri* [a man of one book].[7]

Of course we know that Wesley read many other books and also recommended that other people do so, and he published many important books written by himself and others. But, as Skevington Wood says, "The Bible was his constant yardstick." Wesley once said, "My ground is the Bible, Yea, I am a Bible bigot. I follow it in all things, both great and small."[8] Wesley confessed that the Bible influenced even the way he spoke: "The Bible is my standard of language as well as sentiment. I endeavor not only to think but to speak 'as the oracles of God.'" He said he sought to "speak neither better nor worse than the Bible."[9]

Charles Spurgeon had a similar relationship with the Word. He said, "It is blessed to eat into the very soul of the Bible until at last you come to talk in Scriptural language, and your spirit is flavored with the words of the Lord, so that your blood is *Bibline* , and the very essence of the Bible flows from you."[10]

Unfortunately many Christians today feel that the Bible is not as relevant to us as it was to the great leaders of the past, to Luther, Wesley, and Spurgeon. What the Bible says about itself should dispel that idea. "For the word of God is living and active, sharper than any two-edged sword, piercing to the division of soul and of spirit, of joints and of marrow, and discerning the thoughts and intentions of the heart" (Heb. 4:12). This is God's word to the human race, and it speaks pointedly to human need. While many features of human behavior vary from place to place and age to age, human nature has remained basically the same over the millennia.

I presently supervise our Youth for Christ drug rehabilitation ministry. Finding a biblical theology that addresses how the gospel answers the problem of substance abuse is the biggest theological challenge that will occupy my mind for several years to come. Does the Bible really have something concrete and practically useful to say about the problem of drug dependency? I have the responsibility of discipling three young workers of this ministry. One of them is a former drug dependent. One day he told me that when he reads Paul's Epistles, he thinks that Paul must have been a drug addict prior to his conversion! Some of the things Paul wrote, such as his struggle with sin in Romans 7, suggest that he had an intimate knowledge of what a drug dependent goes through. Though I do not think that the type of drug addiction that we have now was found in the time of Paul, his writings are relevant to that situation because they address the challenges that human nature encounters.

STRENGTH AND SECURITY FROM THE WORD

Not only is the Word valuable as our source of authority, but it is also a strength that helps us weather the storms of life and ministry. Given the uncertainty of much that surrounds us, more and more I have come to realize how important it is for us to have solid and stable sources of security for our lives. The Word is a primary source. The Bible describes this security by showing that it is eternally true. Just note this impressive array of verses:

"Forever, O LORD, your word is firmly fixed in the heavens" (Ps. 119:89).

"But you are near, O LORD, and all your commandments are true. Long have I known from your testimonies that you have founded them forever" (Ps. 119:151-152).

"The sum of your word is truth, and every one of your righteous rules endures forever" (Ps. 119:160).

"The grass withers, the flower fades, but the word of our God will stand forever" (Isa. 40:8).

"Heaven and earth will pass away, but my words will not pass away" (Matt. 24:35).

" . . . you have been born again, not of perishable seed but of imperishable, through the living and abiding word of God" (1 Peter 1:23).

This is the Word of the eternal God who is the Lord of the universe, and it is firm and secure amidst all the uncertainties of life. And this "word is a lamp to my feet and a light to my path" (Ps. 119:105). These truths bring great security to our lives. As the psalmist says, "Great peace have those who love your law; nothing can make them stumble" (Ps. 119:165). We will see how important it is for us to go through life and do our ministry with this sense of security.

But before that we will see how being anchored to the Word of God also gives security and firmness to our ministries. The path of obedience in ministry is not very easy to follow, as it often goes against our natural inclinations. Sometimes when we are obedient to God, others might think we are fools, and even we ourselves might wonder. We know that Jesus said that "the gate is narrow and the way is hard that leads to life, and those who find it are few" (Matt. 7:14). But no one likes to feel like a fool! Here are some examples of biblical ways of ministry that have challenged my perseverance.

• Confronting sin (e.g., lying) in the body and enforcing discipline for sin when most prefer to sweep it under the rug because it is so unpleasant to pursue these paths.

• Forgiving those who have hurt us and refusing to hit back in any way when there are opportunities to do so, but loving them instead.

• Being patient with and caring for the weak and wounded even though it seems to hold back the whole movement to do so. It seems so much easier to simply drop this person from the team, forget about him, and move on. But Christians cannot forget those on their team who are in need.

• Actively working for the welfare of those who leave our ministry even though they may criticize the movement as they leave. This is especially hard because those who were faithful to us, who stood by us and defended us during the crisis, now see us going out of our way to help those who had hurt us.

• Using for public ministry only people whose lives "adorn the doctrine of God our Savior" (Tit. 2:10), even though there may be some extremely talented people who do not satisfy this criterion.

• Refusing to let money influence ministry decisions. The possibility may come up of going to a function that would bring our ministry a lot of funds; however, I have agreed to speak to a group of very poor people at the same time. I must be faithful to my commitment to this group that cannot contribute financially.

What gives us the strength to pursue this straight and narrow path? It is the sense that this is the way prescribed in the Scriptures. These Scriptures are trustworthy and eternal and therefore are the surest source of security on earth. Does it not say, "Enter by the narrow gate. For the gate is wide and the way is easy that leads to destruction, and those who enter by it are many" (Matt. 7:13)? But it is not easy to persevere with this narrow path when things seem to be going wrong. There is such a temptation to give in and try an easier way or a way that will bring quicker results. But we resist this temptation, knowing that the Word of God is eternally true. If we follow God's path, we can be eternally sure that God will honor us. Doesn't the Bible say, "And the world is passing away along with its desires, but whoever does the will of God abides forever" (1 John 2:17)? So we have security amidst all the apparent uncertainty, failure, and humiliation.

If we give up biblical principles for quick results or what seems to be an easier way out of our problems, we lose the security of being anchored to the Word. This loss of security is, I believe, a primary cause for burnout in the ministry. We become restless—and start to act out of that restlessness. Our spirits can't handle the strain of such a course for too long. We will lack the strength for long-term ministry.

All around us we see uncertainty. Political movements fail after a time. Economic conditions are fickle. Natural disasters, accidents, and physical problems hit us most unexpectedly and change our fortunes. In the ministry the people we serve are fickle, and their actions inflict deep pain on us. These blows that come in ministry can be very hard on our emotions. To experience such responses after we have sacrificed so much for others can be so hurtful. This is why the ministry is never a good primary source for our security. Burnout is very high in the helping professions. I recently read a report from an affluent country that said that the highest drop-out rate among professionals was among Christian ministers.

There is a special need to emphasize the security that comes from the Word in this era because the church has recently rediscovered the truth that God still speaks to us through things such as prophecy, words of knowledge, dreams, and strong impressions in the mind. While God does speak in these ways, they do not have the authority that the Scriptures have. We can never be 100 percent sure that the message is infallible. Even when someone gives what is claimed to be a prophecy, we cannot be 100 percent sure that there is no human element in it. We can have such assurance only about the Scriptures, which, though transmitted to us through humans, are nevertheless inerrant in all they affirm. So while other ways of hearing from God are helpful in guiding and encouraging Christians, they must never take the place of Scripture. In fact, they must always be checked by the yardstick of Scripture because God will never give a message that does not accord with what the Bible teaches.

Because the Word is eternally true, it gives us a sense of security. This security is the sense that we are following a reliable path that has a proven track record of bringing success to those who have taken it. This gives us courage to go through the tough times, believing that God will honor his Word. As the psalmist said, "If your law had not been my delight, I would have perished in my affliction" (Ps. 119:92).

When things all around us are bleak, the Word gives us the opposite message: God is sovereign and will work his purposes out through the apparent setbacks. This truth is reflected in the prayer the first Christians prayed when Peter and John told them that the Jewish leaders had prohibited evangelism. Most of that prayer is an extended reflection on God's sovereignty based on the Scriptures and on the victory that resulted from the apparent tragedy of the death of Christ (Acts 4:25-28). The psalmist said, "This is my comfort in my affliction, that your promise gives me life" (Ps. 119:50).

The year 1989 was one of the most terrible years in our history. The estimates of the death toll from an attempted revolution (which was different from the war that we have at the moment) run up to as many as 60,000 in that single year. There never was a time when a body was not floating in the river at the edge of our city. Schools were closed for as much as six months at a time. Buses did not run for long periods of time because of threats by the revolutionaries. So if we wanted to keep our office open, we needed to pick up people from their homes in the morning and take them back in the evening. The three of us in the office who could drive took turns doing this three-and-a-half-hour chore.

Many were leaving the country, stating that it was for the sake of their children. My wife and I had decided that we would stay on in Sri Lanka whatever happened. But we needed to think about our children. We decided that the greatest legacy we could give our children was a happy home. So we resolved that regardless of the circumstances, the children should live in a home where there was Christian joy and contentment. But my moods were not matching this resolve as I often got depressed at what was happening in my beloved country.

One day my wife told the children (so that I could hear!), "Father is in a bad mood. Let's hope he goes and reads his Bible!" She had expressed a rich theological truth. Despite the terrible things taking place in the temporal world, we could maintain our peace if we were rooted in the eternal world of which the Bible talks. The God who is sovereign over everything determines the history of that world.

David says that the Scriptures revive the soul: "The law of the Lord is perfect, reviving the soul" (Ps. 19:7). Willem Van Gemeren, describing this reviving function, says, "Its restorative quality gives healing to the whole person."[11] Note that the revival comes because the law is perfect. Going to the solid rock of Scripture when we are drained from the battles of ministry, we are able to restore our energies and find healing as we live in the secure world of the Word of God. In chapter 2 we talked about George Mueller who traveled all over the world as an itinerant evangelist until he was eighty-seven. When he was asked the secret of his long life, one of the three reasons he gave was "the love he felt for the Scriptures and the constant recuperative power they exercised upon his whole being (Prov. 3:2, 8; 4:22)."[12]

The discipline of finding security in the Word amidst the storms of life is well described in Psalm 119:23: "Even though princes sit plotting against me, your servant will meditate on your statutes." This is a decision we make. We discipline ourselves to meditate on the Word when under the pressure of hostility against us.

THE WORD QUALIFIES US FOR EFFECTIVE MINISTRY

Not only do the Scriptures minister to our personal lives, but they also bring enrichment to our ministries. Paul told Timothy, "If you put these things before the brothers, you will be a good servant of Christ Jesus, being trained in the words of the faith and of the good doctrine that you have followed" (1 Tim. 4:6). A good servant, according to this verse, is one who has been "trained in the words of the faith and of the good doctrine" (to us this would be the Scriptures) and who teaches the truth to the believers. People who are not being constantly trained and nourished by God's Word will lose freshness in their ministries. If they are preachers, they will become dry and repetitive when they speak. Even though they may be good speakers, they will leave their hearers frustrated and unfed.

I have seen gifted preachers who, though they do not do much study, depend on their gifts to carry them through in their preaching ministry. It works for a time, but after some years the emptiness begins to show. Spending time in the Word deepens our knowledge even without our realizing it, and that depth will show when we speak. Scottish theologian P. T. Forsyth has said that the effective preacher "must speak from within the silent sanctuary of Scripture."[13]

Many ministers today have come to realize that in order to be relevant they need to be studying materials on practical issues pertaining to ministry and the results of research done on their audiences. Therefore, most books and magazines for Christian leaders today focus on practical topics relating to the work of leadership and ministry. There is very little space given to the Bible and theology.[14] I think the practical studies are very important, but so are the biblical and theological studies. These feed the hungry souls of ministers, help them think God's thoughts while the rest of society moves in the opposite direction, and give God's servants guidelines for the ministry they do. It is not a case of ministry being driven either by the Bible or by contemporary studies. Rather it is a case of using both these effectively, with the Bible always as the primary authority and thus always having priority.

In today's culture it is more difficult than before for Christians to shift from operating in the practical realm to operating in the biblical and theological realm. Because this does not come naturally to us, many Christian leaders don't make this shift. They end up being starved for rich spiritual food. Unless they change and find ways to shift into the realm of the Bible and theology, they will soon become spiritually weak and ineffective in ministry. So they need to discipline themselves to fight their natural tendency and regularly make the shift to the "Bible and theology mode."

Actually, in addition to the Bible and practical and contemporary studies, there is another essential source of knowledge for ministry. This is practical ministry, where we face numerous challenges and learn the discipline of facing the challenges biblically. As we work with people, we find the issues for which the gospel is the answer. Often we are at a loss, wondering how the gospel can impact what we feel is a desperately complex situation. But as we prayerfully seek biblical answers to these situations, we gain highly valuable wisdom about ministry.

Perhaps no one has helped the contemporary evangelical church to be relevant and to penetrate the culture with biblical truth as much as John Stott has. During a discussion on contextualization and cultural relevance at a conference, he was asked what the key requirements are for one to be an effective contextualizer. He started by saying that the first and most important requirement is that a person should know and study the Bible. That study provides the foundation from which to launch into the other cultural studies necessary for this work.

Biblical ministry is the only way to have lasting fruit in ministry. Both in the ministry of Youth for Christ and in our church, the majority of the believers are converts from Buddhism and Hinduism. Most of them came within the influence of our ministry because they believed that the God of the Christians could meet some specific need of theirs. But once they become Christians, a huge worldview shift has to take place. Unfortunately we have found that this shift does not occur in some people. While these people claim to be Christians, they still do the things they did before conversion, such as lying, being unkind to their spouses, and taking revenge. We have found that almost all those who change their behavior are taking part in a small-group Bible study where the Word is studied and applied to their lives. They demonstrate the reality of Jesus' prayer: "Sanctify them in the truth; your word is truth" (John 17:17).

This challenge is very real today in the West too. The worldview of the unchurched in the West is very different from the Christian worldview. Many have been influenced by New Age and pluralistic thinking. When people come to Christ, they too will have to make a huge shift in their thinking. If they are not properly fed with the Word, they will not be sanctified in the truth.

Preachers, in their eagerness to win a hearing among the unchurched, could neglect the task of teaching some of the basic truths of the Christian faith to their congregations. The result would be many people in the church who claim to be born-again Christians but whose lives do not demonstrate true Christian character. Statistics show that this has already happened in the church.

THE SCRIPTURES AS A SOURCE OF DELIGHT

Today the idea of objective truth has come under assault by the postmodern mood that characterizes the social landscape of much of Western society and has influenced the East too. In this environment the thought of spending time with the Word is viewed by many as a duty that is not enjoyable and is rather irrelevant. This attitude particularly affects the way people view the Old Testament. However, the picture of the Old Testament that we get in the Bible is very different. I believe it is urgently important for Christians to discover the truth about the Old Testament, because if they neglect reading it, they will be greatly impoverished. Besides, if this biblical view is accepted by us, we will look forward to reading the Bible and will invariably end up spending more time in it.

The Old Testament describes God's Word several times as a source of delight. Perhaps the most striking is the description in Psalm 119 (see also Ps. 1:2; 19:8, 10; Jer. 15:16). In various ways the psalmist exults in excitement about the Word, as the list below shows:

- Delighting in the Word: ten times (vv. 4, 16, 24, 35, 47, 70, 77, 92, 143, 174)
- Loving the Word: ten times (vv. 4, 48, 97, 113, 119, 127, 159, 163, 165, 167)
- Longing for the Word: three times (vv. 20, 40, 131)
- Rejoicing in the Word: twice (vv. 111, 162)
- Clinging to the Word: once (vv. 31)
- The Word is better than thousands of gold and silver pieces: once (v. 72)
- The Word is sweet to the taste, sweeter than honey: once (v. 103)
- The Word is wonderful: once (v. 129)
- Praise God for the Word: once (v. 164)
- Sing of the Word: once (v. 172)

What an impressive list this is! Thirty-one references expressing excitement over the Word. Often in these references the psalmist delights over the

law. C. S. Lewis in his book *Reflections on the Psalms* says that he can understand people respecting the law. But he says that it is a mystery to him that
people can rejoice in the law. After delving into possible reasons for this, he
concludes, "Their delight in the law is a delight in having touched firmness;
like the pedestrian delights in feeling the hard road beneath his feet after a
false shortcut had entangled him in muddy fields."[15] This brings us back to
the security of the Word, about which we talked above. It is delightful amidst
all the uncertainty in this world to know that God's Word is a stable,
unchanging "rock."

The idea of truth being delightful is an alien idea in postmodern society.
We live in a sensual world that defines pleasure only in terms of what can be
felt by the five senses: sight, touch, taste, smell, and hearing. The Christian
knows an even deeper joy, the joy of truth. In his autobiography the eminent
American theologian Carl Henry mentions a statement his professor, Gordon
Haddon Clark, made when he was a student at Wheaton College: "A satisfac-
tory religion must satisfy. But satisfy *what* and *why*? The Greek mysteries satisfied the emotions; brute force can satisfy the will; but Christianity satisfies the
intellect because it is *true*, and truth is the only everlasting satisfaction."[16]

One of the saddest consequences of the recent trend of downplaying the
value of objective truth is that the church has lost the joy of truth. And what
a thrill it is missing! In fact, I fear that many consider the emphasis on truth
boring. What a need there is to recover this sense of the practical usefulness
and desirability of the Word. Today this task may be more important than
the battle for the inspiration of Scripture. Many who claim to believe that the
Scriptures are inerrant and the final authority for all matters of faith and practice betray that belief by not using Scripture as if it were the supreme authority. We have to demonstrate to the church that the Scriptures are relevant,
exciting, and desperately needed for a happy and holy life.

There is an urgent need today to emphasize the pleasure associated with
Bible study because ours is a society where pleasure reigns supreme. If people think that the Bible is a boring book and that reading it is a burdensome
duty, they will not be inclined to delve into it. Demonstrating the delightful-
ness of the Word will, I believe, motivate more people to read it.

SPENDING TIME IN THE WORD

If the Bible is what it claims to be, then the Christian minister should be
spending a lot of time with it. The advice about the law that Moses gave
Joshua is true for every believer and therefore doubly true for every minis-

ter. He said, "This Book of the Law shall not depart from your mouth, but you shall meditate on it day and night, so that you may be careful to do according to all that is written in it. For then you will make your way prosperous, and then you will have good success" (Josh. 1:8). The two basic teachings of this verse are that 1) a leader must spend a lot of time in the Word and think about it all the time, and 2) the obedience that results from such exposure to the Word is the key to the leader's success. This is why I have no hesitation to tell young ministers that if they do not spend unhurried time in the Word (and in prayer) daily, they have no future in terms of effectiveness in ministry.

How easy it is for us to keep ourselves busy with things we think are important without lingering in the Word. This practice could be a sign of a serious spiritual malady. Perhaps we have lost our security in Christ and are now finding security through busy activity. Though we have so many study aids and study Bibles today to aid us, I think our generation is spending much less time in the Word than the preceding ones.

As today's ministers are very busy and are called to serve in a fast-paced society, they could say that they don't have time for Bible study. But this is not an acceptable excuse, for we will find time for what we have decided are our priorities. People aren't eating less today because they live in a fast-paced society! Perhaps lingering in the Word is simply not part of our cultural and personal orientation. Therefore, our theology should address our orientation and motivate us to obedience. I think this matter is essentially a lordship issue. If Jesus were truly the undisputed Lord of our lives, we would somehow find a way to do what he asks. The fact that we are not spending as much time in the Word is a sign that we find more satisfaction from our own agenda than God's—a serious problem indeed.

Most of us in the ministry have schedules that change daily. We also have to face emergencies that suddenly crop up, making it difficult to find time for Bible reading and prayer according to a regular pattern. I like to have my prayer and Bible reading time daily before leaving home for work. But sometimes this is not possible. So to handle this uncertainty in my schedule, I have developed the habit of deciding each night at what time I will read my Bible and pray the next day. If I have to change my plan because of an emergency, then as I know about this change, I choose an alternate time for Bible reading and/or prayer. I go into the other activity with the firm resolve that I will somehow spend time with the Lord, which is the most important thing I do each day.

The following extended quotation from Dietrich Bonhoeffer vividly describes what I am trying to get at. Here is the first part of his answer to the question, "Why do I meditate?":

> *Because I am a Christian.* Therefore, every day in which I do not penetrate more deeply into the knowledge of God's Word in Holy Scripture is a lost day for me. I can only move forward with certainty upon the firm ground of the Word of God. And, as a Christian, I learn to know the Holy Scripture in no other way than by hearing the Word preached and by prayerful meditation.
>
>   *Because I am a preacher of the Word.* I cannot expound the Scripture for others if I do not let it speak daily to me. I will misuse the Word in my office as preacher if I do not continue to meditate upon it in prayer. If the Word has become empty for me in my daily administrations, if I no longer experience it, that proves I have not let the Word speak personally to me for a long time. I will offend against my calling if I do not seek each day in prayer the word that my Lord wants to say to me for that day.[17]

Until the day we die, we can keep learning new things from the Scriptures, and these insights will enrich our lives and ministries. Time in the Word becomes an exciting adventure of discovery for us. Each day we can go to the Scriptures with the anticipation of the psalmist, who prayed, "Open my eyes, that I may behold wondrous things out of your law" (Ps. 119:18). John Chrysostom, acknowledged as the greatest Bible expositor of the early church, said, "It is a great thing; this reading of the Scriptures. For it is not possible ever to expand the mind of the Scriptures. It is a well that has no bottom."[18] Martin Luther said regarding Bible study, "We must ever remain scholars here; we cannot sound the depth of one single verse in Scripture; we get hold but of the ABC and that imperfectly."[19]

Let me say something here on behalf of inductive Bible study—that is, study that observes what is written so carefully that it draws out from the Bible what it teaches rather than letting other external factors tell us. There are so many study Bibles and other aids today that I have a great fear that Christian leaders are not really studying the Bible itself anymore. We are not used to grappling with literature in what some are calling this "post-literate society." The publishing world is serving us a huge menu of resources that are supposed to take the sweat out of Bible study. But sweating at Bible study can be exciting! It gives us the joy of discovering "wondrous things out of [God's] law" (Ps. 119:18).

I always read the Bible, even for my devotions, with a pencil in hand. I usually write with "2B" lead, rather than the more common "HB" lead, because 2B is soft and does not harm the thin Bible paper. I write down summaries and titles of chapters, paragraphs, or verses. I underline verses and give numbers if there are lists. I indicate relationships between the different sections with symbols indicating cause or result or reason, etc. This process helps me to stay alert and to look for what the passage is really saying.

But I find that sometimes I too can fall into the trap of depending on secondary sources without trying to find the meaning of the text for myself. Some years ago I was studying the book of Galatians for a series of expositions that I had to give at a conference. Toward the start of this process, I spent two days in the home of my mentor for my graduate studies, Dr. Daniel Fuller, who has taught me a lot about the inductive study of the Bible. Knowing that he had done a lot of work on Galatians, I asked him a few questions. He took his Bible and began to subject the text to rigorous scrutiny. Soon I was horrified to realize that when I had wanted to see the trend of Paul's thought or when I faced a problem text, I had gone to a commentary without grappling with the text myself. I had been affected by the mood of my age that has no time or inclination to do hard thinking. And I fear that this is a major problem with Christian leaders in general.

Bible commentaries, study Bibles, and other study aids can be very helpful to us. But we must use them only as secondary sources. That is, 1) they could be used to get some fresh ideas after we have carefully studied the text. 2) They also could be used to check whether our study has missed something or, 3), is on the wrong track. (4) They also help us solve problems that we still face after we have struggled long with a text.

For one who is looking for an introduction to inductive Bible study, I know of no better book than Robert A. Traina's *Methodical Bible Study*, published by Zondervan. I studied the content of this book at Asbury Seminary under Dr. Traina himself, and now I use what I learned there every day of my life.

BOOKS THAT TEACH THE SCRIPTURES

Over the years my most important way to be fed from the Word has been direct inductive Bible study. But I have also found great refreshment from books that teach the Scriptures. These include biblically based theological and devotional books and books of Bible expositions. Among my favorite authors of such books are Robert Coleman, Kent Hughes, Stanley Jones, Martyn Lloyd-Jones, Leon Morris, J. I. Packer, John Piper, A. T. Robertson, Oswald

Sanders, and John Stott. The published compendia of messages given at the Annual Keswick Conventions in England have also been a favorite source of spiritual food for me over the years.

The value of these books is that when we read them, we are fed by the Word rather than by the ideas of the writers. Some of these books have impacted me markedly and caused me to change my thinking on some topics or to include some completely new concepts as major themes in my counseling, discipling, preaching, and teaching.

As a young seminary student, I was greatly helped by a piece of wisdom the great missionary scholar Bishop Stephen Neill gave us when he visited at Asbury Seminary. He recommended that we take a meaty book and slowly go through it over a period of weeks, finding time to read whenever possible. I have done this with scores of books over the years. When I am reading such a book, I take it with me to many places so that I can squeeze in a few minutes of reading if some time opens up. The books may take several months to complete. Sometimes I do not even complete them. After slowly and meditatively reading a major portion of a book, I may sense that I have acquired its main message, and thus I move on to another book.

Roy Pearson has said, "When a minister stops studying, he simply stops."[20] Bishop Gerald Kennedy said, "Men who die mentally in the ministry are not murdered. They commit suicide."[21]

I heard about a minister who left the ministry and went into other work burned out and discouraged. He had even left his library behind in his last church. When his successor at this church came and went through the library, he found that most of the ex-pastor's earlier books were on Bible and theology while most of the books he had acquired more recently were books on practical topics. The ex-pastor was a typical product of our pragmatic age. Possibly his pragmatism did not give him the resources to remain fresh in ministry over a long period. How sad it is that many Christian leaders who used to spend long hours with the Scriptures in their early years as Christians do not do so anymore. And how dangerous that is for themselves and for those they lead.

HELPING OUR PEOPLE LOSE THEIR FEAR OF THE BIBLE

Another challenge we face today is that of helping our people to lose the fear of the Bible. Given the present-day negative attitude toward books, we can expect to find that the Bible intimidates many Christians. In many churches now hymnbooks have been replaced by the overhead projector, which is much more efficient, especially with contemporary styles of worship where one song follows immediately another. So books are getting scarce in the church, and many Christians are strangers to the Bible!

I can think of many things that we can do to address this problem.

• I usually announce a reading and wait till the audience finds the passage before starting to read. If there are new Christians in the audience, I will give some hints on how to find the passage. Sometimes I will have the audience read alternate verses so that they are all involved in the reading of the Bible. If I find that the version of the Bible I was planning to use is different from the Bible on the pews, I will use the pew Bible version instead. All this gives the audience a chance to handle the Bible. The more they do that, the more familiar they will become with it.

• I try to preach expository messages whenever possible. In this way they are able to see how the Bible is studied and applied, and they see biblical authority in practice. Such messages also give them a taste of the joy of Bible study. Several times people have told me after an expository message that they never realized that the Bible is such an exciting book. I try to give the audience time to look into the text when I am expounding it, so that they can follow with me as we go from verse to verse.

• Even when preaching topical messages, I try to buttress every major point I make from Scripture. Then the people will observe what we mean when we say that the Bible is the supreme authority for faith and practice. This type of topical preaching can actually be called expository preaching, as John Stott has pointed out, because it is derived from the Bible. In fact, Stott says, "all true Christian preaching is expository preaching."[22] A lot of topical preaching today simply takes a text from the Bible and uses it as a springboard to dive into a discussion of a topic the speaker wants to cover. The points made in those messages are not derived from the Bible.[23]

• Often while preaching I ask people something like, "What does this verse say?" Usually I find that many do not immediately look into the text to find an answer to that question. They are not used to keeping their minds so alert during a sermon as to respond to that immediately. So I wait until someone answers. When the people see me waiting, they are forced to look down and read. My hope is that many such experiences of reading will result in their Bible becoming familiar to them.

• The most effective means I know of developing "Bible Christians" is the small-group Bible study. Many small groups today give a lot of time to sharing, praying, and a message but very little time to getting the members to really study a Bible text for themselves. Sometimes the leader has the members quickly read a passage and then asks, "What does this passage say to you?" The authority has shifted from the Word to the reader. This is typical of the reader-centered hermeneutics advocated by postmodern thinkers. Here the subjective response of the reader to the text is more important than the objective content the writer wants to convey. A leader who is always asking questions from the text forces the members to look into the text to find out what it says. The ensuing discussion on how the text applies to the lives of members really helps the Bible to come alive and enables lives to be transformed by the Word.

Let us pray and work until once again evangelical Christians will be known as "Bible Christians," the term John Wesley liked to use to describe the early Methodists.

7

FACING WILD ANIMALS

IMMEDIATELY AFTER THE RECORD of the temptations of Jesus, Matthew and Mark report that the angels ministered to him. Mark adds a note about Christ being with the wild animals: "And he was with the wild animals, and the angels were ministering to him" (Mark 1:13).

WHAT ARE THESE WILD ANIMALS AND ANGELS DOING?[1]

In the Bible wild animals are frequently presented as being in league with the forces of evil. Ezekiel 34:5 says of the Israelites who were let down by their leaders: "So they were scattered, because there was no shepherd, and they became food for all the wild beasts." When warning against false teachers who lead believers astray, Paul said, "Look out for the dogs, look out for the evildoers, look out for those who mutilate the flesh" (Phil. 3:2). Similarly, here we could regard the animals as hostile forces. Also we notice that Jesus is in the desert. In the writings of the intertestamental period, the desert was often presented as a haunt for demons.

Commentators are divided about the role of the wild animals in this story. Some think that the animals were favorably disposed to him. Then this verse would be symbolizing the tranquility of the Messianic kingdom after the defeat of Satan. That is how it was before Adam and Eve sinned and how it will be in the future Messianic kingdom when the wild animals and other beings will live in harmony with each other and the rest of creation (Isa. 11:6-7; 65:25). According to this view, the verse under consideration would be a declaration that the Messianic kingdom has come.

I prefer to take the other view that the animals mentioned here are still hostile. Satan has not yet been defeated once and for all. He will come back later to assault Jesus and Christians. But if these animals represent a hostile presence, in the midst of the hostility the angels minister to Jesus. Actually either view does not change the ultimate meaning much, as the animals represent hostility in both views, though in one the hostility is over. As we look at our lives and ministries, we still face hostile forces.

Angels and wild animals appear together in Psalm 91. Verse 13 says, "You will tread on the lion and the adder; the young lion and the serpent you will trample underfoot." But verse 11 had already said, "For he will command his angels concerning you to guard you in all your ways." I believe that in the Mark passage this combination of wild animals and angels is similar to that in Psalm 91. Mark 1:13 is essentially a proclamation that though Jesus faced the powers that humans dread, the angels were there to minister to him.

The verb translated "ministered" (*diakoneō*) is often used in connection with feeding, providing food, or serving at meal tables (Luke 12:37; 17:8; Acts 6:2). The angels provided food for Elijah in the desert (1 Kings 19:5-8). Some commentators think that the ministry of the angels was that of providing Jesus with food. Whatever the exact meanings of these two figures of angels and wild beasts may be, what we can take for our lives and ministries is that we too will have to face hostile and sometimes terrifying forces, but God will minister to us through his agents.

EXTREME SITUATIONS AND GOD'S MINISTRY

The battle against hostile forces went on throughout the ministry of Jesus, especially as he faced the anger of the Jewish authorities who finally succeeded in putting him to death. He fought his biggest battle just before his death. This time it was not in a desert but in a garden. Luke describes his turmoil vividly: "And being in an agony he prayed more earnestly; and his sweat became like great drops of blood falling down to the ground" (Luke 22:44). Paul's explanation of the death of Christ gives us a hint as to why Jesus suffered so much in the garden: "For our sake [God] made him to be sin who knew no sin, so that in him we might become the righteousness of God" (2 Cor. 5:21). The one who is "of purer eyes than to see evil and cannot look at wrong" (Hab. 1:13) is being made to become sin! Thankfully none of us would ever face such turmoil. We are sinners and thus are incapable of being repelled by sin as Jesus was. Moreover we will never be asked to bear the sin of the world.

Luke says that at this time of deep turmoil, an angel ministered to Jesus in the garden: "And there appeared to him an angel from heaven, strengthening him" (Luke 22:43). But unexpectedly this reference to the angel's ministry comes *before* the reference to his agony. The angel's ministry did not remove his agony, but it gave him strength to face it—an ominous sign to Christ's followers that angelic ministry will not eliminate conflict from our lives and ministries.

In Acts angels again appeared in extreme situations to minister to the apostles. Peter and John were rescued from the public prison in Jerusalem (Acts 5:19), and Peter was rescued again from Herod's prison in Caesarea (Acts 12:7-10), each time by an angel. Paul was surely in an extreme situation after several days on a ship in a storm-tossed sea. He may have hardly eaten for days and thrown up whatever he ate. Considering what I experienced once after about three hours in a much less severe storm at sea, I can imagine that Paul's situation would have been deeply depressing. Suddenly an angel stood beside him and said, "Do not be afraid, Paul; you must stand before Caesar. And behold, God has granted you all those who sail with you" (Acts 27:24).

In each of these cases angels serve as agents of God in extreme situations. To be sure, angels have other roles in the Bible. In the birth narratives of Jesus and John and in the conversion stories of the Ethiopian eunuch (Acts 8:26) and Cornelius (Acts 10:3), angels are messengers and guides. In the death of Herod (Acts 12:23) and many other times, they are agents of judgment.

Do we encounter angels today? Hebrews 1:14 says that one of the ministries of angels is to serve believers: "Are they [angels] not all ministering spirits sent out to serve for the sake of those who are to inherit salvation?" "Serve" here is a rendering of the noun *diakonia*, which is related to the verb *diakoneö*, translated "ministered" in Mark 1:13. As John Wesley puts it, angels serve us "in numerous offices of protection, care, and kindness."[2] Perhaps angels have ministered to us without our being aware of it. Many people have had experiences after which they were clearly aware that angels had ministered to them.[3] Hebrews 1:14 convinces me that even though we may not see angels working on our behalf, they do serve us in our times of need.

There are two themes that we can apply to our lives as we look at the ministry of angels to Jesus and the apostles. First, we will also have extremely trying experiences in our lives and ministries, and, second, we too will have the specific ministry of God to our needs. This ministry gives us sufficient strength to face our trials. In fact, if we are aware of and anticipate God's ministry to us, we would have the strength and confidence in times of crisis to overcome the temptation to sin, to give up, to panic, or to use wrong methods.

I wish I could tell young people entering the ministry that their lives will be all excitement and joy. Indeed, they will be exciting; people surely won't be bored if they are serving Jesus. But often along with the joy will come conflicts and fears, heartaches and tears.

Many of God's choice servants have had to live with or suddenly face situations of extreme crisis. William Carey's wife went insane on the field sometime after her infant son died. Helen Roseveare was raped and held by rebels, and during a wave of anti-Western sentiment, she had to leave Congo—the country she had served so faithfully and sacrificially. George Mueller's orphanages often ran out of money to carry on and to provide food for the children. But God always provided through some highly unexpected means. John Wesley had a wife who did not understand his ministry, suspected him, and even worked to discredit his ministry. But all these people continued to serve God and experience God's sufficient grace and provision. Throughout the centuries those trying to evangelize the lost have faced severe disappointments, frustrations, and persecutions. But churches have grown amid these obstacles, sometimes after God's servants had left the field after faithfully preparing the ground for a rich harvest.

One of the saddest stories I have heard is about a successful pastor whose secretary accused him before the church board of trying to have an affair with her. The church believed the secretary, and he had to leave the ministry with great shame coming to him and his family. Several years later the secretary confessed that it was she who had wanted to have an affair with him and that he had resisted her advances. What she had said earlier was an angry response to being rejected by him. But because of her accusation, he was out of the ministry in shame for many years.

All the instances I have mentioned above are things we can really fear. We have no assurance in Scripture that such things won't happen to us. Perhaps some of them could have been avoided if the ministers had been wiser. But, if we are obedient to God in this fallen world, crises will come even though we are very wise in everything we do. The assurance we do have is that with God's help we can come out of these crises as "more than conquerors" (Rom. 8:37)—better off than we were before the crisis.

GOD'S MINISTRY TO OUR LIVES

I like the verb "minister" (*diakoneö*) used by Mark to describe the work of the angels. It usually takes the following meanings: "serve, wait on; care for, see after, provide for; serve as a deacon."[4] The corresponding noun, *diakonia,* is used in Hebrews 1:14 for the ministry of the angels with believers.

These are words that are often used of our ministries. So what we, as ministers of Christ, try to do to others, God does to us in abundant measure.

A similar idea is conveyed in 2 Corinthians 1 where Paul talks about how he faced an extreme situation in Asia. Here's how he described the crisis: ". . . we were so utterly burdened beyond our strength that we despaired of life itself. Indeed, we felt that we had received the sentence of death" (2 Cor. 1:8-9). But God helped him out. Paul says, "He delivered us from such a deadly peril, and he will deliver us. On him we have set our hope that he will deliver us again" (2 Cor. 1:10).

It is interesting that when Paul introduces the section about the crisis in Asia, he does it with a surprising spontaneous outburst of praise to God. This praise immediately follows, rather abruptly, the customary greeting with which the letter starts. He says, "Blessed be the God and Father of our Lord Jesus Christ, the Father of mercies and God of all comfort, who comforts us in all our affliction, so that we may be able to comfort those who are in any affliction, with the comfort with which we ourselves are comforted by God" (2 Cor. 1:3-4). Next he goes on to expand on the idea that the comfort that we have received enables us to have a ministry of comfort to others (vv. 5-6). Paul was obviously in raptures about the comfort of God whom he calls "the God of all comfort." His pain is not forgotten, but it has lost its sting, and the anger and fear has been replaced by joy over God's comfort.

A few verses later Paul will go into a rapturous exposition of the glory of the ministry (2:14—6:18). The problems have not made him bitter about the ministry. The comfort has compensated for the pain, and he has come out as more than a conqueror—filled with joy.

There is an extremely important lesson to learn about ministry here. The comfort or ministry of the Lord to us takes away the bitterness we experience over the way we have been treated by people and circumstances. When I turned fifty, I made a list of the biggest battles I face in my life and ministry. High up on that list was the battle with anger over the way people have treated me. After we have sacrificed so much in ministry, it is really tough to hear the accusations people make against us and to face the crises that come. But the comfort of the Lord takes away bitterness. And, thank God, he does comfort more than adequately.

One of the saddest sights in the church today is that of Christian workers who are angry—angry over the way they have been hurt by others, by circumstances, and sometimes, they feel, even by God. And there are many ministers and leaders in this condition today. Perhaps the pain and disappointment that some people have carried from the time they were children is so severe that these blows add to already existing wounds, cause these to resurface, and add to the sense that life has been hard on them. How I wish that they would go to God and receive his healing. I have sometimes talked with leaders who I felt did not want to be healed, for that would take away their reason for anger. We sometimes think that we can punish the people who hurt us by remaining hurt and angry! We don't want victory over our pain, for that would seem to reduce the severity of the wrong done to us.

Trying to help such people has been one of the hardest challenges I have faced in my life. I do not know whether I have been very successful. But this I know: God does comfort. We must go to him in our desperation and cling to him. As we linger in his presence, we become like a frightened child with his head on the lap of his mother. In this position the Lord strokes our head, like the mother does, until our fear and anger subside. A ray of light creeps through the dark clouds. We reason, "God has acted on my behalf." We are no longer overwhelmed by the problem.

If we pursue this light, soon we will realize that God's love is greater than the wickedness of the people who hurt us. Then we will realize that because he is sovereign, he will turn this situation into something good (Rom. 8:28), that we will be "more than conquerors" (Rom. 8:37). The pain, of course, may remain, for the loving heart must hurt when others do evil, but the bitterness is gone. If God's love is greater and he is turning this evil into good, we have no reason to be bitter. In fact, we have a good reason to forgive the persons who hurt us.

The comfort of the Lord comes in more tangible ways too; thus the phrase "angel unawares" came into use. We are sometimes amazed by the specific way in which God ministers to us. It may be through an act of kindness by somebody, a check that comes in the mail, reading the Scriptures, hearing a message, or reading a book. These actions are clear evidence that God has seen our need and intervened on our behalf.

Not only does the bitterness leave us, but this experience becomes an aid to helping others with similar problems. Paul says in 2 Corinthians 1:4-7 of the comfort he received: God "comforts us in all our affliction, so that we may be able to comfort those who are in any affliction, with the comfort with which we ourselves are comforted by God" (2 Cor. 1:4). Today the term "wounded healer" is used of Jesus and also of effective ministers. But before they can be effective in healing wounds, they themselves should be healed (or comforted) by God.

So we will all face wild beasts in our lives and ministries. But, thank God, he knows what we need and will minister to us. As I close this chapter, may

I make a passionate plea to you? I have seen too many good people whose lives are ruined by the actions of bad people. Those bad people should not be allowed to have such a powerful impact upon us! God's grace is adequate to minister to you. Perhaps that grace is going to be mediated by someone else. If so, seek that help as a matter of urgency. Don't let a day pass without waging this war against bitterness by utilizing the sufficient grace and comfort of God.

8

BEARING GOOD NEWS

MARK BEGAN HIS GOSPEL with the words: "The beginning of the gospel of Jesus Christ, the Son of God" (1:1). But he does not mention the birth and boyhood of Jesus. In keeping with Mark's "vivid and fast-paced writing"[1] style, he seems to want to get to the main point at once—the ministry of Jesus.

THE LONG-ANTICIPATED GOSPEL

When we read the first few verses of Mark, we sense that he is heading in a particular direction. He wants to show that Jesus is the long-anticipated one. Immediately after the first verse, he goes on to describe the ministry of John the Baptist, focusing on his role as the forerunner to Jesus. Verses 2 and 3 say that his role was to "prepare the way of the Lord." John himself knew that. So he talks glowingly of the coming Christ. He proclaims his unworthiness in comparison to Jesus: "After me comes he who is mightier than I, the strap of whose sandals I am not worthy to stoop down and untie" (1:7). And he shows how much greater Jesus' ministry is than his own ministry: "I have baptized you with water, but he will baptize you with the Holy Spirit" (1:8).

If Mark's description of John's ministry indicates an anticipation of Jesus' ministry, Mark's description of the start of Jesus' ministry expresses this anticipation even more strikingly. Mark writes, "Now after John was arrested, Jesus came into Galilee, proclaiming the gospel of God" (1:14). Mark's mention of the arrest of John suggests that the era of John's spectacular ministry is now over and that Jesus' ministry replaces it in God's agenda. The next verse summarizes Jesus' message: "The time is fulfilled, and the kingdom of God is at hand; repent and believe in the gospel" (1:15). There is a sense here that what people had been yearning for has finally come. Larry Hurtado points to an ancient Jewish prayer: "May God establish his kingdom in our lifetime." He says, "Jesus' announcement is to be heard in the context of the hope reflected in that prayer."[2]

This yearning anticipation for the coming of the gospel is mentioned several times in the New Testament. Jesus said, "But blessed are your eyes, for they see, and your ears, for they hear. Truly, I say to you, many prophets and righteous people longed to see what you see, and did not see it, and to hear what you hear, and did not hear it" (Matt. 13:16-17). Peter said, "Concerning this salvation, the prophets who prophesied about the grace that was to be yours searched and inquired carefully, inquiring what person or time the Spirit of Christ in them was indicating when he predicted the sufferings of Christ and the subsequent glories. It was revealed to them that they were serving not themselves but you, in the things that have now been announced to you . . . things into which angels long to look" (1 Peter 1:10-12). The Christmas carol "O Holy Night" describes this anticipation well: "Long lay the world in sin and error pining, till Christ appeared and the soul felt its worth."

The words of Mark 1:14-15 tell us a lot about what our work is. We too, like Jesus, are "proclaiming the gospel of God." We too proclaim, "The time is fulfilled, and the kingdom of God is at hand; repent and believe in the gospel." The word translated "gospel" (*euangelion*) in these two verses means "good news." This word represents a good summary of what we have said above. Our task is indeed a wonderfully significant one that should fill us with joy over our call. The reformer and Bible translator William Tyndale (c. 1494-1536) expressed his excitement over the gospel in the preface to his New Testament. He said that the word *gospel* "signified good, merry, glad and joyful tidings, that makes a person's heart glad, and makes him sing, dance and leap for joy."[3] Tyndale gave his life for the sake of that gospel at the age of forty-two. Such good news is so important that it is worth dying for.

Psychologists say that if people sense that what they are doing with their life is significant, then they will be happy. Joy is one of the rewards of Christian ministry. Despite the many problems, we can feel good about what we do because, whether people accept it or not, we are proclaiming the most important message that people can hear. Isaiah faced powerful opposition to his message, opposition about which God warned him when he received his call (Isa. 6:9-10). But Isaiah says, "How beautiful upon the mountains are the feet of him who brings good news, who publishes peace, who brings good news of happiness, who publishes salvation, who says to Zion, 'Your God reigns'" (Isa. 52:7).

THE COMPULSION OF TRUTH

Realizing the nature of the gospel gives the minister of the Word a sense of compulsion. We realize that this is God's message to fallen humanity; hence the seriousness of our task. Paul expressed this compulsion when he said, "Necessity is laid upon me. Woe to me if I do not preach the gospel!" (1 Cor. 9:16). The Scottish Puritan preacher Richard Baxter (1615-1691) said, "I preach as never sure to preach again, as a dying man to dying men."[4]

This compulsion is well expressed in an episode from the life of Jeremiah. Pashhur, the chief officer of the temple, supposedly the official representative of God, has attacked this prophet of God. Jeremiah is beaten and put in the stocks overnight on the temple premises. After his release, Jeremiah complains to God: "O LORD, you have deceived me, and I was deceived; you are stronger than I, and you have prevailed. I have become a laughingstock all the day, everyone mocks me. . . . For the word of the LORD has become for me a reproach and derision all day long" (Jer. 20:7-8). He considers the prospect of giving up the ministry, but he realizes that he cannot. He says, "If I say, 'I will not mention him, or speak any more in his name,' there is in my heart as it were a burning fire shut up in my bones, and I am weary with holding it in, and I cannot" (20:9). Truth has a way of burning, as the disciples on the road to Emmaus found out. After their encounter with the risen Christ, they said, "Did not our hearts burn within us while he talked to us on the road, while he opened to us the Scriptures?" (Luke 24:32).

Several related reasons are given for such compulsion in the New Testament, and they are all related to the fact that the gospel is true. First, *the gospel is God's revelation.* As Amos said, "The Lord GOD has spoken; who can but prophesy?" (Amos 3:8). The early apostles expressed this attitude when the Jewish authorities "charged them not to speak or teach at all in the name of Jesus" (Acts 4:18). Their answer was, "Whether it is right in the sight of God to listen to you rather than to God, you must judge, for we cannot but speak of what we have seen and heard" (4:19-20). And we, who know these facts to be true, are similarly compelled to preach the gospel.

Second, we are compelled by the knowledge that *the gospel describes what God has done to save humanity.* This type of compulsion is seen in 2 Corinthians 5 where Paul describes his motivation to mission. His strongest expression of compulsion is in verse 14: "The love of Christ controls us." The word translated "controls," *sunechō* (compels—NIV, urges us on—NRSV, constraineth—KJV), is a strong word that refers to a powerful pressure being exerted on Paul. When we consider this verse, we often overlook the fact that

Paul goes on to give a reason for this strong compulsion of love. He immediately says, " . . . because we have concluded this: that one has died for all, therefore all have died; and he died for all, that those who live might no longer live for themselves but for him who for their sake died and was raised" (2 Cor. 5:14-15). The truth of the gospel—the fact that Christ has died for all, and therefore all should be living for him—caused the compulsion of love.

Third, we are also compelled by the fact that *the gospel we preach has the power to bring salvation to people*. Paul expressed his compulsion in three ways in Romans 1:14-16. First, he said, "I am *under obligation* both to Greeks and to barbarians, both to the wise and to the foolish" (1:14, italics mine). Second, he says, "So I am *eager* to preach the gospel to you also who are in Rome" (1:15, italics mine). Third, he says, "For I am *not ashamed* of the gospel. . . ." This verse goes on to give the reason for the compulsion: " . . . for it is the power of God for salvation to everyone who believes" (1:16, italics mine).

Fourth, we are compelled by *the knowledge that those without Christ are lost and without hope*. Paul expressed this compulsion in Romans 9:1-3: "I am speaking the truth in Christ—I am not lying; my conscience bears me witness in the Holy Spirit—that I have great sorrow and unceasing anguish in my heart. For I could wish that I myself were accursed and cut off from Christ for the sake of my brothers, my kinsmen according to the flesh." The passage goes on to show that the reason for this compulsion was the fact that the Jews had rejected the gospel and were thus lost. Jude describes how the awareness of this lostness influences ministry: " . . . save others by snatching them out of the fire" (Jude 23).

The fact of lostness gave urgency to the ministry of some of the great ministers of the past and helped them persevere amidst much hardship. Hudson Taylor said, "I would have never thought of going to China had I not believed that the Chinese were lost and needed Christ." The American evangelist D. L. Moody told an audience in London, "If I believed there was no hell, I am sure I would be off tomorrow for America." He said he would give up going from town to town and spending day and night "urging men to escape the damnation of hell."[5]

So we have a compulsion based on four truth-related features of the gospel. A report in the *London Daily Mail* during one of Billy Graham's early campaigns in England explains this urgency that comes from a conviction that the gospel is the truth. It said, "He has no magnetism; he has no appeal to the emotions. His power—and power he has—is the indivisible conviction that he knows the right way of life."[6]

Such conviction will have a profound influence upon our understanding of mission. We live in an age of religious relativism and pluralism that frowns at the idea of religious conversion. It rejects the idea of absolute truth—that is, truth that is so true, so perfect, so complete, and so important that everybody everywhere must accept it. It is because we believe that God has spoken the definitive word to humanity that we have the audacity to call people of other faiths to conversion to Christ in this pluralistic environment.

I was once traveling by train to a predominantly Buddhist area where we had a ministry. I was seated next to a Buddhist government official with whom I struck up a conversation. When he realized that I, a Christian worker, was going to a Buddhist area, he asked me a question that is in the minds of many in our religiously pluralistic nation. He asked me why we Christians go to Buddhist areas and try to convert Buddhists. He pointed to the disruption that takes place in these villages because of this activity.

I told him that we believe that there is a God who created this world and that this God has provided the answer to the deep problems that plague the world. I said that we have discovered this answer. Now that we know it, we must share it. It would be selfish and unloving for us not to tell others. I do not know what his response to this answer was. But I think he at least understood why Christians are so eager to share their faith with people of other faiths.

Such truth-related compulsion can produce the type of urgency that enables us to persevere amidst hardship; and indeed it can give us a reason for taking on hardship. Jesus often talked about the price we pay because of the gospel. He described those who have "left house or brothers or sisters or mother or father or children or lands, for my sake and for the gospel" (Mark 10:29). In his basic call to discipleship, he said, "For whoever would save his life will lose it, but whoever loses his life for my sake and the gospel's will save it" (Mark 8:35).

If we were to define greatness as the ability to persevere with a difficult but important work amidst much hardship and deprivation, then we could say that the realization of the nature of the gospel should spur Christians on to achieve greatness. It should help those called to work among resistant people to persevere without visible fruit. It should challenge people to refuse the temptation to give up sharing the gospel when persecution and other trials hit them. We have seen many examples of such greatness in the past. Can we expect to see this greatness today?

This sense of the truthfulness of the gospel will also make the gospel something delightful, in the same way that the truthfulness of the Scriptures makes them delightful, as we saw in chapter 6. This reality also gives meaning to our ministry. I have had times when I was so exhausted or discouraged that the last thing I wanted to do was to preach. But that is my job, and I cannot miss appointments saying that I did not feel like preaching. I would drag myself to sit down and go through my notes before preaching. But as I read these notes, I am gripped with a sense that what I am going to preach is true—wonderfully true! The urgency returns, and the tiredness and discouragement are forgotten in the excitement of being able to preach such a wonderful message.

We could see how such an approach to truth could help us to keep ministering over a long period without losing our enthusiasm. Gypsy Smith (1860-1947), a powerful British evangelist, was born in a gypsy tent and had very little education. He preached the gospel from the age of seventeen until he died at sea at age eighty-seven on his way to America for a preaching mission. Someone asked him the secret of his freshness and vigor even in his old age. Smith replied, "I have never lost the wonder."[7]

COMPULSION AND THE POSTMODERN MOOD

I think there is a major hindrance today to fostering the type of compulsion I have described above. All four reasons presented for compulsion were objective truths about the gospel. But we live in the postmodern age where people are not naturally inclined to be as motivated by objective truth as in previous ages. The postmodern revolt against the objective is a reaction to the heavy emphasis on the rational that characterized the modern era. Postmodernists think that factors outside of people (objective factors) such as authoritative truths and doctrines and the demands of productivity and profitability tyrannized them, deprived them of expressing essential aspects of their nature, and left them incomplete and unfulfilled. So there is a greater emphasis on subjective or personal truth, which has its focus on the subject (me), rather than objective truth, which has its source in an object outside of us (such as God or the Bible).

While most evangelical Christian workers will subscribe to the supreme authority of the Bible, most of us have been affected by this mood. We have been influenced by our environment to devalue our understanding of the power and relevance of objective truth. Therefore, we may not think that preaching and the Word of God are as relevant and powerful to change lives and attract people as ministers of a previous generation did.

There is a shift in styles. A somewhat isolated society, which places high value on physical work, may regard relatively fat but physically strong women as very attractive. Gradually, with influence from the outside world and technological advances, that value may change drastically. Thinner women, who were once considered unattractive, become highly valued. Similarly those heavily influenced by a society that places high value on subjective factors would gradually lose some of their sense of the value of objective truth. I believe this has happened to many Christians.

Consequently, a major feature that attracted people to the gospel in previous generations—the urgency coming from the sense that it is absolutely true—would be much less a feature of the church. It seems that in place of urgency, some growing churches are attracting people through entertainment. Growing churches generally serve a high-quality program that is attractive and entertaining. As one involved in youth ministry, I can testify to effectiveness of entertainment in attracting people outside the church so that they come within the sound of the gospel.

But entertainment must always be a servant of truth. Unfortunately, given our pragmatism, we may sometimes neglect some important objective truths such as the Atonement, the reality of judgment, and the need for holiness because those concepts are not very entertaining. These doctrines don't seem to produce good subjective feelings, and that factor may, in practice, be more influential in determining a church program than the fact that a given truth is a biblical doctrine. So we could produce a generation of Christians who do not include many unpleasant doctrines in their worldview (their basic approach to life). The result will be an unhealthy church.

Today we have a great challenge to be both relevant and true to the Scriptures. We need to restore our trust in the value of truth and then "not shrink from declaring . . . the *whole* counsel of God" (Acts 20:27, italics mine), including the tough doctrines. Trust in the value of truth will also give us an urgency that, I believe, can still attract people to Christ, as it did in earlier generations. The urgency would spur us on to find the most relevant means of communicating the eternal, unchanging truth of the gospel. If entertainment is such a means, we will use it, within the confines permitted by Scripture.

The church in every era needs to be countercultural in areas where the culture clashes with biblical emphases. The biblical emphasis on the primacy of the absolute truth of the gospel certainly clashes with the postmodern distaste for objective truth and rejection of the idea of absolute truth. The biblical emphasis on the importance of authentic spirituality and subjective experience, however, touches on a felt need and interest of postmodern people. Our challenge is to present the gospel in such a way that our hearers understand that it is based on objective truths and also that it gives rise to deeply satisfying subjective experiences.

THE GOSPEL OF THE KINGDOM

Mark's description of Jesus' message in 1:15 includes four features. First Jesus said, "The time is fulfilled," and we looked at that above under the heading, "The Long-Anticipated Gospel." Next Jesus said, "and the kingdom of God is at hand." The third and fourth features represent the human response to the message. We are to "repent and believe in the gospel."

The Kingdom of God

The coming of the kingdom indicated that God has begun to establish his rule over this world, which many devout Jews at that time viewed as being under the tyranny of Satan and evil.[8] It is of course true that the kingdom of God was always here even in Old Testament times. But the coming of Christ brought God's rule in a way that could be said to have inaugurated the new "age to come," for which the Jews were waiting. So Jesus said, "But if it is by the finger of God that I cast out demons, then the kingdom of God has come upon you" (Luke 11:20).

Jesus gave several parables that explain how this kingdom will grow from small beginnings until it finally conquers the world (see Matt. 13). This consummation, when the kingdom takes on its full power and glory, will take place only after Christ returns to complete the destruction of these enemies (1 Cor. 15:23-28). At that time the righteous will fully inherit the kingdom (Matt. 25:31-34).

In the meantime we live in the present age where features of the new age have mingled with the features of the old age. We await the consummation but experience "a foretaste of glory divine." On the one hand we are filled with peace and joy, so that Paul says, "For the kingdom of God is not a matter of eating and drinking but of righteousness and peace and joy in the Holy Spirit" (Rom. 14:17). On the other hand Paul says, "We . . . who have the firstfruits of the Spirit, groan inwardly as we wait eagerly for adoption as sons, the redemption of our bodies" (Rom. 8:23). In recent years few people have helped the church understand the meaning of the kingdom as much as the American New Testament scholar George E. Ladd. The title of one of his many books on the kingdom expresses this mingling of the old age and the age to come well. The book is called *The Presence of the Future.* [9]

During this present age we must always be vigilant, for we do not know when the Master will return. Therefore several times in the New Testament we are asked to be watchful and ready for his coming (e.g., Matt. 24—25; Luke 12:35-48). One way to be vigilant is to pursue a life of holiness (Titus 2:12-14; 2 Peter 3:11-12). Another way is to be doing the work that has been entrusted to us (Matt. 24:46). Jesus reiterated this point using various parables (e.g., Matt. 24:45-51; 25:14-46).

We even have a part to play in bringing in the consummation of this kingdom. In fact, Peter said that we can hasten the coming of this day (2 Peter 3:12). Jesus gave a clue as to how we can do this when he said, "This gospel of the kingdom will be proclaimed throughout the whole world as a testimony to all nations, and then the end will come" (Matt. 24:14). G. E. Ladd says, "Perhaps the most important single verse in the Word of God for God's people today is . . . Matthew 24:14."[10] This is because it presents what should be the most important agenda in the church's program: the taking of the gospel to the whole world.

Interestingly, Paul does not mention the kingdom much in his Epistles, and neither does Luke in Acts. It could be that the early church refrained from using this word too much (though it does appear a few times in Acts and Paul's Epistles), as it may have been misunderstood as referring to an earthly kingdom. Then the Christians could be accused of treason against the Roman Empire. Both Acts and the Epistles use the word *Lord* for Jesus many times. This word is used often in the Gospels too (though less frequently). It seems that what is intended by the king and the kingdom in the Gospels is communicated with the use of the word *Lord* in the Epistles.

Repentance

The third and fourth features of the announcement of Jesus in Mark 1:15 show how people can enter the kingdom: They are to "repent and believe in the gospel" (Mark 1:15). Jesus explained this more clearly when he said, "Whoever humbles himself like this child is the greatest in the kingdom of heaven" (Matt. 18:4). So radical is this entrance to the kingdom that Jesus described it as being born again (John 3:3).

Jesus' message includes a call to repentance, similar to John the Baptist's (Mark 1:4). Donald English warns of the danger of understanding repentance too narrowly, as evangelical preachers have often done. He says, "Fundamentally it means 'a changing of direction,' 'turning back,' 'change of mind.'"[11] When we respond to the gospel, we change the direction of our lives from trusting self and other idols to trusting in God.

Yet both John and Jesus were quite specific about the things that people need to repent of. John told different categories of people the different ways in which their repentance should be expressed. He said to the crowds, "Whoever has two tunics is to share with him who has none, and whoever has food is to do likewise." He asked tax collectors to collect no more than they were authorized to take. He told the soldiers, "Do not extort money from anyone by threats or by false accusation, and be content with your wages" (Luke 3:7-14). Jesus told the rich young man to sell what he had and give it to the poor, and then come and follow him (Luke 18:22-25). Specifics help people to understand what is involved in repentance.

Both John and Jesus were also forthright in warning their hearers of the consequences of not repenting. We know that most of the statements about hell in the Bible come from the lips of Christ. Paul says, "Do you not know that the unrighteous will not inherit the kingdom of God? Do not be deceived: neither the sexually immoral, nor idolaters, nor adulterers, nor men who practice homosexuality, nor thieves, nor the greedy, nor drunkards, nor revilers, nor swindlers will inherit the kingdom of God" (1 Cor. 6:9-10).

Today many of our hearers would react very negatively if we spoke the way Jesus and Paul did. We have developed such an attitude toward our private lives that when preachers specifically mention sins that require repentance, they are accused of meddling and somehow doing something inappropriate.

The failure to be specific in our call to repentance could result in people not realizing that Christianity cannot coexist with some terrible sins. I think this is why many evangelical churches have had a bad record in terms of social sins committed by their members. When preachers called people to repentance, they mentioned personal sins such as drunkenness, sexual immorality, and dishonesty, but they did not mention sins such as treating people as inferior, prejudice, and underpaying workers. The result was that people who stoutly defended orthodoxy were guilty of these social sins, and many of them were not told that Christians don't do such things or have such attitudes.

Ministers in every era need to look through the eyes of Scripture at their cultures and see what sins they need to be alert to. I can think of several such areas that are important today. Paul's list above from 1 Corinthians 6 mentions that people indulging in sexual immorality, adultery, and homosexual practice cannot inherit the kingdom. Considering how many churchgoers are indulging in sex outside marriage, we need to be warning our hearers that such cannot go to heaven!

The Old Testament in particular talks a lot about the sin of exploiting the poor, but that is still happening, especially in poorer countries, where even Christian businesspeople underpay their workers. It has been shocking to note how often in history Christians have been guilty of racism and prejudice. Is this because the preachers did not warn them about the seriousness of these sins? In Sri Lanka, where we suffer daily as a result of an ethnic conflict, preachers very rarely speak of the sin of ethnic prejudice! Sometimes the way preachers speak shows that even they have not overcome their prejudices.

In Sri Lanka we find that many Christians have imbibed the cultural practices of the people among whom they live. Husbands sometimes exploit their wives. Mothers go abroad in search of money for the family, leaving their children for long periods so that they are sometimes woefully neglected and subjected to abuse. In our preaching we need to be bringing up such issues and warning our people not to be carried away into conformity with the society in which they live.

Belief

The fourth feature Jesus mentions in his summary in Mark 1:15 is "believe in the gospel." This feature is mentioned often by Jesus, but it is Paul who gives the fullest exposition of it. Belief is the other side of the coin to repentance. When we turn from sin, we see God waiting to accept us based on what Jesus has done for us, and we run to his arms and ask him to look after us. That is what belief is like. After we repent from trying to run our lives, we entrust our lives to God, believing that what he has done for us in Christ is indeed sufficient for our salvation.

THE MINISTER'S AUTHORITY

The first chapter of Mark clearly demonstrates the authority of Jesus. He had the authority to call people to repent and believe in order to enter the kingdom of God (1:15). Then we see his authority to call some fishermen to leave their nets and follow him (1:16-20). Then he goes to Capernaum and teaches in the synagogue, "and," says Mark, "they were astonished at his teaching, for he taught them as one who had authority, and not as the scribes" (1:21-22).

And we too have something of this authority. Certainly it is not an authority inherent to us, for in that sense Jesus was in a class by himself. Paul says we are merely "jars of clay." But he also says that in these jars is the treasure of the gospel (2 Cor. 4:7). Jesus entrusted us with the task of proclaiming this gospel to the ends of the earth. He told his disciples, "As the Father has sent me, even so I am sending you" (John 20:21). It is interesting that in Matthew, prior to giving the Great Commission, he says, "All authority in heaven and on earth has been given to me" (Matt. 28:18). This is followed by the Commission: "Go therefore and make disciples of all nations, baptizing them . . ." (28:19). The one who has all authority has entrusted us with a commission, and we are to proclaim this message with confidence based on his authority. We are to attempt to preach this gospel everywhere in the world. Even when people do not want the gospel preached in some areas, we will attempt to do it because the Lord of the universe has asked us to do so, and his authority is higher than that of all other earthly authority.

Preachers, especially evangelical preachers, have been accused of arrogance because of the authority with which they proclaim their message. Therefore it would be good for us to reflect on the nature of our authority. Paul's statement in 2 Corinthians 4:5 explains: "For what we proclaim is not ourselves, but Jesus Christ as Lord, with ourselves as your servants for Jesus' sake" (2 Cor. 4:5). The word Paul used here, *doulos,* is better translated as slave or bondservant.[12] We are slaves of our hearers. Slaves in those days had a lot of responsibilities. Sometimes they were even more educated than their masters. But their status did not allow them to be arrogant. So we cannot be arrogant either.

We are preaching about the one who is Lord of the universe, and we know that this message is true. Therefore we can preach with authority. But as to our lifestyle, we must be known as humble servants. I believe that one of the greatest challenges facing the church in this pluralistic age is for Christians who preach the unique and authoritative gospel to also demonstrate radical servanthood.

We must also remember that our commitment is not to authority but to the truth that is in Jesus. Some preachers are afraid to say that they do not know or are not fully certain of the answers to some questions. Some are afraid to admit that they may have been wrong about certain things they have said. They fear that such uncertainty will undermine their authority. But ultimately by refusing to admit faults and uncertainties, they may end up undermining their authority anyway. When something that they proclaimed with authority is proved to be wrong, then their hearers begin to despair of the possibility of being certain about anything at all.

Teaching people to respect the authority of the Bible and proclaiming what the Bible clearly teaches with authority is a much safer route to take. When we are uncertain of what the Bible says about a topic or whether the

Bible says anything at all about that topic, we should simply state that. Then people would continue to respect the Bible as their authority, while being aware that there is much more to learn and grapple with in their spiritual pilgrimage.

If we make a mistake in something we say, we will correct ourselves, because we do not want our message to be spoiled by untruth and because truth is more important than our reputation. I am very careless with numbers, and sometimes this weakness surfaces in my preaching. Shortly after giving a number, I may realize that the figure I gave was incorrect. For example, I may say, "There was a big audience at the meeting," when actually there were only about a hundred people there. Then I would need to correct myself immediately by saying something like, "Well, actually it was not a big audience. There were about a hundred there." This is a bit humiliating, and I find that often the audience laughs when I make the correction. But it is so important that we preachers speak the truth that the humiliation is worth facing in order to protect the integrity of our message. We are servants of truth. The authority is there!

We can be thankful that the Bible does have something authoritative to say about all the issues of life that are of eternal significance. So we can speak with passion, conviction, and authority about these things without compromising our integrity.

Preachers then do have authority, but it is a derived authority. First it is *derived from the Scriptures on which we base our message.* For this reason when preachers lose their confidence in the Word, they also often lose their passion. I know some godly ministers in Sri Lanka who were once passionate preachers. They went for theological studies, and during this time they discarded their belief in the infallibility of Scripture. They remained godly people, and I still admire and respect them for this and would like to learn from their example. But they lost their passion, and with that their preaching lost much of its power.

So preachers need to grapple with doubts they have about the authority of the Bible. Many great preachers have gone through such doubts. But they have grappled with them until they came through with their confidence in the Word restored. Older Christians must be sympathetic with those who have these battles, and they should try to help them without condemning them for asking difficult questions. Often the insensitive responses to doubters frustrate the doubters and make wholesome wrestling with problems difficult to do. But there is so much at stake in this battle that those who struggle with doubt must do so to a finish.

Billy Graham had such a battle when he was thirty years old. There were questions his friend and fellow Youth for Christ evangelist Charles Templeton (who later abandoned Christianity[13]) and others were asking that he could not answer. Billy was deeply troubled by doubts. It all came to a head at a conference under the leadership of the great Bible teacher Henrietta Mears, held at Forest Home, a retreat center in California. One night he came to the point of saying that he was going to accept what the Bible says "by faith," even though he could not answer some of the questions his friends were raising.[14]

Graham says this step "gave power and authority to my preaching that has never left me. The gospel in my hands became a hammer and a flame. . . . I felt as though I had a rapier in my hands and through the power of the Bible was slashing deeply into men's consciences, leading them to surrender to God."[15]

The great British Bible expositor G. Campbell Morgan also had such a battle. He was a young man when he read authors such as Darwin, Huxley, and other progressive thinkers. He then began to question some of his beliefs. The result was what has been called three ambivalent years. He read many books for and against belief in the Bible and what it teaches.

This is how his daughter-in-law and biographer Jill Morgan explains what happened: "At last the crisis came when he admitted to himself his total lack of assurance that the Bible was the authoritative Word of God to man. He immediately cancelled all preaching engagements. Then, taking all his books, both those attacking and those defending the Bible, he put them all in a corner cupboard." After locking the door of the cupboard, he went to a bookstore and bought a new Bible.

Returning to his room, Morgan said to himself, "I am no longer sure that this is what my father claims it to be—the Word of God. But of this I *am* sure: If it *be* the Word of God, and if I come to it with an unprejudiced and open mind, it will bring assurance to my soul of itself." He gave himself to reading the Bible. "That Bible *found* me!" he said. "I began to read and study it then, in 1883. I have been a student ever since, and I still am [in 1938]."[16]

Now everyone may not solve their problems about the Scriptures in the same way that Graham and Morgan did. I did not have serious doubts about the authority of Scripture in the same way (my biggest doubts were about whether some of the things that the Bible taught really worked). But I encountered strong skepticism about the Bible in my church in my teenage years, and I encountered battles among Christians regarding the extent of the Bible's infallibility when I was a theological student.

My first Christmas vacation as a seminary student was the decisive time for me. I was in the home of my elder brother, and I carefully went through J. I. Packer's book *"Fundamentalism" and the Word of God.* I became convinced that there was an intellectually sound case for believing in the infallibility of the Scriptures. And I see that as a decisive step in my pilgrimage as a preacher.[17]

Today we find that some Christians are very proud of their doubts and do not attempt to resolve them. Perhaps this is a reaction to the shallow dogmatism and easy-believism often seen in evangelical circles. Yet I believe that some people are using these problems as an excuse for intellectual and spiritual laziness. When confronted by others about their uncertainty, they say they are "working on it." But in reality they are not waging an all-out battle to find an answer to their problems. That uncertainty will leave them ineffective and without a real message to give to the world.[18]

Second, our authority is *derived from the call we have received from God to preach the Word.* The Bible says that all believers have gifts that can be used for God's service. When these gifts are used in the body, then each one in the body becomes equally important (1 Cor. 12). But it also says that the gifts have been carefully apportioned by God (Rom. 12:3; 1 Cor. 12:11; Eph. 4:7). Therefore all are not called to preach.

Those who become vocational preachers should have a conviction that they have been called to preach. How often Paul mentioned the fact that he was called and/or set apart for his work (Rom. 1:1; 1 Cor. 1:1; Gal. 1:15-16; 1 Tim. 1:12-16). This conviction comes in different ways. Indeed there will be times of discouragement when we will have doubts about our call. But one who is called to the ministry will have an abiding impression that this is the work that God has given him or her to do.

Dennis Kinlaw, in his powerful book *Preaching in the Spirit,* tells the story of the first time a great preacher of an earlier generation, John R. Church, preached. This is how Church described it: "The first sermon I ever preached had thirty-six points in it, and when I stood up I couldn't remember a single one of them. I had to sit down in total humiliation; my mind was a complete blank. It was a little country church in the mountains of North Carolina, and as soon as the service ended, I went running out of the door. My father finally caught up with me. He came down the dirt road with his lantern and walked beside me in solemn silence for a few minutes. Finally, he said, 'God knows you can't preach. I know you can't preach. Now the whole community knows you can't preach. For God's sake, don't put the family through that again.'"

Church's reply was, "'Dad, I'm sure you know I can't preach. I know I can't preach. But if God knows I can't preach, why doesn't he take the burden off me? Dad, I've got to preach.'" That young man had a call to preach![19] I wrote this section in the home of my friend Philip Brooks, who had heard Church preach shortly before he died. Philip told me that even in his old age, Church was a brilliant preacher with an amazing gift of oratory!

Third, our authority is *derived from the Holy Spirit who anoints us to preach*. We looked at this aspect in chapter 2.

So as for our lifestyle, we will strive to be humble servants of the people we serve. As for our message, we will proclaim it with passion and conviction because we know that the gospel is true.

GROWING IN A TEAM

IMMEDIATELY AFTER THE RECORD of the start of Jesus' preaching ministry in Mark 1.15 is a description of the calling of the first disciples (vv. 16 20). The fishermen Simon and his brother Andrew were casting their net into the sea when Jesus told them, "Follow me, and I will make you become fishers of men" (v. 17). This is followed by the call of two other fishermen, James and his brother John (vv. 19-20). From this point on, right until the Ascension, the Gospels give a prominent place to the disciples of Jesus. Among the last things Jesus did before his death was to spend an extended time with these disciples. And after the Resurrection he seemed to spend his time on earth almost exclusively with them.

We will look at the way Jesus trained these disciples in the following two chapters. Here we will look at how Jesus built his disciples into a team and at some of the implications for our lives of this understanding of team ministry.

TEAM MINISTRY IN THE NEW TESTAMENT

It is clear that team ministry was the standard model of ministry in the New Testament. The twelve disciples were the basic team with which Jesus did his ministry. Sometimes the group was subdivided into smaller teams. When Jesus sent out his twelve apostles and seventy disciples, they were sent out two by two (Mark 6:7; Luke 10:1). The context of the team was also his model for training ministers. A large portion of Christ's teaching in the Gospels is given to the Twelve.

This group ended up as his friends. Toward the end of his life he told them, "No longer do I call you servants, for the servant does not know what his master is doing; but I have called you friends, for all that I have heard from my Father I have made known to you" (John 15:15). Here is a beautiful example of the way friendship became the environment for making disciples. And the heart of friendship, according to this passage, is that Jesus shared with them all that he knew.

The pattern of team ministry is also seen in the book of Acts. When Peter rose to speak on the day of Pentecost, he stood up "with the eleven" (2:14). When he talked of his witness, he said, using the plural, "We are witnesses of this" (3:15; cf. 2:32; 5:32). He was not a lone voice, but he had a ministry team backing him when he spoke. Peter and John are seen ministering as a team at the start of the church (Acts 3 and 4) and later on too (8:14). When Peter went to the home of Cornelius on his historic visit, he took six brothers with him (Acts 10:23; 11:12).

When the first missionary team for Gentile evangelization was commissioned, the Holy Spirit wanted two people, Barnabas and Saul, set apart (Acts 13:2). When this team broke up, both Paul and Barnabas took others along to form their own teams (15:39-40). We know that Paul almost never traveled alone. He had his traveling Bible school where he trained "interns" such as Timothy and Titus. Even when Paul went to Rome as a prisoner, Luke was with him (27:2). When from prison he wrote his last letter in the Bible to Timothy, Luke was still with him, and he told Timothy to join him quickly and to bring Mark along (2 Tim. 4:9, 11).

We are not always told how the teams operated as far as the responsibilities of the members were concerned. The record of the way Peter and John and Paul and Barnabas ministered shows that Peter and Paul respectively did most of the public speaking. Paul presents his team members as his coauthors in eight of his thirteen letters. Mentioned are "all the brothers who are with [him]" (Gal. 1:1), Sosthenes (1 Cor. 1:1), Timothy (2 Cor. 1:1; Phil. 1:1; Col. 1:1; 1 and 2 Thess. 1:1; Philem. 1), Silvanus (1 and 2 Thess. 1:1). Paul asks that Mark be brought to him "for he is very useful to [him] for ministry" (2 Tim. 4:11). We can expect that the teams worked according to the giftedness of the members as described in 1 Corinthians 12.[1]

WHEN WE DO NOT CHOOSE OUR TEAM MEMBERS

Unlike Jesus, we do not always have the luxury of choosing the members of the team we lead. What if we do not like some of the team members we "inherit"? Say, a senior pastor is appointed from outside a church. He inherits the ministry team already there. There is one person on this team who makes him feel uneasy. Perhaps he thinks that he will have conflicts with this person or that this person would not respond well to his leadership style. Perhaps he has doubts about the person's abilities.

What should the new pastor do? Some would say that he should ask the person to leave. Such a response comes from the highly individualistic theology found especially among evangelical Christians, which, I believe, violates the biblical teaching of corporate solidarity within the people of God. This theology gives certain people the freedom to change churches when they don't like a new pastor. There isn't a sense of being committed to a body "in sickness and in health; for richer, for poorer." Actually such an attitude is what causes people to immediately think of divorce when serious problems appear in a marriage.

We can imply from the teaching of Paul in 1 Corinthians 1 that he would have been revolted by this lack of permanence in the commitment we have to fellow Christians. In the body of Christ we do not reject people because we do not like them. Our theology of the body addresses our personal feelings in such situations. In the most important things in life the leader is united, as members of one body, with this person that he does not like. Since this is so, there is an adequate foundation to pursue a relationship with the people we do not like. Here is one of Paul's lists of such unifying factors: "There is one body and one Spirit—just as you were called to the one hope that belongs to your call—one Lord, one faith, one baptism, one God and Father of all, who is over all and through all and in all" (Eph. 4:4-6). In light of these powerful unifying factors, the differences between Christians pale into insignificance. With this theological backing we pursue our relationship with the one we do not personally like.

Perhaps the tragedy with the evangelical church is that feelings overcome theology very often in determining the way we decide and act. The biblical Christian says, "Whatever my feelings are about this person, I will accept him because God wants me to do so. And I will ask God to give me the grace to work harmoniously with him." Our theology says that this effort at working with this person will succeed, even though our feelings may give another message. Our theology drives us to work hard at this relationship. We pray for the person and about our relationship with him. We meet him regularly. We seek to show Christian love to him and do all that we can for his personal welfare. We develop dreams for what this person could achieve through the team.

I have had a few situations in Youth for Christ and at church when I've needed to work closely with a person whom I would not have chosen. Once or twice the person initially seemed to imply that he did not want to work under my leadership. Most often I have found that, after some time, I have come to like the person. I pray almost daily for the people with whom I work closely, and when you pray for someone so regularly, you automatically develop a special affinity for that person. Usually, after some time, I have also come to recognize great value in the person. I do not see this as some unusual achievement. I simply see this as an aspect of doing my job! We cannot drop those we dislike. We have the responsibility to care for everyone entrusted to us. So as part of doing our job, we work hard at developing God-honoring working relationships with those we initially dislike.

THE VALUE OF TEAM MINISTRY

Some years ago, while in the United States on a sabbatical to write a book on the doctrine of hell,[2] I was so concerned about what I perceived as a lack of some aspects of biblical community life in the church that I wrote an additional unplanned book, *Reclaiming Friendship*.[3] There I mention in detail several reasons why we need others as our friends or team members as we do ministry. Here I will mention three areas particularly relevant to Christian workers that point powerfully to this need.

Help with Our Weaknesses

All of us have weaknesses that are very much a part of our personalities. Because of this, when we fall in these areas, we cannot expect to immediately be over the problem by the simple process of confessing the sin and receiving forgiveness. As these weaknesses are a part of our personality, there is a strong likelihood that we will fall again into the same sin. Here are some examples of such weaknesses:

- Carelessness with our use of time (e.g., habitually late);
- Carelessness with our use of money (e.g., using church funds for personal needs with the intention of replacing them sometime);
- Carelessness about noting down official expenditures;
- Carelessness about eating habits or about getting exercise;
- Losing one's temper with family members or ministry coworkers;
- Lack of discipline with devotions, especially because of a heavy schedule;
- Working hard but not giving sufficient time for the family;
- Sexual sins such as viewing unclean material on television or the Internet;
- Serious pre-conversion weaknesses such as addiction to a chemical substance, homosexuality, or sexual abuse—to which temptations can come later on in one's Christian life.

Let me describe a common scenario. A Christian worker commits a sin springing from his weakness. He is deeply sorrowful about it and confesses the sin to God with tears and receives God's forgiveness with gratitude. Feeling free again, he goes back to his routine of ministry. He seems to be effective until a situation arises that becomes a temptation in his area of vulnerability. He falls again, and the process of confession is repeated. The problem is that there is no guarantee that he will live in an environment where he will be totally immune to these temptations. He could keep on falling over and over again until his behavior becomes a huge scandal.

The Bible recommends that we get help in our areas of weakness. Paul describes how we can be vessels fit for the Master's use in 2 Timothy 2. He first says we must cleanse ourselves from what is dishonorable (v. 21). Then he says, "So flee youthful passions and pursue righteousness, faith, love, and peace, along with those who call on the Lord from a pure heart" (v. 22). I preached on this text in my preaching class in seminary and talked about the need to flee youthful lusts and pursue the virtuous qualities Paul mentioned. After the sermon my professor, Dr. Jerry Mercer, remarked that I had not dealt with what is possibly the most important point in this verse—that we do the fleeing and the pursuing "along with those who call on the Lord from a pure heart." I represented the typical evangelical distortion of Christian holiness by turning it into an individualistic rather than a corporate matter. God intends for us to battle for holiness along with fellow Christians.

Hebrews 10:24 explains one way in which fellow Christians help us along the path to godliness: "Let us consider how to stir up one another to love and good works." The word translated "stir up," *paroxusmos,* which is used here in the sense of encourage, can be translated as "sharp argument or disagreement."[4] This text is describing a sometimes unpleasant prodding in the direction of godly living. The prodding ideally takes place in the context of an accountability group, which is what a ministry team should be.

Many Christian workers have had experiences prior to conversion that have left wounds that did not automatically disappear when they became Christians. These wounds remain as weaknesses in their lives. After they were converted, they grew steadily and became effective in service and gradually came to positions of leadership. But the weaknesses still affect their lives, and they need help in overcoming them.

Take the case of a woman who was treated in a very unfair way at home during her childhood. She could not do anything to prevent herself from being exploited, even by her parents. The thought of it still fills her with anger. Then she encounters a situation in the ministry where it seems as if her group is being unfairly treated. Her Sunday school classroom is given to another group, and her group is sent to a less suitable room. She explodes in anger, and a situation that could have been easily settled through some reasoned discussion becomes a huge problem. The result is dishonor to God and to the staff of the church.

When several similar incidents occur, her supervisor realizes that there is a weakness here that could easily ruin her testimony. The supervisor talks with her and finds out about the background prompting the problem behavior. The woman too realizes the reasons for her behavior. She is brought to the point of accepting the truth that because God is sovereign, no injustice could ultimately harm her. So she has strength to forgive her parents for their injustice. She can now look at this painful past with gratitude to God for his promise that he will bring something good out of it. In this way she is aided in overcoming her weakness through a process of accountability and by taking preventive measures.

Here is another Christian worker who, after straying a few times into some unclean sites on the Internet, finds that he is strongly compelled to go to pornographic sites. Thousands of Christians are struggling with this today. But this worker has an accountability group. He shares his problem with the group, and they set several guidelines for him, including the requirement that he regularly report to the group about his activity in this area. Now whenever he is tempted to stray, he remembers that he has to report everything to his group. He knows that he may have to face disciplinary action over his failings. There is a check in his spirit that pulls him away from the path of temptation. In time this process will free him from the stranglehold of pornography.

This type of procedure is helpful for several other weaknesses, such as irregularity with devotions and irresponsible use of funds. Sometimes it is necessary to take disciplinary action against the persons so that the pain of the discipline acts as a deterrent when they face the same temptation again. I have spoken to a few Christians who have committed sexual sins, confessed them, and then gone back to ministry, but who have succumbed to temptation again when they faced a similar situation. The memory of a painful discipline process would trigger a resistance to the temptation when it assails them with great force. Sometimes when a team member has a serious problem that requires specialized counseling, the team could ensure that this help is made available to him or her.

Also under the category of weakness is the effect of sexual abuse during childhood or youth upon adult Christian workers. A man finds that his fiancée reacts coldly to physical touch or that his wife is somewhat unresponsive during sexual intercourse. Sometimes this behavior results from traumatic sexual abuse or wrong teaching about sex, especially if the person grew up in a strict religious environment. Now it may not be a team member who can help here, but often it is. The problem may surface when a leader asks the young staff worker he is discipling about his personal life. Thereafter the leader can take steps to solve the problem. One of those steps may be to refer that person to someone who is more skilled at helping him.

My point is that many of our personal weaknesses and problems are best solved with the active involvement of the body of Christ. I believe there are many Christian workers today who are fighting a losing battle with these problems with no help from anyone in the body. That is tragically wrong. The Bible teaches that we can and must get help from the body in order to grow and be made whole.

Help When We Are Vulnerable

Aside from our weaknesses, there are also situations when we are vulnerable, and we would really be aided by the guidance of our friends here. When our friends see us going in a wrong direction, they can warn us and, by so doing, save us from making a huge mistake. Sometimes we are so blinded by our emotional attachment to our plans, desires, and actions that we do not realize some of the folly in them. The Bible says, "The way of a fool is right in his own eyes, but a wise man listens to advice" (Prov. 12:15). This proverb applies to several areas in our life.

Since the Bible talks clearly of the need to receive advice before making important decisions, it is really strange that many Christians do not seriously go for advice from trusted brothers and sisters in the choice of a marriage partner. This is particularly strange because it is generally accepted that love has a certain blinding effect on us, as expressed by the statement "Love is blind!" Surely then we should be getting the help of our accountability group when making this decision. John Wesley urged his workers, "Take no step toward marriage without first acquainting us with your design."[5] I think individualism has so gripped us that we think that this is an area where we must go it alone for it to be truly romantic! There are so many sad stories of Christian workers who married the wrong person. We should be rethinking the way we handle this area.

The same principle applies when a person is offered an attractive job or ministry opportunity. He or she may be unaware of many of the issues or be blinded from seeing them because of the attractiveness of the proposal. Friends can help this person see the other side of the story and perhaps save him or her from making a serious mistake. I have seen so many ministers who have lost their effectiveness because they neglected their primary work, which was not public and glamorous, in order to take more glamorous assignments. Soon they failed in their primary work, and with that they lost their credibility as ministers of the gospel. As a result, they began to get fewer invitations for the more glamorous assignments.

Recently we have seen many instances of Christian workers who got into an inappropriate relationship with a member of the opposite sex without ever planning to do so. Perhaps the relationship was with someone the worker was counseling or someone who worked alongside him or her who needed some help. Perhaps it was a friendly colleague who simply enjoyed chatting with the worker. Gradually, unnoticed by the two people, an emotional tie was developing. But because the relationship started in such an honorable way, they kept denying the existence of this unhealthy emotional tie—until it was too late, and people were hurt on all sides.

Often others saw what was happening. Though the two people ignored the danger signs, others saw the way the eyes connected, the way the two talked to each other, or the way they moved toward each other in company. Those who observed realized that there was something deep and unhealthy developing. Unfortunately these observers did not feel they had the freedom to talk about it. So they kept quiet, and finally good people were deeply hurt, and God's name was dishonored.

Some people are not happy when others get involved in their lives in this way. People especially resent the use of rebuke and discipline. Rebuke and discipline should be regular features in a healthy Christian organization. I read a biography of John Calvin recently, and I have been reading through the journals of John Wesley over the past several months. I have been surprised at how much disciplining of Christians took place in the ministries of these two leaders.

But we have to create an organizational culture in our groups where loving and sensitive confrontation is appreciated and valued. We will talk about that later. One feature of that culture is that team members have genuine personal concern for each other's welfare as expressed in the leader/team member paying the price to "be there" when he/she needs help. It is essential for me to be with my colleagues at special times in their lives—when they move, when their children are very sick, etc. When a colleague of mine was arrested on suspicion of being a terrorist, I felt it was necessary for me to take his lunch every day to the police station where he was held for forty-five days. We may think that something like this takes us away from our work. But this *is* part of our work as leaders. Time will show how these time-consuming diversions develop deep ties that ultimately help bring much relief to us through the dedicated service of these team members.

People who are urgent about the gospel and about holiness will find disciplining and rebuking to be a necessary, though painful, means of achieving their passion to please God. Primarily describing God's discipline, Hebrews 12:11 says, "For the moment all discipline seems painful rather than pleasant, but later it yields the peaceful fruit of righteousness to those who have been trained by it." The Bible is harsh in its critique of those who refuse to submit to such discipline: "Whoever loves discipline loves knowledge, but he who hates reproof is stupid" (Prov. 12:1).

Help When We Are Discouraged

All of us will face failure and disappointment in ministry. Projects fail; programs end up as flops; people we invested in at much personal cost betray us; we make silly mistakes; those we serve reject us—the list can go on and on. The great danger at such times is that we can become really discouraged. Because a project failed, we think *we* are failures. But life is more than just a project. These are the times we value close friends the most, for they help us to look at our problems more realistically. Ecclesiastes says, "Two are better than one . . . if they fall, one will lift up his fellow. But woe to him who is alone when he falls and has not another to lift him up!" (4:9-10).

After Hudson Taylor had been in China for a little less than two years, he was deeply discouraged. His missionary society had not kept its promise to support him. The established missionaries in China were critical of his unorthodox methods. His fiancée in England had written to say that she feared she did not love him. The British consul had ordered him to stop work in one of the towns he was focusing on. He wrote to his mother, "My heart is sad, sad, sad. . . . I do not know what to do."[6]

At this stage a godly Scottish missionary named William Burns, about twenty years his senior, befriended Hudson Taylor. They traveled, preached, and prayed together for seven months. Burns was God's answer to Taylor's discouragement. Biographer John Pollock says, "Burns saved Taylor from himself."[7] Taylor went on to found the China Inland Mission (now called Overseas Missionary Fellowship), whose impact provides one of the most exciting stories of recent missionary history.

Here are six ways our friends help us when we are discouraged:

• Just the simple act of sharing with friends takes a huge burden off our backs and gives us much relief.

• The act of articulating our problems becomes a means of helping us to think reasonably about them.

• Our friends usually help us realize some of the positive things about our lives and situations and thus reduce the extent of the gloom we feel.

• The love of friends helps heal the pain of the rejection we have experienced.

• Their love also helps us combat bitterness. It is hard to be angry at the world when some of its inhabitants are so kind to us!

• Friends also help us avoid making rash and foolish decisions in response to a crisis, such as resigning from our job or making foolish public statements. They help us find the wisest way to respond. At such times we need people who are not too emotionally affected by the problems to help us view things realistically.

These are just a few of the benefits of ministering in a team of friends. There are many more, such as increased fruit through the combining of the different gifts that each one brings.

No THEOLOGY OF GROANING

A few weeks before writing this chapter I spoke at a conference of Christian ministers in Sri Lanka about the need for those in ministry to have friends to whom they are accountable and with whom they could share their struggles and joys. The overwhelming response to what I said was that this is good theory, but it is impossible to practice. Many said they have been so hurt as a result of confiding in others that they will not do it again. For days I grappled with this question: Why is it that so many Christian workers who strongly believe in the total authority of Scripture do not have close friends even though Scripture clearly shows that such relationships are a necessity for the Christian life?

While I was studying a book on ministering to drug addicts (more on that later) a few days after this conference, I suddenly realized that the growing church in Sri Lanka may be having a theological problem. We may be presenting Christianity in such a way as to leave no place for the biblical concept of groaning.

The typical growing evangelical church today has a strong theology of the necessity for *growth*. This is surely a biblical concept when the growth takes place through the lost coming to Christ. The book of Acts rejoices over those who are saved, often talking about the numbers of those added to the church, showing that God is concerned with its numerical growth (2:42, 47; 4:4; 6:7; 11:1; 14:1).

The church also has a strong theology of *praise*. So testimonies are given to what our powerful God has done in people's lives, and affirmations are made about what the Bible says about the blessings God gives. The result is exultant praise, which also is biblical. Does not the Bible have a whole, large book, the Psalms, whose Hebrew title is *tehillim,* meaning "songs of praise"?

Then our churches have a strong theology of *power*—of God's ability to meet the needs of people and to defeat their foes. This too is a biblical concept. We see in the Gospels and Acts and in isolated references in the Epistles that God arrested people's attention and made them receptive to the gospel by meeting, often miraculously, the needs of individuals. We will discuss this in chapter 12.

But theologies of church growth, of praise, and of power can give rise to serious aberrations if they are not balanced with a theology of groaning. I have taken the term "groaning" from Romans 8:23, which says, " . . . we ourselves, who have the firstfruits of the Spirit, groan inwardly as we wait eagerly for adoption as sons, the redemption of our bodies." Earlier Paul said, "the creation was subjected to futility" as a result of the Fall (8:20). So we do not get everything we want; nor do we experience the fullness of perfection that God intends to give us in heaven. But we have a foretaste of it, for we "have the firstfruits of the Spirit" (8:23). So things will go wrong in our lives—we will be harmed by accidents, we will get sick, and we will have persons who dislike us and hurt us. Despite our desire to be like Christ, who was perfect and sinless, we will make mistakes and commit sin. Our thirst coming from the foretaste of heaven will clash with the reality of living in a fallen world, and the result is that we will groan sometimes.

In the Bible groaning can coexist with praise. In fact, the Bible has a whole genre (category of literary style), called the lament, to give expression to this groaning. Laments are raw, painful expressions of hurt and sorrow. About fifty of the 150 songs in Psalms (the book of praises) are classified as laments. These expressions are found in other Bible books such as Lamentations and Jeremiah too. Old Testament scholar Chris Wright describes the content of a biblical lament this way: "God, I am hurting; and, God, everyone else is laughing. And, God, You are not helping very much either; and how long is it going to go on?"[8]

Another Old Testament scholar, my friend Dr. David Baer of Costa Rica, told me of a helpful distinction that some scholars are making between laments and complaints. Laments are said to represent the hopeless cries of devastated people. But complaints are the cries of those who believe that God is good and cannot now see this goodness in what they are experiencing. They cry out to God, but these cries are tinged with hope. If we were to accept this distinction, the biblical passages that we have called laments should more accurately be termed complaints.

Biblical characters, then, were not afraid to groan. If the Holy Spirit inspired so many laments (or complaints) to be recorded in the Bible, then groaning must surely be part of the Christian life too.

Those who have a theology of lament will have a place for emphasizing honest expressions of struggle. And that place can exist alongside an emphasis on growth, power, and praise. I think that sometimes we are so eager for growth that we have become like advertisers who give only the positive side of the product and avoid talking about its drawbacks. I find that nowadays advertisers are required to read out the negative aspects of products. And they usually do it softly and fast. I think many churches have not caught on to that practice yet! They know that people will be attracted to the church if the message presented shows all the wonderful things that God can do. For marketing reasons the problems Christians face are neglected. And that has happened for so long that many people do not have a place for groaning in their understanding of the Christian life.

When some talk about their problems in this environment, the other Christians don't know what to do. Sometimes those who share honestly face rejection and blame for not being good Christians. Therefore, they learn to live without talking about their problem, unless it is the type that could become a prayer concern and be exposed through prayer to God's wonderworking power. So they will ask for prayer for healing and guidance and provision of a job or funds, but not for overcoming a hot temper, a bad habit, or discouragement.

In a sense this situation gives evidence of a defective understanding of grace. The biblical understanding is that grace is so great that Christians do not need to fear facing up to their sin. Indeed sin is never justified in the Bible and therefore must always be condemned. But grace is greater than sin, and grace cannot be applied unless we admit that we have sinned. Therefore, if we desire the fullness of God's grace in our lives, we will be eager to confess our sins so as to open the door to a rich experience of grace. This confession is not done in a flippant or light way, for we are grieved by sin. But we are so eager for cleansing that we will eagerly face up to the problem and seek forgiveness.

First John 1:5—2:3 presents this paradox powerfully. John says, "My little children, I am writing these things to you so that you may not sin" (1 John 2:1a). So sin is never condoned. But he goes on to say, "But if anyone does sin, we have an advocate with the Father, Jesus Christ the righteous. He is the propitiation for our sins, and not for ours only but also for the sins of the whole world" (1 John 2:1b-2). God's grace in Christ is so great that we do not need to fear to face up to sin. In fact, we fear not facing up to it, for we know that "if we walk in the light, as he is in the light, we have fellowship with one another, and the blood of Jesus his Son cleanses us from all sin" (1 John 1:7). We dread the prospect of losing the fellowship and the cleansing by not walking in the light. So we will be eager to "confess our sins" (1 John 1:9).

Defective theologies of groaning and grace can join to cause a church where people are afraid to express their deep hurts and struggles to other Christians. So, for example, when there are problems between members, they do not talk about it. They do not have the assurance that God's grace is sufficient for this challenge, and they do not have a theology of groaning that can accommodate the temporary unpleasantness that will arise from bringing up the issue. So they choose to ignore it. They continue to praise God and, through concentrating on God's goodness, have satisfying experiences of worship. Because of the emphasis on power, this church will also attract many needy people and thus will grow. Outwardly the leaders may hug and smile at each other, but inwardly there will be hidden frustrations and anger over unresolved problems. They will work together until the problems get so big that they can't bear them anymore. Then they burst out in an unpleasant confrontation. Often the church breaks up, and a group leaves.

NEW TESTAMENT TEAMS: LIFE IN THE RAW

What a contrast to the above scenario is the description in the Gospels of the life of Jesus and his twelve-man team of disciples. There we find what I am calling "life in the raw." There is no hiding of the problems of the disciples. Not only did they face up to their failures, but the Holy Spirit also had these problems recorded in Scripture so that we could learn something from them.

We find them asking foolish and selfish things. At the Transfiguration Peter wanted to build tents for Jesus and Moses and Elijah, and Luke adds that he didn't know what he said (Luke 9:33). James and John, at their mother's instigation, asked to sit on either side of Jesus when he entered glory (Mark 10:37). The other disciples heard this and "began to be indignant at James and John" (Mark 10:35-41). But this episode prompts the rich and

deep discourse by Jesus about the nature of servant leadership and the revelation of himself as the servant who came to give his life as a ransom for many
(10:42-45).

Elsewhere we are told that they argued among themselves about who was
the greatest among them. Yet that argument elicited from Christ the statement: "He who is least among you all is the one who is great" (Luke 9:48b).
They argued about this even during the Last Supper, after he had donned the
garb of a servant and washed their feet. But that dispute triggered a wonderful
discourse on true greatness and on the rewards of service (Luke 22:24-30).

The disciples rebuked the persons who brought children to Jesus, even
though he wanted them to come so that he could lay hands on them. But from
that episode came the memorable words: "Let the little children come to me
and do not hinder them, for to such belongs the kingdom of heaven" (Matt.
19:14). The disciples "were indignant" when the woman poured the expen-
sive ointment on Jesus' head, and their protests prompted Jesus to elaborate
on the "beautiful thing" she did to him (Matt. 26:10-13).

This was a community where the members were not afraid to admit their
ignorance and their doubts. After Jesus had told them that if they saw him,
they saw the Father, "Philip said to him, 'Lord, show us the Father, and it is
enough for us'" (John 14:8). This request prompts a gentle rebuke from Jesus,
followed by a masterly and irrefutable defense of his absolute uniqueness
(14:9-11).[9] When the disciples told Thomas that Jesus had risen from the
dead, he refused to believe without more tangible evidence. But that incident
also elicited a gentle rebuke and an important comment about saving faith
(John 20:24-29).

In the Garden of Gethsemane the disciples were sleeping when they
should have been praying. They needed this crucial preparation for the arrest
that soon took place, followed by the terrible events that led up to their
Master's death. But out of that embarrassing incident came the critical statement: "The spirit indeed is willing, but the flesh is weak" (Matt. 26:41). And
when Jesus was arrested, "all the disciples left him and fled" (Matt. 26:56).

Peter, the leader of the first church, did not fare very well in the Gospels.
Jesus called him "Satan" when Peter tried to rebuke him for talking about
his death (Matt. 16:23). That situation prompted the great statement by
Christ on the cost and rewards of following him (16:24-28). After bravely
launching on a sea walk, Peter suddenly grew afraid and cried out, "Lord,
save me." But that incident resulted in one of the first acknowledgments in
the Gospels of the deity of Christ when the disciples worshiped him and said,
"Truly, you are the Son of God" (Matt. 14:33).

Only a handful of such incidents are mentioned in all four Gospels, and one of them is Peter's denial of Christ. But the denial and Peter's subsequent remorse gave rise to the beautiful way in which he was restored and re-commissioned. When the angel asked the women to tell the disciples that Jesus was risen, only Peter was mentioned by name (Mark 16:7). John chose to close his Gospel with a description of the touching conversation where Jesus spoke to Peter about his love, the call to feed Christ's sheep, his martyrdom, and the call to follow Christ (John 21:15-23).

What a long list this is! We can make up a similar list for the leaders of the early church too. Mark left the team of Paul and Barnabas (Acts 13:13) in what Paul viewed as a desertion (Acts 15:38). Paul and Barnabas had "a sharp disagreement" over whether to take Mark on their next journey, and they parted company (Acts 15:36-40). But they seemed to have become colleagues again later on (1 Cor. 9:6), demonstrating that people could work together even after serious disagreements. Toward the end of his life Paul, writing from prison, told Timothy, "Get Mark and bring him with you, for he is very useful to me for ministry" (2 Tim. 4:11). Mark, of course, became the author of the second Gospel and probably pioneered the preaching of the gospel in Egypt. That nation was soon to become the intellectual center of the church. These events demonstrate powerfully how people who fail at first can make a comeback and be used mightily by God.

Then there was the sad situation in Antioch where both Barnabas and Peter gave in to pressure from the circumcision party and withdrew from table fellowship with the Gentiles. This action resulted in Paul's public rebuke of Peter (Gal. 2:11-14). But this situation and other events surrounding it prompted Paul to write his great letter to the Galatians. Second Corinthians (like Galatians) includes raw, painful expressions of hurt and sorrow like the laments/complaints. But out of the pain and its healing came a matchless and lengthy reflection on the glory of the ministry (2 Cor. 2:14—6:13). Paul faced up to problems and grappled for solutions without giving up on people and without leaving room for division in the church.

The beautiful thing is that after each of these blunders, wonderful insights into the mind of God emerged. The first Christian churches were communities that blundered a lot. But by facing up to their blunders without sweeping them under the carpet, they gave an opportunity for God to minister to them deeply. The result is theological insight and also depth in spiritual and community life. A community that does not come to grips with the shortcomings of its members will always be a shallow community.

The New Testament then has raw representations of the first teams of disciples. They and the New Testament writers were not afraid to acknowledge their weaknesses. But this practice of acknowledging weaknesses fits in with the teaching of Jesus. He showed that the one who admits his or her sins and weaknesses is great in the kingdom. His kingdom manifesto begins with four statements extolling the value of acknowledging one's need. It says that the poor in spirit, those who mourn, the meek, and those who hunger and thirst after righteousness are the ones who are truly blessed (Matt. 5:3-6). He tells the story of how a self-righteous Pharisee and a sinful tax collector went to the temple to pray. After the Pharisee had waxed eloquent on his faithfulness to God's law, "the tax collector, standing far off, would not even lift up his eyes to heaven, but beat his breast, saying, 'God, be merciful to me, a sinner!'" (Luke 18:13). Yet Jesus said that it was this man and not the Pharisee who went home justified (18:14). He said that the greatest in the kingdom are those who turn, humble themselves, and become like children (Matt. 18:3-4).

Jesus is the only one in the Bible without sin, but the Gospels show even Jesus struggling at times. We see him weeping at the funeral of Lazarus (John 11:35). Later as he contemplated his own death, he confessed, "Now is my soul troubled. And what shall I say? 'Father, save me from this hour'? But for this purpose I have come to this hour" (John 12:27).

The Gospels do not hide the fact that Jesus really struggled with the will of God in the Garden of Gethsemane. Matthew says he was "sorrowful and troubled" (Matt. 26:37); Mark says he was "greatly distressed and troubled" (Mark 14:33). Luke is the most expressive on this: "And being in an agony he prayed more earnestly; and his sweat became like great drops of blood falling down to the ground" (Luke 22:44). The reason for his agony was that he was finding the will of God for him (bearing the sin of the world on a cross) difficult to accept. He prayed, "Father, if you are willing, remove this cup from me. Nevertheless, not my will, but yours, be done" (Luke 22:42). Strengthened by the angel, Jesus marched so triumphantly to the cross that those who came to arrest him "drew back and fell to the ground" when he introduced himself to them (John 18:6)!

Do we not also often wish to avoid something that we know we should do? Well, Jesus' frank confession of his feelings to God gives us the courage to express our apprehensions. And when we do so, the others in the community should not judge us but sympathize with us and help give us the courage to be obedient. Our expression of need provides the trigger for God's work of strengthening us for our tough challenges. The important thing is to be obedient. Those who never express their fears sometimes end up disobeying God because they have not really grappled with the problem and also because they have no one to encourage them at their time of need.

So a healthy team encourages its members to be open about their faults and fears. Their desire for all of God and their belief in the sufficiency of grace will urge them to confront sin and problems fearlessly and to look for God to use that to purify, teach, and deepen the community. A community that deals with problems openly and biblically will become a community with a deep spirituality because God is able to minister and teach his deep truths through the grappling that takes place to solve the problems.

Now it is time to tell you how this train of thought was triggered by my study on how to minister to drug dependents. I was reading that drug dependents resort to drugs when they have difficulty handling what the author calls "heavy emotions." Heavy emotions include anger, discouragement, pain, sorrow, remorse, and jealousy.[10] These emotions signal a situation that could be addressed with proper responses and relationships. But people see that step as too painful, and, fearful of taking it, they opt for faster relief by resorting to drugs.

Most drug rehab programs use group activity and therapy in their attempts to help drug dependents avoid this process of going back to drugs. The participants become part of a group where they bare their souls and express their hurts and fears without being rejected. The hope is that through this means they will learn to use positive and helpful relationships and responses when feeling down instead of resorting to drugs. Most drug rehab programs use recovered and recovering drug dependents as the members of these groups. These are fellow sufferers; they will understand and will not reject the persons who share the terrible things going through their minds.

Many drug rehab workers have despaired of trying to incorporate their members into outside groups, as they feel that the Christians in these groups do not make an effort to understand these people and do not have the patience to try to learn what they are going through. Therefore, when drug dependents share their problems, they feel judged by the others, become hurt, and withdraw from the group. Because of this, some ministries are starting their own churches consisting almost exclusively of recovered and recovering drug dependents. I believe we must work really hard to incorporate these people into regular churches. At the same time we can have small groups for them where they know they will be understood and not judged and rejected.

I think Christian workers face a similar situation. They have a peculiar set of problems, and no one seems to understand them. They are expected to help suffering people, but they do not have anywhere to go when they suffer.

If they do share their problems with other Christians, these people would be so surprised or upset that they could cause damage to the ministry.

The drug rehab workers are afraid to send their members to regular churches, as these people could face rejection there. In the same way Christian workers are afraid to share their problems with the groups they are a part of, as they have had painful experiences of rejection when they have done so. We need to have groups that enable Christian workers to share their problems without fear—groups that they are accountable to. I believe that these groups would need to have such a strong theology of grace and of groaning that they will be able to accommodate what I have called "life in the raw."

ACCOUNTABILITY FOR THE CHRISTIAN WORKER

A "serious man" told John Wesley early in his Christian walk, "Sir, you wish to serve God and go to heaven? Remember you cannot serve him alone. You must therefore find companions or make them." This is what I would urge all Christian workers today. *Find* companions or, if you can't find them, *make* them. Wesley followed this advice for himself and for the Methodist movement he founded.

Wesley developed a community life that had four different types of groups. The first was the "society," which is the equivalent of the modern congregation. This was where Bible teaching and worship was done. The next type was the "class meeting," which was a neighborhood group consisting of about twelve people from the same area. This was a heterogeneous group consisting of men and women, married and single people, and people of varying ages. The function of this group was to apply the teaching they had received in society meetings to their daily lives. The fourth type was the "specialized band," a group of people with a common goal, who met to be helped to achieve this goal. For example, there were groups for backsliders seeking restoration and for believers seeking entire sanctification.

The third type of group is of most significance to this discussion: Wesley called this group the "band," which was equivalent to an accountability group. It was a homogeneous group, with groups divided according to sex, age, and marital status. By restricting the groups in this way, Wesley was able to encourage the members to share private things about their personal lives. Wesley's "Rules of the Bands" states, "The design of our meeting is to obey that command of God, 'Confess your faults one to another, and pray for one another that ye may be healed' (James 5:16)." Here Wesley listed six things that would be done at this meeting. Two are of special concern to us:

4. To speak to each of us in order, freely and plainly, the true state of our souls, with the faults we have committed in thought, word and deed, and the temptations we have felt since our last meeting . . . .

6. To desire some person among us to speak his own state first, and then to ask the rest in order, as many and as searching questions as may be, concerning their state, sins, and temptations.[11]

I believe that all ministers should be part of the equivalent of Wesley's band—a group of people to whom they are accountable. Today there is a tendency among Christian leaders to have as members of their accountability group people who do not work together with them. This can be effective if the different members of the group can be frank and can confront another in the group with weaknesses, sins, and other challenging issues. The disadvantage is that the members do not see each other in the natural setting in which they work.

Those who live or work together are able to see what is really happening in each other's lives. This can be a great asset, given our natural tendency to rationalize our faults and withhold some of the truth when reporting about our own weaknesses to others. We can give our accountability groups an unrealistic picture, and they would have no way of knowing whether we are telling them the whole story. Boards with members who are not actively involved in a ministry suffer from this disadvantage. Usually the only worker on the board is the leader, and what members will hear at the meetings are the leader's perspectives on the issues.

Also, other people may observe weaknesses that the person himself or herself may not recognize. Those working together have a much better opportunity to observe one another and thus discover both strengths and weaknesses.

For the above reasons I think the ideal accountability group consists of the members of a team. This is the type of group that Jesus developed with his disciples. I know that many pastors and Christian workers today do not have people in their congregations or organizations with whom they can share their deepest thoughts. I believe they must pray and work to build such a team; they must *make* friends. And the way to do this is by investing in people, just as Jesus invested in the disciples. We will discuss this in the next two chapters.

I think that friends who have a long history together can also constitute a good accountability group. Even though they may not work together, they have over the years developed an openness with each other, which makes accountability possible. It is difficult to bluff people who know you so well. They know your weaknesses and therefore can be alert to these in their efforts to help you. I have seen some effective groups of this type consisting of people who served together in their church youth fellowship. They are no longer youths, but deep ties developed in their younger years, and that made it possible for them to help each other in their adult years too.

Ideally pastors could have the other ministers of their denomination or organization who work in the area as an accountability group. This is what John Wesley did with his preachers. But sadly most Christians today are afraid to share their problems with these fellow workers, as they cannot be sure that the hearers won't use this information in a way that will hurt them. All I can say about this is that it is a terrible tragedy. Jesus would surely not have intended the leaders of his body to have such an attitude toward each other. We should pray and work to remedy this situation.

Today we are seeing like-minded pastors and Christian workers, who belong to different organizations but serve in the same geographical area, meeting for prayer and fellowship. This is a wonderful development and should be encouraged everywhere. Some of these groups have become places of accountability for these workers. This too is very good, especially if these workers do not have people in their own groups to be their friends. But it is not the ideal accountability structure for the reasons given above. While such workers should continue to meet, they should also work on developing trusted friends from within their own ministries.

I have two groups that I am seriously accountable to. I say "seriously" because there are other groups that I am accountable to also, such as the leadership team in my church. In fact, in my traveling ministry I consider the church or group I am ministering with at a given time as a group I am accountable to.

But for help with the many personal decisions and activities of my life, I go to two main groups. The first consists of five friends who worked together in Youth for Christ (YFC). We have been close friends for more than thirty-five years. Two of them are former YFC staff colleagues and are now in other ministries. One is still a YFC staff colleague, and another has been my board chairman for the twenty-six years I have served with YFC. All five members are board members in YFC. We meet about once a month.

The other group consists of my fellow leaders in YFC, and we usually meet once every two weeks. The members of this group are much younger than I am, but they are the ones I work closely with and, therefore, in some ways are the more important group in my life.

When we meet, we ask each other the following questions (which were selected and adapted from a larger list of questions that one of my colleagues got from a website).[12] The questions are more appropriate for men, but I believe they will give guidelines for women also who seek to develop such a group.

1. Have you spent time with God on a regular basis?
2. Have you compromised your integrity in any way?
3. Has your thought life been pure?
4. Have you committed any sexual sin?
5. Did you put yourself in an awkward situation with a woman?
6. What significant thing did you do for your wife and/or family?
7. Have you shared your faith this week? How?
8. Have you been truthful in everything we have discussed?

I cannot adequately describe how helpful these groups have been. We pray about our weaknesses. We discuss our struggles and challenges, our joys and discouragements. We talk and pray about our children. We sometimes talk theology and politics. I give them a report of my behavior after each trip I make abroad. They know the areas of vulnerability in my life, and I report to them on those areas. And how many times the wisdom of these friends has saved me from some very foolish things!

I should say something about teams that include both men and women. It is certainly possible for such teams to enjoy friendship and most of the blessings of team life. The one area where they will need to be careful is about the sharing of intimate details, which can foster unhealthy emotional ties between members of the opposite sex. What I have seen is that if the women are in a minority on such teams, they often miss out on sharing some of the private struggles that they cannot talk about in front of the men on the team. The leaders must ensure that the women are adequately ministered to. When a woman has a personal problem, I usually will have a first appointment with her and then do one of three things: I may meet with her along with my wife; I may ask my wife to meet with her; I may hand her over to the care of another trustworthy woman. These are situations where we must overcome our messiah complexes and accept the fact that others would do a better job than we can in helping these people.

Whatever the constitution of the group may be, one person in the group has to be responsible for ensuring that the group meets regularly. Most ministers have so many urgent demands on their time that it is easy to overlook this meeting. In the age-old battle between the urgent and the important, victory comes when someone is proactive to ensure that the meeting takes place.

Before I close this chapter, I must say that for those of us who are married, our spouses are our most important accountability partners. This is a relationship that has to be nurtured, and, as with any other deep relationship, that takes time. There are few things as important in the life of a married Christian worker as unhurried time spent talking with a spouse. Christian workers who are too busy to have long chats with their spouses are simply *too busy!*

Proverbs 18:24 says, "A man of many companions may come to ruin, but there is a friend who sticks closer than a brother." We are in a "people profession." Therefore, our work requires that we have many acquaintances. But even so, we can be lonely. And as this proverb warns us, we could ruin our lives. May we all find or make friends who will stick closer to us than a brother.

DISCIPLING YOUNGER LEADERS

IN THE LAST CHAPTER we saw that Jesus worked with his disciples as a team. During the time he spent with them, he nurtured and trained them and saw them grow into mature and effective ministers of the gospel. The work of Christian leaders to help other Christians become disciples of Christ I am calling the ministry of discipling. I am calling the leader who cares for the trainee the *discipler* and the trainee the *disciplee*. The words *discipler* and *disciplee* (as opposed to *master* and *disciple*) point to the fact that we are raising up disciples of Christ rather than of ourselves. Robert Coleman called the discipling ministry of Christ *The Master Plan of Evangelism*, which is the title of his classic and unsurpassed book on the topic.[1]

The leaders of the New Testament church also adopted the strategy of nurturing through discipling, as we saw in the last chapter. Paul always traveled with faithful assistants, such as Timothy and Titus, each of whom he described as his "child." Six times for Timothy and once for Titus and Philemon he uses this tender Greek word *teknon*,[2] which has been described as "a term of endearment."[3] There was an intense love for these people in his heart, as is evidenced by the following statement to Timothy: "I remember you constantly in my prayers night and day. As I remember your tears, I long to see you, that I may be filled with joy" (2 Tim. 1:3-4). He had such an intimate relationship with Timothy and trusted him so much that he was able to say about him: "He is my beloved and trustworthy child in the Lord. He will remind you of what I teach about Christ Jesus in all the churches wherever I go" (1 Cor. 4:17 NLT). Paul had a wide public ministry, but he did not neglect the personal ministry of discipling younger workers. Peter calls Mark his son

(1 Peter 5:13; Greek: *huios*), indicating that he had a discipler-disciplee relationship with the young man.

This topic is so vast that one could easily write a whole book on it. And
I would recommend the one by Robert Coleman mentioned above to anyone
looking for such a book. Wondering how to tackle this topic within the lim-
ited scope of this work, I decided to use Jesus' prayer for the apostles in John
17:1-26 because that passage describes well the care he had for them and how
he went about discipling them. This passage is the longest recorded prayer of
Jesus, and it can be divided into four parts. First he prays for his own glori-
fication (17:1-5); then he prays for his disciples (17:6-19); then he prays for
others who will believe in him (17:20-23); finally he prays again for the disciples (17:24-26). Seventeen out of twenty-six verses in this prayer are for the
disciples.

Here we will look primarily at verses 6-19. This part of the passage
reveals the way Jesus cared for his disciples, and it presents a model of spiritual parenthood. But it also gives very helpful principles on how parents
should care for their physical children. In fact, I believe there are several principles here that would help leaders in secular situations too. We see nine features of spiritual parenthood in this and the following chapter.

JESUS REVEALED GOD

Jesus begins this section by saying, "I have manifested your name to the people whom you gave me out of the world" (John 17:6a). By "name" here is
intended the nature of God. The disciples found out what God was like
through Jesus. He repeats this idea in verse 26: "I made known to them your
name, and I will continue to make it known, that the love with which you
have loved me may be in them, and I in them." Jesus would have imparted
this knowledge in two ways—by his life and by his teaching.

Revealing God by His Life

We find several statements in John to the effect that Jesus revealed God to the
disciples by his life. John said, "No one has ever seen God; the only God, who
is at the Father's side, he has made him known" (John 1:18). Jesus said,
"Whoever sees me sees him who sent me" (John 12:45; see 14:9). He said
that when he speaks, it is actually God speaking: "The words that I say to
you I do not speak on my own authority, but the Father who dwells in me
does his works" (John 14:10).

Now obviously we will not be able to be the image of God in the way that Jesus was. But we are called to reflect God by our lives. Jesus said, "Let your light shine before others, so that they may see your good works and give glory to your Father who is in heaven" (Matt. 5:16). Paul tells us that we are to conform to the image of Christ (Rom. 8:29; 2 Cor. 3:18).

John Selwyn, missionary Bishop of Melanesia, had a boy in training with him from one of the most barbarous islands of the South Seas. One day the bishop had to rebuke him for his stubborn and defiant behavior. The boy flew into a rage and struck the bishop a blow on the face. The bishop said nothing but turned and quietly walked away. The behavior of the boy went from bad to worse until he had to be sent back to his own island as incorrigible.

Many years later a missionary on that island was summoned to visit a sick man. It was Bishop Selwyn's old student. He was dying and desired Christian baptism. The missionary asked him by what name he would like to be known. The dying man replied, "Call me John Selwyn because he taught me what Christ was like that day when I struck him."[4]

Jesus closes his prayer saying, "I made known to them your name . . . that the love with which you have loved me may be in them, and I in them" (John 17:26). He seems to suggest that they had come to understand and experience the love of God the Father by the way Jesus loved them. In the same way we too could by our parent-type love help people to understand the love of God the Father. Many people find it difficult to accept the fatherhood of God because they have not had good experiences of the loving concern of an earthly father. Their inner wounds have made them so numb that they are unreceptive to the committed love that characterizes the relationship between father and child. In order to protect themselves from further hurt, they may close themselves to the possibility of trusting anyone to love them as a father should.

Perhaps one of the ways they will come to understand the father-love of God is by experiencing parent-love from a spiritual father or mother. Through this they come to believe that they are indeed lovable. And that opens their mind to the thought that God does love them in this deeply committed way. Once they believe this, they can open their lives to accepting and experiencing God's love.

There is a leadership crisis in society and in the church today, and I have seen this especially as a youth worker. Young people have found their leaders to be so unreliable in terms of practicing what they preach that they do not trust anyone anymore. The result is that holiness has become an unnecessary thing to them! They have seen unholy leaders take nations along the path to economic prosperity, and they have come to feel that if a leader brings a country into such prosperity, that person is a good leader even though his behavior may be immoral.

I have been surprised by the fact that millions of devotees from all over the world follow gurus in India whose personal behavior has been morally scandalous.[5] Then I realized that to many people morality is not an important issue. These gurus have miraculous powers, and that is what people want from them. In fact, spirituality has been defined almost exclusively in terms of power—over anxiety, over the future, over sickness, over poverty, etc. People will follow leaders who can give them that power even if the leaders' moral behavior is found to be wanting. So spiritualists, witches, psychic readers, gurus, and the like are growing in popularity. Recently there have also been some unfortunate instances of serious moral failure among prominent Christian evangelists who have been exhibiting miraculous gifts in their ministry.

But in biblical Christianity power without holiness is useless and unacceptable (1 Cor. 13:1-3). The God of the Bible is not like other gods who supposedly can be appeased and grant favors if devotees follow certain magical rituals. The God of the Bible is a holy God, demanding total commitment from people in every area of life. Therefore, in biblical religion holiness is so important that all our success would be worthless without it. Holiness is clearly one of the primary qualifications for leadership. This is why in the list of fifteen qualifications for overseers that Paul gave Timothy (1 Tim. 3:2-7), only one has to do with ability ("able to teach"). The rest have to do with character, reputation, maturity, and family life. All these are qualities related to godliness.

Later Paul warns Timothy, telling him not to be hasty about appointing leaders (1 Tim. 5:22). Immediately after that he adds, "nor take part in the sins of others." This warning suggests that when a leader that Timothy appoints sins, Timothy participates in that sin. The situation of leaders sinning is so serious that the person who appointed them to leadership bears some of the responsibility for the ensuing scandal. James says, "Not many of you should become teachers, my brothers, for you know that we who teach will be judged with greater strictness" (James 3:1).

Paul told Timothy that the way to overcome the rejection that he faced in the church because he was young was to "set the believers an example in speech, in conduct, in love, in faith, in purity" (1 Tim. 4:12). Paul told Titus, "Show yourself in all respects to be a model of good works, and in your teaching show integrity, dignity, and sound speech that cannot be condemned, so that an opponent may be put to shame, having nothing evil to say about us" (Titus 2:7-8). Three times in his Epistles Paul asks his readers to follow his example. To the Corinthians he said, "Be imitators of me, as I am of Christ" (1 Cor. 11:1; see also Phil. 3:17; 2 Thess. 3:7).

So one answer to the worldwide problem of unholy leadership in society and the church is to present examples of godly leadership. When Christians are tempted to lie, to give a bribe, to take revenge, to be prejudiced against someone, or to act in a dishonorable way, the lives of their leaders should act as a deterrent. Seeing the way their leaders behave should give people such a thirst for God that they will be ashamed of sin and earnestly desirous of holiness. If leaders are not holy, the members have an excuse for unholiness. They reason, "If my pastor lies, why can't I lie?" "If my pastor slanders others, why can't I?" We have the great challenge today of creating an atmosphere where such actions are simply not tolerated and where positive examples of godly leadership are plain for all to see. Such standards would act as a strong deterrent to ungodliness.

As I said earlier, we live in a pragmatic society that overlooks ungodliness if the ungodly person is powerful in achieving some needed immediate goals. In such an environment one can see how capable but ungodly people can come into leadership even in the church because of their usefulness to the church's program. This is why Paul asked Timothy not to be hasty in appointing leaders (1 Tim. 5:22). In this area we cannot afford to compromise.

Of course, we all fail and sin. When we do, we must face up to the consequences. Then, as people see the seriousness with which we regard our sin, something of the glory of God that was lost by our sin would be restored. Paul said, "As for [leaders] who persist in sin, rebuke them in the presence of all, so that the rest may stand in fear" (1 Tim. 5:20). When the church sees how the leader's sin has been dealt with, they realize that holiness is vitally important to the Christian life. Though such action humiliates the rebuked leader, he has the consolation of knowing that some measure of the glory of God, which was lost by his sin, has been restored. If his primary aim in life is the glory of God, then he will be satisfied amidst his pain.

D. L. Moody was greeting people at the end of a service when a man approached him and deliberately insulted him. "Moody pushed the man away, only to send him tumbling down the stairs to the lower vestibule." When Moody went to the platform shortly after that to preach at the next service, he said, "Friends, before beginning tonight, I want to confess that I yielded just now to my temper, out in the hall, and I have done wrong. . . . If that man is present here, . . . I want to ask his forgiveness, and God's. Let us pray."[6]

Unfortunately, today we sometimes do not respond adequately to the sins of leaders, as we are afraid of the uproar that could result. So we often have situations where most of the people know that the leader has done something wrong. They may talk about it privately, but they will not bring it up publicly. The leader does not lose face, and an external calm is maintained. But revival is stifled, God's glory is removed from the church, and a huge disincentive to holiness exists in the church.

Robert Murray McCheyne (1813-1843), who was mightily used by God to bring revival in Scotland though he died at age twenty-nine, said, "My people's greatest need is my personal holiness." Always our biggest battles in ministry are with ourselves. Only our disobedience can thwart God's desire to bless us and make us fruitful. Other causes will threaten to take away the blessing from our lives, but they will succeed only if we respond to these attacks in an ungodly way. God in his sovereignty can turn attacks against us into good. In the Introduction to this book I presented D. L. Moody's statement that he had more trouble with D. L. Moody than with any other person he had met!

Revealing God by Teaching

The other way Jesus revealed God to the disciples was by his teaching. He mentions or implies this means several times in the prayer of John 17. In verse 6b he says, "Yours they were, and you gave them to me, and they have kept your word." To keep God's Word they should have heard it from Christ. Other verses are more explicit: "For I have given them the words that you gave me" (17:8a); "I have given them your word" (17:14a).

The extended discourse in John 13—16 is a good example of the teaching Jesus gave his disciples. R. T. France thinks that Jesus must have taught his disciples in an extended way like this several times. France points to the fact that Jesus would deliberately withdraw with the disciples to lonely places for retreats away from the crowd during which he would have taught them (Mark 6:30-32). Mark 9:30-31 is a good example: "They went on from there and passed through Galilee. And he did not want anyone to know, for (*gar,* because—NIV) he was teaching his disciples."[7] In the Synoptic Gospels his teaching during the latter portion of his ministry "is devoted to the disciples."[8]

Getting people into the Word is the primary means of bringing them along the path to holiness. Later in his prayer Jesus said, "Sanctify them in the truth; your word is truth" (17:17). One of the pitfalls of a discipling ministry is making people too dependent on us. And one of the best ways to avoid that problem is to get them into the Word so that they can get their strength through it directly. Then, whether we are there or not, whether we live up to their expectations or not, the Word can always be trusted to be the sure source of authority for their lives. So not only do we teach them the Word, but we train them to be people of the Word, people who know how to handle the Word aright. Such a person, according to Paul, is a good worker for God. He tells Timothy, "Do your best to present yourself to God as one approved, a worker who has no need to be ashamed, rightly handling the word of truth" (2 Tim. 2:15).

So leaders must teach the Word to those they lead. The early church felt that the apostles should be set apart to concentrate on prayer and the ministry of the Word (Acts 6:2, 4). Therefore, we should not be surprised when we find that of the fifteen qualifications for overseers, the only ability-related qualification given is that of teaching (1 Tim. 3:2).

Some of the teaching takes place in a formal setting. Such training is structured and systematic and thereby helps us come close to giving our people "the whole counsel of God" (Acts 20:27). Jesus did a lot of this type of teaching. He would go to the synagogue on the Sabbath when people expected to be taught. He would go to special spots such as the beach or a mountain where people came to him specifically to have him teach them. The Sermon on the Mount (Matt. 5—7) and the teaching he did seated on the boat by the beach are examples of this type of teaching (Matt. 13:1-9).

Another way to get people into the Word is through informal theological conversation. A lot of the teaching found in the Gospels consists of informal discussions triggered by some incident. Jesus' discourse on wealth and following him (Luke 18:24-30) was sparked by the encounter with the rich young ruler. The story of the Good Samaritan came as a result of the question, "Who is my neighbor?" that a lawyer asked in the middle of a conversation (Luke 10:25-37). Jesus' great discourse on the last things (Luke 21:6-36) was triggered by his hearing some people "speaking of the temple, how it was adorned with noble stones and offerings" (Luke 21:5).

Similarly when we are traveling together, at our team meetings, and as we face crises, we simply chat about the things of the Lord. This is one reason why team meetings should not be rushed (another reason is that informal chatting helps deepen fellowship). When we chat theologically about the things we face, we get our people into the discipline of applying the Bible to everything they do. That is a key to nurturing people to become biblical Christians.

An important theme of the John 17 prayer of Jesus is that he was leaving these disciples, and he was sending them into the world (John 17:11-18).

His teaching was to prepare them for that mission. Verse 18 says, "As you sent me into the world, so I have sent them into the world." In the same way our teaching will need to be geared toward helping those we lead to go into their particular world.

Whenever I have responsibility for discipling a volunteer in Youth for Christ, I will meet with him regularly. And during our appointment we spend a lot of our time talking about the challenges he faces in his home and school or workplace. This is where he has to live the Christian life, and we need to talk about how he can respond Christianly to the various situations he will face.[9] When I am with paid staff, the conversation will be about such things as their ministry, their family life, and their relationships with their in-laws and neighbors. Of course, with both groups we will talk about their personal spiritual life, devotional life, and the battle with temptation.

JESUS WAS A STEWARD

We Don't Own Anyone

What Jesus said about his relationship with the disciples implies that he was saying that he did not own them. They belonged to God. He described them as "the people whom you gave me out of the world" and says, "Yours they were, and you gave them to me" (John 17:6). Later he says, "I am praying . . . for those whom you have given me, for they are yours" (17:9). If Jesus, the Lord of all creation, could speak as he did about the Father owning the children, how much more should this be true of us. We do not own anyone, even our own children. They belong to God, and they have been entrusted to our care for a time. So our relationship with them could be described as stewardship rather than ownership.

Though Jesus did not use any words that directly mean "steward" in this prayer, he communicated that idea. A steward is "one to whose care is committed the management of the household (Gen. 43:19; Luke 16:1)."[10] This definition can be broadened to the idea of a master giving a responsibility that is to be faithfully fulfilled. Those we lead have been entrusted to our care. We try to help them as much as we can, but we do not own them.

The Bible often uses the parent-child metaphor when referring to the relationship between leaders and those they lead, as we saw at the beginning of this chapter. I believe it is a good metaphor, for it carries the idea of caring for one's children. If I were to give one word to describe the discipling process, it would be *caring*. Interestingly, however, Jesus said, "And call no man your father on earth, for you have one Father, who is in heaven" (Matt. 23:9).

The context of that statement shows that Jesus was talking not about the function of parenthood but about the status and honor that the Pharisees had claimed for themselves by allowing the people to call them "father." When it comes to status and honor, we are servants. When it comes to function and responsibility, we are parents. Leadership does not have to do with status; it has to do with responsibility.

The concept of stewardship leaves room for role reversals. In the record of the partnership between Paul and Barnabas in Acts, Barnabas is always mentioned first at the start, indicating that he, as the senior man, was the leader (Acts 11:30; 12:25; 13:1, 2, 7). But in the middle of the record of the first missionary journey, the order changes, and it becomes Paul and Barnabas (13:43, 46, 50; 15:2, 22, 35, 36). This shift probably indicates that Paul became the prominent member of the team and that he did the public speaking.

Interestingly, in two places the order is reversed again. In Lystra Barnabas is mentioned first. The people of Lystra identified Barnabas with Zeus, the patron god of the city, and Paul with Hermes, who would have been the divine spokesman (Acts 14:12). It seems that the people of Lystra saw Barnabas, who must have been older and looked more distinguished, as the leader even though Paul, as the speaker, was the prominent one. The other place where Barnabas appears first is in the record of the Jerusalem Council (Acts 15:12, 25). In Jerusalem Barnabas was the more respected leader, and it would have been more appropriate for him to take the lead.

Some years ago in India I had the wonderful privilege of ministering together with James Hudson Taylor III. He was for many years the head of Overseas Missionary Fellowship (OMF), the organization that his great-grandfather Hudson Taylor founded. Recently I met him in Hong Kong where he lives and works. I asked him about his son Jamie, and the father proudly said, "He's my boss!" After retiring from the post of general director, the father had pioneered a specialized OMF ministry to mainland China. Then he had stepped down from the leadership of that ministry and handed it over to his son.

As we pursue this understanding of discipling, we can see that we could have different spiritual parents at different stages of our lives. This seems to have been the case with John Mark, who must surely have been mentored by Barnabas. Later Peter calls him "my son" (1 Peter 5:13). I have had different people I consider as spiritual fathers and mothers at different stages of my life. My mother was perhaps the most influential in laying the foundation for everything that followed in my walk with the Lord. I consider my pastor during my teenage years, an Irish missionary named George Good, as a spiritual father. Then I came under the influence of our Youth for Christ director Sam Sherrard. At Asbury Seminary Robert Coleman became like a father to me. And then at Fuller Seminary my mentor Dan Fuller took on this role.

Today I can see how each of these people has influenced my life and ministry markedly. There are others that I regard as my mentors. For example, my missions professor J. T. Seamands and preaching professor Donald Demaray took a personal interest in me and taught me many, many important things.

Now the disciples may have had only one primary mentor: Jesus. But Jesus was perfect, and so he would have given them a complete training. Since we are not perfect, I believe it is advisable for people to be mentored by more than one person so that one could compensate for the weaknesses of another.[11] I am weak in handling the areas of administration and finance. People I supervise and disciple need help and supervision in these areas too. Therefore, we have arranged for others who are more competent to help them in these areas. This may cause a little confusion in terms of our organizational chart, but it helps get the job done and ensures that our workers are given adequate supervision.

We must always be ready to release the people we disciple. We must be careful not to cling to them or have them as a primary source of satisfaction. Indeed, we will rejoice when they do well and mourn when they suffer. But our primary source of security must always be God. Then if it is best for our disciples to work under someone else's leadership, we will gladly release them, as we want the best for them. If we cling to people and try to control them, soon the relationship will turn sour as they mature and seek more independence. And often there will be an unpleasant parting that leaves both parties hurt. We could end up stifling their potential too. Our primary fulfillment should always be from God and never from any aspect of our ministry. This is one of the many reasons why we should never sacrifice our time with God for ministry.

Gradual Growth in Understanding

Jesus said, "Now they know that everything that you have given me is from you" (John 17:7). By using the word *now* (*nun*, meaning now or at the present[12]), Jesus suggested that they did not understand earlier who he really was. It was like saying, "At long last they understand." He said something similar earlier that same evening: "If you had known me, you would have known my Father also. From now on you do know him and have seen him"

(John 14:7). In that same conversation he mildly rebuked Philip saying, "Have I been with you so long, and you still do not know me, Philip?" (14:9). They had made some progress after three years of intense discipling, but they still had more to learn. So after his resurrection he tells the two disciples on the road to Emmaus: "O foolish ones, and slow of heart to believe all that the prophets have spoken!" (Luke 24:25).

If Jesus, after being with his disciples almost continuously for three whole years, found that they took a long time to understand his teaching, we should not be surprised when progress is slow in our attempts to disciple people. Those of us who work with new converts will especially find this to be true because many who come to Christ have not grown up under the influence of the Christian worldview. I think this problem is going to be increasingly encountered in ministry in the West too. So we mustn't get discouraged when those we disciple act in ways that seem to betray all that we have taught them. We must persevere in teaching them the Word, knowing that this is what will ultimately effect a change in their thinking and attitudes.

Of course, in this era we have the benefit of the more personal ministry of the Holy Spirit. This is why on this same evening Jesus said, "It is to your advantage that I go away, for if I do not go away, the Helper will not come to you. But if I go, I will send him to you" (John 16:7). He then goes on to explain the special advantage of having the Spirit: "And when he comes, he will convict the world concerning sin and righteousness and judgment" (16:8). So we will teach the Word, and we will look to the Holy Spirit to do his work of conviction. And if the disciplees are receptive to this dual ministry, they will grow in the knowledge of God.

Special Responsibility for a Few People

As the prayer proceeds, we see that the relationship Jesus had with the disciples while he was on earth was a special one: "I am praying for them. I am not praying for the world but for those whom you have given me, for they are yours" (John 17:9). As the Savior of the world, he cares equally for everyone in the world. That is why he came down to save the world (John 3:17). But when he accepted the limitations of humanity, he took on a special responsibility for a few people, whom he trained to carry out his work after he left the world.

We can carry this principle through for our lives also. We do care for the world and do what we can to make it a better place. We have a greater responsibility toward our neighborhood and the church. But our greatest responsibility is for those entrusted to our care—family members and others with whom we work closely. For leaders that would mean those whom they directly supervise and, even more specially, those they disciple. If we try to look after the whole world, we will die of exhaustion. We cannot even fully look after everyone in the church or organization we lead. As leaders we must ensure that everyone is looked after, but we may not have to do it all ourselves. In fact, our primary task may be to work with the team that will look after each person in the group.

Freshness in Ministry

Few things keep us fresh in ministry as much as the ministry of discipling. It brings desperation into our prayer lives as we yearn for our disciplees to do well in life. It brings deep perplexity over their failures, which drives us to our knees. It challenges us to find answers to the questions and problems that they are facing, and that helps us to learn much and grow in our knowledge of theology and ministry. Discipling also challenges us to be spiritually alert, for we know that we cannot help them to be holy unless we ourselves are holy. Sometimes I find that a young staff worker I am discipling struggles with some of the same things that I am struggling with. What an incentive for me to get my life straightened out so that I can help him!

Discipling brings freshness to our lives in another way too. Sometimes when I am very busy and under a lot of stress, I may not naturally think of having an appointment with a young staff worker. There are so many urgent things to attend to. But an appointment of an hour has been slotted into the schedule. If I keep in mind that I am going to spend a whole hour with that person, that hour can be like an oasis of rest in the midst of a maddening schedule. God can use the time to bring his healing refreshment to our lives.

Servanthood Is Commitment to People

Today there is a lot of talk about leadership as servanthood. We are not only servants of God, but we are servants of the people we minister among (2 Cor. 4:5). I like to define servanthood as the commitment to do all we can for the welfare of the people whose servants we are. In fact, I would include this in my list of the three most important roles of a leader.

Some leaders feel that, as CEO of the organization/church, they must look at the big picture and cannot afford time to work toward the fulfillment of God's best for individuals. They leave that to the human resource development (HRD) people in the organization. That is not the biblical model. The organization or church will not suffer because leaders are devoted to those they lead. God brought these people to the organization/church. God's best for them should dovetail with God's best for the organization/church, for he has a wonderful plan for both. So when an individual grows into achieving God's best for his or her life, then the group to which he or she belongs also grows toward God's best for it.

If God's best for a person does not fit in with the goals of the group, then out of concern for both the person and the group, the leader will try to help that person find a more suitable position. True, we may lose a good worker, but we will not ultimately suffer by acting in the best interest of the individuals entrusted to our care. We will trust God to look after us and concentrate on doing what we know to be in keeping with scriptural principles. Then we will find God's blessings according to the principle that when we lose our life, we will find it. If we sacrifice a valuable worker because another place is better for him or her, we can trust God to compensate.

Giving adequate time to care for a few individuals becomes a big challenge as we grow in leadership. Public ministries can crowd out the time we used to have for personal discipling. We need to make some tough decisions to ensure that we give discipling priority. As we grow in leadership, we need to be constantly reminding ourselves of our primary callings. In order to meet the demands of those callings adequately, we will need to cut off other areas of involvement. Very high up on our priorities should be caring for the people we lead.

When you are a leader, you cannot expect to spend time with those you lead unless you carefully include it in your schedule. I think we should make regular appointments with these people and keep those appointments rigidly. Most leaders are so busy that they shouldn't expect automatically to have quality time with close coworkers. Therefore, they must make some firm decisions to ensure that they meet with them. I think we have the same challenge when it comes to giving time to the home. If we don't make tough decisions about this, we will find that we have unconsciously slipped into neglecting the family.

I try to ensure that I do not cancel my appointments with those I lead when I am very busy with a big program. Sometimes we may need to postpone the meeting because of emergencies. But just like our time with the Lord, if we miss it due to unavoidable circumstances, we will have it another time during the day rather than cancel it. There is no substitute for unhurried times spent with those we lead. In fact, spending such time is one of our primary aims as leaders. According to Mark, when Jesus chose the Twelve, he intended to achieve two things with them—be with them and send them out for ministry. Mark 3:14 says, "And he appointed twelve (whom he also named apostles) so that they might be with him and he might send them out to preach."

JESUS PRAYED FOR HIS DISCIPLES

A Biblical Priority

We have already said that the longest part (seventeen verses) of the longest recorded prayer of Jesus (twenty-six verses) consisted of prayer for his disciples. The only time Jesus mentioned his prayer life outside the words of a recorded prayer is when he said that he prayed for Peter that his faith would not fail (Luke 22:32). Within Jesus' high-priestly prayer that we are studying, Jesus said that he particularly prayed for the disciples: "I am praying for them. I am not praying for the world but for those whom you have given me, for they are yours" (John 17:9).

In ten out of his thirteen Epistles Paul says that he prays for his recipients. In two letters he says he prays night and day. He says he prays night and day over his desire to go to Thessalonica (1 Thess. 3:10). Then he tells his spiritual child Timothy, "I remember you constantly in my prayers night and day" (2 Tim. 1:3). Here again we see concentrated prayer for the person for whom he had a special responsibility.

We preachers often have people tell us, "Please pray for me." Sometimes we hear these requests as we greet the audience after we have finished speaking. If three out of the 100 people who shake hands with us ask us to pray for them, how can we remember? Usually when such a request is made of me, I pray for the person at once, and so fulfill the promise I made. Sometimes I may remember to pray again. Sometimes I may put the prayer request on my prayer list.

But we cannot pray in such an ad hoc manner for those for whom we have a special responsibility—family members and those we disciple or supervise. I try to pray for these people daily, usually making it about five times a week for my colleagues and each day for my family. To ensure that I remember, I have them on my prayer list, and I also have written down some specific things in their lives and ministries to pray about. I also have their pictures in the place where I pray in my room.

The Scudder family name is a very distinguished one in the South Asian church. Dr. Ida Scudder founded the famous Vellore Medical College and Hospital. Ida's grandfather, John Scudder, first came to Sri Lanka (then called

Ceylon in the languages of the colonial rulers) as a missionary and then went to South India. He had nine children, and all of them became missionaries. He is reported to have said that all his children were literally prayed into the kingdom by their mother. In fact, it was her practice to spend their birthdays in fasting and prayer for the particular child whose birthday it was.

Following Paul's admonition to "pray without ceasing" (1 Thess. 5:17), we can send what are called "flash prayers" or "arrow prayers" for people at different times of the day. Here is a father whose son is at a party, and the father is concerned about how the boy will respond to the temptations he will face there. The father can continuously send up flash prayers for his protection. He is battling for his son spiritually while the boy is at the party. A mother could be praying during the time that her spiritual or physical daughter is taking an exam. A pastor can be in prayer at home while his new youth director is having his first meeting with the youth fellowship committee. This reminds us of the battle that Joshua led against the Amalekites, where victory was won through the prayers of Moses, with Aaron and Hur holding up the hands of Moses (Exodus 17:10-13). Of course flash prayers will come out of a background of time spent alone with God and should never be a substitute for one's quiet time, as we shall show in chapter 14.

I have come to believe that praying for those I lead is the most important thing that I do as a leader. This belief is based on what the Bible says about the power of prayer. The church in Jerusalem set a precedent by giving the apostles the opportunity to "devote" themselves "to prayer and to the ministry of the word" (Acts 6:4). In keeping with this principle, the first item in my official job description as director of Youth for Christ is that I pray for YFC and its people. Moses' times of intercession for Israel are well known (e.g., Exod. 17:10-12; Num. 12:13-15; 21:7; Deut. 33:6-17; Ps. 106:23). Samuel told the people of Israel, "Moreover, as for me, far be it from me that I should sin against the LORD by ceasing to pray for you" (1 Sam. 12:23). W. E. Sangster has said, "When we go to heaven and realize all that prayer did on earth, we'll be ashamed that we prayed so little."

If prayer is the most important thing that we do, then we should work at developing our prayer life. This may involve bringing freshness to it by occasionally trying out new ways of praying. W. E. Sangster said that anyone who takes intercession seriously would soon find that he or she needs a prayer list. Such a list helps us to remember the things we want to pray for. We will keep revising our prayer list so that it reflects current prayer needs. I have photographs pasted all over my office at home, arranged according to categories. And I find this an excellent aid to intercession. Just as professionals seek to improve their skills in their field of specialization, so Christian leaders should work on improving their skills in prayer. I think our prayer list is an excellent project to work on during our annual leave or vacation.

Tell Them You Pray for Them

Both Jesus and Paul told people they were praying for them. I think we should too. That could be a real encouragement. For example, if a child who is doing something difficult, such as taking an examination, knows his father is praying for him, he would be encouraged. The student might also be spurred on to persevere without giving up when discouraged. I think that a great security and hope come to people when they know that others are praying for them. This benefit would be compounded if they knew that one of those praying for them is their leader.

Prayer Is an Exercise in Hope

The prayer of Jesus for the disciples was actually an exercise in hope. In a short time they would all flee in fear. Peter would deny knowing him with cursing and swearing. But Jesus looked in hope beyond those setbacks. This is particularly true of his prayer for Peter. Jesus said, "Simon, Simon, behold, Satan demanded to have you, that he might sift you like wheat, but I have prayed for you that your faith may not fail. And when you have turned again, strengthen your brothers" (Luke 22:31-32). He looked beyond the failure to the time when Peter would be strengthening other Christians.

Clement of Alexandria headed a Christian training school in the Egyptian town of Alexandria during A.D. 190-202. He tells the story of how the apostle John prayed for a young convert who had wandered off to be the leader of a band of robbers:

> "Why do you flee from me, child?" John cried out. "You still have hopes of life. I will give account to Christ for you." When the young man wept and embraced him, John interceded for him with abundant prayers, struggled along with him in continual fasts. . . . Nor did he depart, so they say, until he had set him over the congregation, setting a great example of true repentance and a great token of regeneration.[13]

Sometimes it may be our prayers that carry people through during a tough time. Some years ago I went to Singapore for about eighteen days. My plan was to preach during weekends and write during weekdays. At that time I was leading a Bible study with two new Christians in their twenties. One had been a heavy drinker and the other a drug addict before they came to Christ through our church. While I was in Singapore, I felt a strong burden to pray for these two people, and I prayed for them even more than I usually do.

When I returned, I found that the former drug addict had gone back to drugs. I was grappling with some serious problems in the ministry at that time, and I felt that this was the last straw. How was it that one of them should fall so badly even though I had prayed for them at what I felt was the prompting of the Lord? That happened about eight years ago. Now both of these people are fine Christian leaders. I have come to think that my prayer was like the prayer of Jesus for Peter. It did not prevent him from falling, but it may have helped keep him from falling so badly that he could never come back.

There is great value in persevering prayer, which unfortunately has been somewhat obscured recently as a result of the new emphasis on strategic praying as part of spiritual warfare. We are finding people going and proclaiming the victory of Christ over places and situations. There is, of course, some truth to this emphasis, but it should never detract from the call to patiently persevere in prayer for people and things over a long period of time.[14] Jesus told the parable of the persistent widow and the uncaring judge "to the effect that they ought always to pray and not lose heart" (Luke 18:1).

Paul climaxes his description of the nature of spiritual warfare in Ephesians 6 by saying, " . . . praying at all times in the Spirit, with all prayer and supplication. To that end keep alert with all perseverance, making supplication for all the saints" (Eph. 6:18). We note here the emphasis on perseverance in prayer.

Sometimes all we can do for some people is to pray for them. They may have rebelled against what we taught them, and they are not in a position to listen to our advice. Though they may not allow us to talk to them about God, we can talk to God about them! God surely listens to the prayers of a heartbroken mother over a prodigal son.[15] We must persevere in prayer.

Early in his ministry George Mueller covenanted to pray for the conversion of five people daily. The first of these five people came to Christ eighteen months after he started his daily prayers. The second came five years after the first was converted. The third came six years after the second. Once he wrote that he had been praying for the other two for thirty-six years, and they had not yet come to Christ. The fourth came shortly before Mueller's death, and the fifth a few years after his death.[16]

JESUS WAS GLORIFIED THROUGH THEM

The next point mentioned by Christ in his prayer has to do with a reward of discipling. Jesus said, "All mine are yours, and yours are mine, and I am glorified in them" (John 17:10). I think we should be careful about thinking that we too are glorified through our disciplees as Jesus was through his disciples. Certainly this is not something we look for. All the glory must be directed to Christ. But because we are one with Christ, we also share some of it.

We should not try to use glory from our disciplees to push ourselves forward. We should not brag about them in a way intended to focus attention upon our success in discipling. Charles Spurgeon was converted through the preaching of a layman who spoke that Sunday because the scheduled preacher had not come. Spurgeon never told who this lay preacher was, but many have claimed to have been the one!

I feel uneasy when I hear people say things like, "He's my spiritual child," or "He's my Timothy." Such statements can take glory that is due to Christ and deflect it in our direction. We saw above that Paul and Peter said something like that, but in these cases they were calling Timothy, Titus, Philemon, and Mark their children in order to lift the children up, not to lift up themselves. What I am cautioning about is the habit of using our disciplees to boast about ourselves.

But the fact remains that when people we have invested in do well, it brings us immense joy. Robert Coleman says, "The glory of the teacher is to sit at the feet of the student and learn from him." This is the reward of discipling. Many will not make it, and as we loved them dearly, their failure will break our hearts. But some will make it, and their success makes the toil worthwhile.

Of course, some of us may see the fruit of our labors only when we get to heaven. We may be called to plough hard ground and make it ready for someone else to reap the harvest. Therefore, we should not base our evaluation of our ministry purely on the level of success we see.

But when those we invest in do make it, our hearts are filled with joy. Paul addressing the Philippians said, "Therefore, my brothers, whom I love and long for, my joy and crown . . ." (Phil. 4:1).

11

LAUNCHING DISCIPLES
INTO MINISTRY

IN THIS CHAPTER we continue with our discussion on discipling, using principles gleaned from the high-priestly prayer of Jesus when he prayed for his disciples (John 17:6-19). In the previous chapter we saw that disciplers reveal God to the disciplees, act as stewards, pray for the disciplees, and find some fulfillment and joy through their successes.

JESUS PROTECTED THE DISCIPLES AND PREPARED
THEM TO BE WITHOUT HIM

In verses 11 and 12 Jesus described in prayer how he prepared them for his departure. He said, "And I am no longer in the world, but they are in the world, and I am coming to you. Holy Father, keep them in your name, which you have given me, that they may be one, even as we are one. While I was with them, I kept them in your name, which you have given me. I have guarded them . . ." (John 17:11-12b).

In verse 11 Jesus asked God to "keep them in your name." The word translated "keep" (*tereō*) appears four times in this prayer. The first time it is used to indicate "keeping the word" and takes the sense of "observe" or "obey" (17:6). The other three times it takes the sense of "keep under guard" or "keep in custody." In verse 12 Jesus said, "I kept them in your name." In verse 15 Jesus prayed, "I do not ask that you take them out of the world, but that you keep them from the evil one." In verse 12 Jesus used another word (*phulassō*), which means "keep under guard,"[1] and says, "I have guarded them."

We Protect Them First

Let's try to visualize the background of these statements. Jesus is about to leave this world with its multitude of evil influences. While he was with the disciples, he guarded them. Now not only is he going to leave them, but also he is going to send them into that world. So he asks God to look after them. How much like leadership and parenthood this is! In the early times of discipling and parenting, we have to give special protective care to our spiritual and physical children. Later we can release them from our grip to live more independent lives.

Children must be protected from things they are not equipped to handle, such as explicit sexual images on the Internet and on television. There may be prostitutes on the street that the children see regularly. But the parents may not be too descriptive about who they are and what they do. However, when the children get to be young people, the parents will need to tell them more and warn them and also give a Christian perspective on prostitution.

Similarly new believers often find the enthusiastic and authoritative teaching of the cults with their appeal to Scripture very attractive, especially if these converts are beginning to see things that they do not like in their church. They need to be warned.

A pastor may not tell his small children about the way a respected leader in the church has hurt him. They would find it difficult to understand that such things happen in the church and especially that the source of this pain is such a respected leader.

Leaders will also need to equip their children to face the dangers in the world. Young people should go into the world with their eyes open and with an understanding of some of the challenges they will have to face. They must have some guidelines on how Christians can respond to such challenges.

There are two essential ingredients to such preparation. One is a warning of danger. I traced two Greek words that have the idea of "warning" in the Gospels, and I found that they take this sense twenty times. The first word, *prosechō*, appears ten times and has the idea of "pay close attention to, be on guard, watch, be careful." The other word, *blepō*, appears sixty-six times in the Gospels. It usually means "see," but it can take the meaning "beware of," and it appears in this sense ten times. These twenty references show us that Jesus often warned people about the dangers they would face in this sinful world.

Obviously the discipler has to know something about the world of the disciplee. Over the years I have led vastly different divisions of Youth for

Christ in Sri Lanka. As teenagers love music, I need to examine the music they are listening to and discuss with them things such as lyrics and the body movements and attire of the musicians. As a youth movement we discuss TV programs popular with teens and critique these from a Christian viewpoint, mentioning both good and bad content. I think parents should do that with the programs children watch on TV. We also discuss controversies in the field of sports and politics, issues that seem to excite the whole nation, so that teens won't be carried away by popular opinion, but think in a Christian way about these topics.

It is also important for us to discuss the Christian response to special challenges our people face. For example, we need to show why Christians do not watch and read pornography. It is not only because porn is sinful. If that were the only reason we gave, the temptation would still have a lot of force. People could reason that though it is sinful, porn offers real enjoyment. The Christian view is that pornography is ultimately not enjoyable. In fact, it takes away real sexual enjoyment. So young people stay away from it because they are committed to enjoying sex! In this world with so many warped images of sex, we need to develop a healthy biblical attitude among Christians toward sex as a beautiful thing that God created. We will also need to really grapple with the reasons why sex outside of marriage is sinful and terribly dangerous, especially because much of society views this behavior as something quite normal.

I have given challenges here that youths face as an example. We need to know what the challenges are for the group that we lead. We need to warn people in our care about these and then direct them toward a Christian response.

The Level of Protection Changes

Just as Jesus released his disciples to go into the world and committed them to the care of God, we release our spiritual and physical children. First we will see that with time the extent to which we direct them changes. Earlier we supervised them closely, but after some time we let them out on their own and pray for them as they are in the field. Jesus followed this practice with his disciples whom he sent out as groups of two on at least two mission trips.

Earlier we cared for our disciplees like babies, but later we come to view them as peers. During his Last Supper conversation, Jesus told the disciples, "No longer do I call you servants, for the servant does not know what his master is doing; but I have called you friends, for all that I have heard from my Father I have made known to you" (John 15:15). Now that Jesus had given them the knowledge they needed, he related to them as their friend.

This is one of the delights of both leadership and parenthood. Those who were once treated like children have also become friends. As a youth worker, I find that my physical children are now my "consultants." I often ask them for guidance on how I should apply a certain truth I am going to speak on to the lives of teens. As we said in the previous chapter, great delight comes to teachers when they can sit at the feet of their students and learn from them!

Of course, as friends they will provoke each other to live godly lives (Heb. 10:24-25). We never stop being blessed by others, though sometimes the ways in which the blessings come are different.

Once, after I had spoken on the idea of leaders being friends of those they lead, a pastor in the audience came up to me and told me that he had been taught that that idea was wrong. Such a friendship would be a hindrance to leading and to exercising authority. I directed him to John 15:15 where Jesus, the Master leader, said that he was the friend of the disciples.

I have often thought about what this pastor said. I came to see that he was reflecting an attitude common among contemporary Christian leaders whose relationships with those they lead focus primarily on the job that must be done and not on the needs and feelings of those doing the work. Job descriptions are written and compliance is expected. To be talking in such a way that workers open up about what they feel is considered too time-consuming and impractical in this efficiency-oriented age.

Yet Paul had deep friendships with those he led. The closeness of his relationship with Timothy is reflected in the following statement: "As I remember your tears, I long to see you, that I may be filled with joy" (2 Tim. 1:4). This indicates that an emotional tie existed between Paul and Timothy. Paul had allowed Timothy to observe him closely. He said "You, however, have followed my teaching, my conduct, my aim in life, my faith, my patience, my love, my steadfastness, my persecutions and sufferings" (2 Tim. 3:10-11a). Such relationships are forged through much time spent together.

I believe that if today's leaders spend the time to cultivate warm ties like this with those they lead, the result would be a powerful sense of comradeship in the gospel within our ministry teams. The time spent together helps create an environment where the team members are free to share what is on their minds. Workers can clear up misunderstandings and resolve their objections to the course of action proposed by the leader. The result is an atmosphere where high motivation could result if the team has a passionate mission to achieve. With such motivation, you will find the team members working very hard and really sacrificing to see the common goals achieved. Such hard work results in increased efficiency as these motivated workers complete more work, and spiritual power is unleashed by your unity. So the time spent forging a team of friends is more than compensated for by the final results.

Protection Results in Unity

It is most interesting that Jesus mentions unity as the result of the protection he was asking God to give the disciples. Jesus prayed, "Holy Father, keep them in your name, which you have given me, that they may be one, even as we are one" (John 17:11). The word translated "that," *hina*, means "so that" or "in order that." Unity is being clearly presented as a result of the protection he talked about in the previous verses. Several things can cause disunity in a Christian community. Disunity is one of Satan's greatest strategies against the church, and sometimes this problem results from his direct attack. Leaders need to be alert and do all they can to overcome such attacks, through prayer, through talking with the hurt parties, and through any other means.

John says that walking in the light spiritually is a prerequisite for Christian fellowship: "But if we walk in the light, as he is in the light, we have fellowship with one another, and the blood of Jesus his Son cleanses us from all sin" (1 John 1:7). This verse suggests that sometimes unity is broken because one or more members are living in sin or are not open about their problems.

The causes for disunity vary, and leaders who take Christian community life seriously will be alert to this area. Putting into practice Paul's admonition to be "eager to maintain the unity of the Spirit in the bond of peace" (Eph. 4:3) will soon become one of their primary responsibilities. Peter O'Brien explains that the verb (a participle here) translated "eager to" (*spoudazō*) "has an element of haste, urgency, or even a sense of crisis to it."[2] Like Paul, Jesus is very clear about the urgency of the need to deal with unity issues. "So if you are offering your gift at the altar and there remember that your brother has something against you, leave your gift there before the altar and go. First be reconciled to your brother, and then come and offer your gift" (Matt. 5:23-24).

I am amazed at how often Christians today fail to use this approach when there are unity problems. They will write letters, they will speak to others, they will boycott meetings, but they won't go and speak to the person with whom there is a problem. Sometimes they will go to a lawyer before they go to the brother or sister to whom they need to be reconciled.

Now this is hard work. Often before unity is restored, the conversation may go on for several hours. Leaders are usually very busy people. Can they afford to spend so much time? The interaction is usually unpleasant. Those angry with us may be much younger and with much less experience. They may say things that seem to be disrespectful. If so, we need at some time, preferably later, to confront them about this. But isn't it demeaning for the leaders to subject themselves to such treatment? Leaders are servants of the people and of the groups they lead. Whether it is time-consuming or not, demeaning or not, we undertake urgent tasks because we have caught the urgency of Jesus and Paul about the need to solve unity problems.

The distinctive of Christian love is a willingness to go against our natural inclinations and take that extra step to bring Christ's love into an otherwise irredeemable situation. As leaders persevere in doing that, they will be able to see true Christian community at work. I can say that in my twenty-five years as leader of Youth for Christ in Sri Lanka, "maintain[ing] the unity of the Spirit in the bond of peace" has been the most absorbing challenge I have had. This past year when our pastor was on sabbatical leave abroad, I had a lot of extra responsibilities in our church. There, too, maintaining unity was the greatest challenge that we faced.

If we take this challenge seriously and strive for unity, a wonderful depth will come into our community life. If we ignore divisions or try to sweep them under the carpet, we will never know the richness of community life that God intended for us. That Jesus presented unity as the key result of protection shows how important it was for him. In the same way Christians leaders also should give a high place to unity in their list of priorities.

JESUS COMMUNICATED HIS JOY TO THEM

The next thing Jesus was eager for his disciples to have before he left was his joy. So in his prayer he went on to say, "But now I am coming to you, and these things I speak in the world, that they may have my joy fulfilled in themselves" (John 17:13). Note the emphasis on the abundance of joy: He talked about joy being "fulfilled" (*plëroö*) in them. The New International Version translates this request as " . . . that they may have the full measure of my joy within them." Once before on this same night he talked about a full joy when he said, "These things I have spoken to you, that my joy may be in you, and that your joy may be full" (John 15:11). Note how in both these verses Jesus connected the joy with himself and also presented it as a full joy. Twice on this night he also spoke of giving his disciples his peace (John 14:27; 16:33). It seemed to be important to Jesus at that crucial hour to pass on his joy and peace.

As we are not the Saviors of the world, we cannot give people our joy in the same way Jesus did. But we can reflect the joy of Jesus, exemplify it, and help our disciples along the path to joy. Joy is, of course, presented many, many times in the Bible as a basic feature of Christianity. It is the second fruit of the Spirit (Gal. 5.22). It is commanded of us in Philippians 4:4: "Rejoice in the Lord always; again I will say, Rejoice" (Phil. 4:4). The repetition accentuates the importance of joy as a basic feature of the Christian life. Christians then must be joyous people, and leaders must be examples of joy.

If we are to be leaders then, we should make the pursuit of joy an important aspect of our lives. This is part of our homework. True, we suffer for the gospel. We pay a huge price to be faithful to God and his principles. But those things are done out of a lifestyle of joy. In fact, just after saying, "These things I have spoken to you, that my joy may be in you, and that your joy may be full" (John 15:11), Jesus went on to say, "This is my commandment, that you love one another as I have loved you. Greater love has no one than this, that someone lays down his life for his friends" (John 15:12-13). The joy must come first, and out of its strength we launch into sacrificial service.

In chapter 3, in the context of pursuing God's affirmation, we looked at how we can cultivate joy in our lives. Once in a New Year's address George Mueller said, "The welfare of our families, the prosperity of our businesses, our work and service for the Lord, may be considered the most important matters to attend to; but according to my judgment, the most important point to be attended to is this: above all things to see that your souls are happy in the Lord." He goes on to say, "other things may press upon you; the Lord's work even may have urgent claims upon your attention," but this pursuit of joy is "of supreme and paramount importance. . . . Day by day seek to make this the most important business of your life."[3] The joy of the Lord is a wonderful treasure. We must not leave home without it!

John Stam and his wife, Betty, were missionaries in China who were martyred in 1934 when they were twenty-seven and twenty-eight years old. Their tragic deaths motivated many young people to go into missionary service. John once said, "Take away everything I have, but do not take away the sweetness of walking and talking with the King of glory."[4]

Of course we are talking about the joy *of the Lord*. There are other types of joy that we will lose because we love God and people. A few paragraphs before Paul urged the Philippian Christians to "rejoice in the Lord always," he told them, "Complete my joy by being of the same mind, having the same love, being in full accord and of one mind" (Phil. 2:2). He had lost some joy because they were not fully united. Later he was more specific when he wrote, "I entreat Euodia and I entreat Syntyche to agree in the Lord" (Phil. 4:2). Anyone who truly loves this world will be hurt and even angry at seeing the pain and problems here.

Yet if we are bitter people, without the joy of the Lord, we will not help solve these problems. In fact, we will become part of the problem. As I said in chapter 7, one of the saddest things I see today is the number of angry Christian workers in the church. Perhaps the church has hurt them. They have had their share of problems from difficult people. But we must not give bad people the power to ruin our lives. And, for two very good reasons, we don't need to.

First, the Bible is clear that however bad people have been to us, *God's love is greater than their wickedness.* Paul says, "God's love has been poured into our hearts through the Holy Spirit who has been given to us" (Rom. 5:5). That word translated "poured" (*ekcheö*) is often used of liquids, and it can even take the idea of "floods," which is how Moffatt translated it.[5] "The word denotes both abundance and diffusion."[6] The great commentator Albrecht Bengel (1687-1752) used the Latin word *adundantissime* to describe it.[7] God's love is inexhaustible, and it is there in abundance for us to tap into. After that love has had its desired impact on us, the pain, the sorrow, the heartache, and even the righteous anger may remain, for these emotions can coexist with love. But bitterness cannot. We must wage war on bitterness through letting God love us, and we must not let go of God until we sense that he has ministered his comfort to us. Jacob wrestled all night with God saying, "I will not let you go unless you bless me" (Gen. 32:26).

The second reason we cannot be bitter is that *God is greater than our problems.* If we let him, he can and will turn the terrible things that happen to us into good as he has promised in his Word (Rom. 8:28). Ultimately, then, not only do we conquer, but "we are more than conquerors through him who loved us" (Rom. 8:37). The expression "more than conquerors" comes from one word, *hupernikaö*, which has the idea of "over-conquer." "It suggests a lopsided victory in which the enemy or opponent is completely routed."[8] Someone may have wanted to harm us, but we have ended up better off than we were before his action because God turned the evil intended into some-thing good. We can say with Joseph, "As for you, you meant evil against me, but God meant it for good, to bring it about that many people should be kept alive, as they are today" (Gen. 50:20). This verse gives us the strength to for-give these people, and, with that conscious step of forgiveness, the burden leaves our lives. We can minister in the freedom of the Spirit with no hin-drance to the love and joy of God filling our souls.

I read a rather nasty review of one of my books by a respected Christian leader and scholar whom I had held in high esteem. His criticisms hit a sen-sitive spot in my life, and I struggled with anger over this for a long time. I would forget it, and then it would come back to torment me. One day as I was riding my bicycle (for exercise) and thinking and praying, I was able, through a conscious and definite act, to forgive this brother. Though this hap-pened many years ago, I still remember it as if it were yesterday. I remember the place on the road where I was and the time of day when it happened. I felt a huge burden fall off my back. I still feel hurt sometimes over the review, but I think its sting is gone. Now, as I look back, I can say that this reviewer helped me immensely to become a better writer, even though I still think he was unfair in what he said. Truly, our critics are sometimes more helpful to us than our friends.

The Christian worker has to wage this type of battle often. As I said above, the joy of the Lord is so great a treasure that we cannot afford to live without it.

JESUS EXPOSED THE DISCIPLES TO THE HATRED OF THE WORLD

Our next point is something that I would not have included in a discussion of discipling, but we are following a passage, and this idea figures promi-nently there. And it is an important point. Jesus said in verse 14: "I have given them your word, and the world has hated them because they are not of the world, just as I am not of the world" (John 17:14). There is a sense in which we are all aliens in this world. Those who fully follow God's agenda will rarely be esteemed by most people. Sometimes we will face their hatred. The gospel is too radical to be loved by all unless we dilute it by removing some of its "hard truths."

It is hard enough when they hate us, but it is so much harder when they hate those we disciple. This is one of the heartaches that accompanies evan-gelistic ministry. We give people the good news of salvation—and that is what it is to those who accept it: good news. But that same gospel is terrible news to the families of some of those who accept it. This reality weighs heavily on me as one working in a ministry that evangelizes primarily non-Christian youth. It is sometimes heart-rending to see families disrupted by the conversion of one member. Of course Jesus predicted that this would happen: "Do not think that I have come to bring peace to the earth. I have not come to bring peace, but a sword. For I have come to set a man against his father, and a daughter against her mother, and a daughter-in-law against her mother-in-law. And a person's enemies will be those of his own household" (Matt. 10:34-36).

We need to balance this aspect of evangelism with the teaching that Christians must honor and care for their parents and relatives. Paul frankly warns Christians about failure to care for their families. He says, "But if anyone does not provide for his relatives, and especially for members of his household, he has denied the faith and is worse than an unbeliever" (1 Tim. 5:8). We urge our young people to show the best behavior possible to their parents after becoming Christians. We advise them to be wise in the way they live at home so that they will be able to both honor their parents and obey God at the same time.

Yet we know that however much we try to be respectful, loving, and considerate toward others, persecution will come. We must prepare our people for it as Jesus prepared his disciples (see e.g., Matt. 10:17-42; John 15:18-25).

JESUS SENT THE DISCIPLES INTO THE WORLD

We have looked at the fact that Jesus was sending his disciples into the world, and we saw how he prepared them to face its evils. Now, toward the end of the prayer, Jesus seems to be focusing on the fact that they are to go into the world as he came into the world—that is, for ministry. Verses 15 and 16 describe the call to go into the world but not to be "of the world": "I do not ask that you take them out of the world, but that you keep them from the evil one. They are not of the world, just as I am not of the world." Verse 18 connects their going into the world with Jesus' coming into the world: "As you sent me into the world, so I have sent them into the world." He came to save the world, and we take the message of his salvation to the world. He says something similar after his resurrection: "As the Father has sent me, even so I am sending you" (John 20:21).

Ultimately only Jesus has the right to commission people to go into the world, but he uses us to actualize this commission. We impart what we know to others and send them out to serve God. And they, in turn, invest in others. We call this the ministry of multiplication, well presented in 2 Timothy 2:2: "What you have heard from me in the presence of many witnesses entrust to faithful men who will be able to teach others also." Four generations of Christians in the multiplication process are described in this verse. Paul represents the first generation, and he imparts truth to Timothy, who represents the second. Timothy, in turn, imparts the truth to faithful men, the third generation, and they will teach the fourth generation.

Jesus' method in preparing the disciples for this mission is very instructive. Robert Coleman's classic, *The Master Plan of Evangelism*, describes the process.[9] Let me mention a few points here.

First, we see that Jesus always had their potential before his eyes. When he called Simon and Andrew, he said, "Follow me, and I will make you become fishers of men" (Mark 1:17). When he appointed the Twelve, there were two reasons for making the appointments, and one was so that they might be sent out as ministers. Mark says, "And he appointed twelve (whom he also named apostles) so that they might be with him and he might send them out to preach and have authority to cast out demons" (Mark 3:14-15).

Second, Jesus taught them, as we saw in the last chapter. A large percentage of the teaching of Jesus in the Gospels is instruction he gave the Twelve.

Third, he sent them on ministry assignments even before they were fully commissioned. The most famous of these are the two occasions when he sent disciples two by two, once the Twelve, and the other time seventy-two, on itinerant ministry assignments (Matt. 10; Luke 10).

Fourth, he commissioned them. The New Testament presents the Great Commission many times. There are the well-known statements in the four Gospels and Acts (Matt. 28:18-20; Mark 16:15; Luke 24:46-49; John 20:21; Acts 1:8). But there are other statements too that imply this commission, such as the verse we are discussing here: "As you sent me into the world, so I have sent them into the world" (John 17:18; see Acts 10:42). Each of the different statements of the commission focuses on different aspects of it. Matthew's version focuses on many points—from the authority needed to the nature of the ministry, to the presence of Christ with those who fulfill it. Mark showed the extent of the challenge: "the whole creation." Luke focused on the message and the power needed for the work. John presented Jesus' coming to the world as the model for this work. Acts focused on the power needed to fulfill the commission and on its geographical extent. Acts 10:42 describes the command to preach and to testify that Jesus is the judge of the living and the dead.

Jesus demonstrates visionary leadership here. He always keeps before the people the grand and glorious work that must be done. This is one of the key requirements of a leader, to place before the people the grand picture. Problems and challenges faced in their own little world can bog them down so that they forget the big picture and lose the vision. Therefore, the leader must always point to the vision.

Some today are reluctant to use the term "Great Commission," pointing to the fact that there were many other tasks Jesus commissioned his apostles to do. However, I believe that the frequent repetition of the commission to preach the gospel and the variety of ways in which it is presented in the four Gospels and Acts indicate that this task is so important that it must always be a priority in the program of the church. This is why I believe that it is still correct to say that world evangelization is the supreme task of the church. Surely, if we believe that people without Christ are eternally lost, then we would realize the urgency of the task of introducing them to Christ.

Those who are involved in evangelizing the unreached know how much hard work that involves. It usually provokes persecution and unpopularity. Often the statistical results are much less impressive than results from other programs. There are so many other urgent needs in the church that it would be easy to overlook evangelism or give it a secondary place. The result would be that though the church is evangelical and often evangelistic in its program, very little or no evangelism is done among non-Christians. So because it is so easy to neglect evangelizing the unreached and because the frequent repetition of the commission implies that this is an urgent task requiring top priority, I believe that the use of the word *Great* in connection with this Commission is justified.

We look at people with hope just as Jesus did. Every believer is a key vessel that the Lord is waiting to use. Jesus looked at the impulsive and somewhat unstable Peter and said that this man was going to be a rock (Matt. 16:18-19). He told the highly discouraged Peter that he would feed Christ's sheep and would be a martyr for the gospel (John 21:15-23).

Paul kept encouraging Timothy to be faithful to his call, and Paul instructed the young man with his ambitions for Timothy in view. Paul told him, "Do not neglect the gift you have, which was given you by prophecy when the council of elders laid their hands on you" (1 Tim. 4:14). Paul looked at Timothy through the eyes of hope that these prophecies would be fulfilled. So as Paul taught his disciple, he kept the prophecies in view. He once said "This charge I entrust to you, Timothy, my child, in accordance with the prophecies previously made about you, that by them you may wage the good warfare" (1 Tim. 1:18). He was training Timothy to become the great person Paul knew (through prophecy) he would become.

So we keep looking at people through the eyes of hope. Even when they do wrong, in the back of our minds is the ambition to see them achieve the wonderful things God has planned for them. If they are timid like Timothy (2 Tim. 1:7), we may need to remind them of the things God has planned for them. People are exposed to a lot of discouragement and rejection from others in this competitive society. May we be people who remind others of their potential under God and help them "fan into flame the gift of God" (2 Tim. 1:6).

Let me say here that there are two ways in which we can look at all the Christians we meet. Every Christian has strengths and weaknesses. Some leaders focus on the strengths and view the weaknesses as things they will work on. When leaders think of these disciplees, their overriding thought is the potential and not the things that annoy them. Other leaders focus on the weaknesses so that the moment they meet these people, they have an urgency to point out these weak points. May I recommend the former strategy to you? Focusing on people's strengths gives them hope, which in turn gives them the courage to work on overcoming or compensating for their weaknesses. I believe this approach is the way to apply Paul's statement: "Love . . . believes all things, hopes all things" (1 Cor. 13:7).

I would confide in and ask for help regarding my weaknesses from someone who appreciates me and sees some potential in me. If a person seems to reject me the moment he or she meets me, I would be reluctant to trust that person to help me in areas of my life that trouble me.

The ambitions we have for people could become regular features of our prayers for them too. We could write these goals in our prayer list so that we will remember to pray for them specifically. Good leaders then look at people through the eyes of hope.

JESUS DIED TO MAKE THE DISCIPLES HOLY

The last statement from the prayer of Jesus that we consider is his somewhat strange comment: "And for their sake I consecrate (or "sanctify" NIV) myself, that they also may be sanctified in truth" (John 17:19). We usually think that the word *sanctify* or *consecrate* refers to being made holy in terms of becoming Christlike, but we know that Jesus is already completely holy in that sense. *Sanctify*, however, can also be used to mean an act of consecration to the will of God. Jesus says he does this "for their sake," which suggests that he is talking about his death for them. Don Carson points out that "the language ["for them," *huper auton*] is evocative of atonement passages (e.g., Mark 14:24; Luke 22:19; John 6:51; 1 Cor. 11:24)."[10] It is clear that the death and resurrection of Christ is the climax to which the Gospel of John is moving (e.g., John 1:29; 10:17-18; 11:49-52; 12:23-26; 18:11; 19:30). So in verse 19 Jesus is talking about his great act of consecration when he will die for the disciples, and for all people.

Jesus says that the result of his death is that the disciples will also be sanctified (John 17:19). As the sanctification of Christ mentioned here is presented as parallel to the sanctification of the disciples, we should probably take the latter here to mean what it meant in connection with Christ—a consecration for the service of God.

Can we follow this path of Christ in dying for the consecration of those whom we disciple? Certainly we cannot die in the sense of being a substitute for the sins they have committed. But that does not absolve us from laying down our lives for the people we are called to serve. In the previous verse Jesus said, "As you sent me into the world, so I have sent them into the world" (John 17:18; see also John 20:21). If we are sent to the world as he was sent, then we should expect to die for others as he died for people. This is also implied in John 10:11-18 where Jesus said that as the Good Shepherd, he has to die for the sheep. In the same way, if we are good shepherds, we should die for those we look after.

Earlier, during the same evening that Jesus prayed his High-Priestly prayer, he presented the principle that Christians die for others more explicitly. He said, "This is my commandment, that you love one another as I have loved you" (John 15:12). Lest we miss the point he goes on to explain how we are supposed to love one another: "Greater love has no one than this, that someone lays down his life for his friends" (15:13). To show that this is an essential aspect of discipleship, Jesus adds, "You are my friends if you do what I command you" (15:14). According to this logic, one of the ways to see whether a person is a friend of Jesus is to see whether he or she will die for others.

Of course, we cannot die for the whole world as Jesus did. In fact, when Jesus described his death as an example to us in John 15:13, he said he "lays down his life *for his friends.*" Earlier he says we are to "love *one another,*" again implying that it is dying for people close to us that is intended. Christians die for "one another," for "their friends" toward whom they have a special responsibility. When we follow the example of Jesus who is the eternal God, we do so in a restricted sense, given our human limitations. What Jesus as God does for the whole world, we do for those for whom we are responsible. Of course, in emergency situations we may die for others. This is not an absolute command; our friends are not the only people we die for.

For example, we may jump into the sea to save a stranger who is drowning and die in the process. We may jump in front of a bullet aimed at a little child. But these are exceptions to the rule.

As we said in the previous chapter, we have a special responsibility toward different groups of people. Most important are the members of our family. Then there are our colleagues in work and ministry, those we lead, and those we disciple. Then there are the members of our congregation, our neighbors, and our friends. We have a responsibility toward those and other groups of people to varying degrees. Pastors, for example, cannot care comprehensively for every member in their congregation. So if they are good leaders, they will divide this responsibility among a group of leaders. While leaders have the responsibility to ensure that everyone in their group or church is looked after, they themselves may not be the ones who look after every person.

It is interesting that Paul says that husbands are to die for their wives: "Husbands, love your wives, as Christ loved the church and gave himself up for her" (Eph. 5:25). Applying this verse helps us explain what we mean by dying for our people. Most wives would say, "I really don't want my husband to die for me. Just ask him to talk to me! He comes home from work tired and in such a bad mood that he won't open his mouth. He even gets annoyed when I try to talk to him." That husband is physically tired and emotionally drained after a tough day at work, and the last thing he wants to do is to talk. But because he loves his wife, he dies to his inclination to remain silent and talks to her. To him at that time, talking is a kind of death!

There are similar situations where a husband dies to his natural inclinations because he loves the members of his family. He may be very busy and rather stressed out with some special challenges at his job. His family has a need that is not urgent but is one of his routine responsibilities as a husband or father. But, as a Christian, he will drop everything to meet that need, for routines are essential features of a stable family. If the family knows that their spouse or parent, who is in Christian ministry, regularly sacrifices his or her convenience in order to serve the family, then they would excuse an occasional situation when he or she is unable to do something that needs to be done.

I have heard family members of ministry workers say that these workers are so caring toward others that they neglect their own families. The workers have no time or energy left to help when the family needs it. This is one reason why the family members of some highly motivated, hardworking, and successful Christian workers are unhappy about that ministry. These ministry workers need to be dying daily to their convenience and inclinations in order to care for their families.

Meeting personally with those they lead or disciple is a very important aspect of a leader's responsibilities. As we grow in leadership, time to do this becomes harder and harder to find. Often there is no urgent matter that needs to be discussed, and so we do not meet. The result is that we meet less and less with the people with whom we work closely. They feel neglected and distant to us even though they may see us every working day. We must discipline ourselves to have our regular appointments with those we lead, however busy we may be. And doing that may be a kind of death.

Sometimes an urgent need of a family member or someone we lead or disciple may suddenly crop up at a time when we are very busy. Or this person may be sick or very discouraged or angry about something. These are situations where you cannot postpone ministering to the person. So we somehow squeeze in time to meet that need and pray that the Lord will enable us to do those other things we have to do. The price we pay here may be missing out on sleep or rest or just becoming exhausted. Here the weariness would be the death we die for these people.

Sometimes, of course, the sacrifice we make for these people will be a more direct one that clearly shows our commitment. Barnabas refused to give up on Mark even though the young man had failed the mission team on an earlier occasion. And Barnabas paid a price for his commitment to Mark (Acts 15:36-41). Today too leaders who believe in someone may need to pay a price for continuing to support that person whose mistakes have brought some shame to the leader.

After a worker sins seriously and is disciplined, the committed leader does not then forget the worker, but may need to spend many hours to help him or her recover from the sin—hours of unscheduled time amidst a busy schedule. If the discipline enacted requires that the worker does not preach for some time, then the organization or church may have to create an interim job description for him. And that may not be easy to do.

A staff worker leaves an organization and is very angry about the incidents that led to her leaving. Perhaps it is best for her and the organization that she works elsewhere. But if she does not handle the anger properly, she will be permanently handicapped in ministry. The leader needs to talk to her at length and give her an opportunity to tell her side of the story. Usually this is very painful for the leader. But this worker is in a vulnerable position, and this is the least we can do for her. Actually even though she may be angry, out of concern for her we may go out of our way to ensure that she has a secure future. That may mean using our influence as leaders to find her another job.

Sometimes we may need to give a lot of time to help younger people with special challenges in their lives. Here are some examples of such time-consuming projects: raising funds for their studies, helping them with the preparation of talks, visiting their parents who are unhappy about their involvement in ministry even though the parents live far away, or spending long hours studying a topic in order to counsel the young people on it.

Dying, then, is an integral part of our approach to ministry. If that is the case, we will make these sacrifices without much hesitation. We won't make a big fuss about this, as we see it as something included in the call to be a Christian leader. If we have a biblical theology of the cross firmly in place, we are not going to complain when the needs of those we lead take enormous amounts of our time and energy.

But in the long run we will see that such expenditures are not a great sacrifice after all. If we don't invest sacrificially in people, we will not develop good leaders. We may have impressive programs and also impress people with our great talents, but soon our credibility will be affected by the way people leave our work and by our failure to truly develop leaders. We will be like the many experts roaming the world today giving seminars on specialized topics but who really do not have a ministry as evidence to back up what they teach.

There is another reward of costly commitment to people, which we have already implied. When leaders die for their people, these people—challenged by the commitment of their leaders—will die for their church or organization. Leaders today complain that they cannot carry out their desired programs because of the lack of commitment among Christians. Churches are arranging seminars, and preachers are preaching sermons to try and remedy this crisis of commitment. Perhaps one of the answers to this problem is for the leaders to pay the price of commitment to these Christians. That would result in these Christians paying the price of commitment to the programs of the church. But there is no substitute for committed leadership here. Commitment begets commitment.

Today rules and staff handbooks are becoming very prominent in the supervision and direction of Christian workers. While these are helpful, they must never replace the much more time-consuming work of pastoral care of staff. Pastoral care is too demanding and messy for driven and results-oriented leaders. Pushing the rulebook to solve problems of dissent and appointing someone to conduct an inquiry when problems surface seem to be much more efficient and much less of a mental strain than spending hours talking with the people concerned. But when leaders adopt such methods and neglect expressing personal concern for those they lead, they often lose the passionate commitment that will make them pay the price to see the program succeed. They will "work to rule"!

We all agree that pastoral care is an important part of a pastor's ministry. But the church must also ensure that pastoral care is provided for the workers. And there is no better person to do that than the one who supervises those workers. Recently we are seeing the phenomenon of the itinerant "pastor to pastors," which is helping to meet this need. This is a welcome trend. There are few things a mature and experienced Christian worker can do that are more strategic than helping other Christian workers. But this development does not absolve leaders of their responsibility to care for those they lead.

I want to close this discussion by saying that the type of commitment to people advocated in the last two chapters is not an outmoded and impractical relic of the past that is incompatible with today's fast-paced life. The ideal organizational culture for an institution in society is governed by the need to achieve a mission. And success in achieving this mission is determined by meeting certain measurable goals. Such thinking can help a church or organization to get out of a rut and to grow. But we must never forget that, at its heart, Christian organizational culture is relational and not project-driven. Loving each other by dying for each other is basic to Christian organizational life. Many in our generation have lost this concept, and the church has paid a huge price because of that loss.

MINISTERING TO THE SICK AND DEMON-POSSESSED

THE THIRD QUARTER OF Mark 1 (1:21-34) describes some specific events that took place on a Sabbath day. Jesus first goes into a synagogue, teaches there, and heals a person afflicted with an unclean spirit (1:21-28). Then he goes into the home of Simon and Andrew and heals Simon's mother-in-law (1:29-31). In the evening he ministers to many people who are brought to him for healing and deliverance from demons (1:32-34). This passage is very helpful to Christian ministers, as we see descriptions of the typical grassroots ministry that he did—especially his ministry on a Sabbath day.

CASTING OUT DEMONS AND MINISTRY IN THE MIRACULOUS

The first specific occasion of preaching that Mark describes is in the synagogue in Capernaum on a Sabbath day. He uses the word *teaching* (*didaskö*) to describe the preaching (Mark 1:21). The people's response is mentioned: "And they were astonished at his teaching, for he taught them as one who had authority, and not as the scribes" (1:22). But most of the space in this narrative is devoted to describing the way Jesus cast out an evil spirit from a man who was there (1:23-27).

Approaches to the Demonic in the Bible and the World

I suppose if it were left to me to choose the topics to be discussed in this book, I would not have chosen casting out demons! One of the values of expository preaching, teaching, and writing is that sometimes we are forced to deal with issues simply because they appear in the Scripture we are studying.

In the New Testament the casting out of demons is a very important topic. I found seven places in Matthew that narrate Jesus' ministry in this regard. That figure is eight for Mark and nine for Luke. In Mark's description of the choosing of the twelve apostles, he gives three basic features of their role. One of these was to "have authority to cast out demons" (Mark 3:15; cf. Matt. 10:1; Mark 6:7; 16:17; Luke 9:1). So the disciples also drove out demons in the Gospels (Mark 6:13; Luke 10:17), and so did an unidentified man about whom the disciples had some queries (Mark 9:38; Luke 9:49). I found four places where this ministry is specifically described in the narrative of Acts (Acts 6:16; 8:7; 16:16; 19:12).

There is nothing to suggest that demons suddenly ceased to exist after the New Testament era. But many churches have nothing in their program that suggests a belief in the existence of demons. In the church today many Christians talk about the dangers of the two extreme positions of demon-mania and demon-phobia. However, I think most churches today can be placed into one of these two groups.

Some Christians seem to find demons everywhere. All sorts of things, from sickness to human weakness to weeds in the fields, are attributed to demons! This can be very dangerous. It may indicate the impatience of our "quick-fix generation." Many difficult situations related to such things as bad habits, troubled relationships, and resistant people require strong commitment on our part before a solution is found. Some are called to persevere in prayer and in faithful ministry, seeing little visible fruit before resistant people respond to the gospel. Some are called to patiently pray and work hard before a stormy marriage relationship is healed. Some in our impatient generation instead go and proclaim Christ's victory over the demonic forces in those places and situations, but they do not have the patience to persevere in the work that may be necessary to change the situations.[1]

Attributing sicknesses, weaknesses, and psychological or mental problems to demons can cause great damage and keep a person from seeking the help he or she needs for the problem. However, many times there is a demonic reason for problems even though conditions do not seem to indicate such a cause.[2] Therefore, much discernment is needed.

I have seen people who have a special gift of discernment, as listed in 1 Corinthians 12:10. We once had an elderly lady in our church who began to lose control of her mind and act in ways that indicated that something serious was going on. She felt that she was under a demonic influence and wanted to see someone who had a gifting in this area. We took her to a minister who exercised a ministry of healing. After hearing her story and praying for her, he told us that he thought this was a mental and not a demonic problem.

This lady was a kind and considerate person who had suffered deeply in silence with no one knowing about her pain for most of her life. Now, in old age, it seemed that she had lost her ability to hide her pain any longer. The medical doctors confirmed that hers was a serious case of depression. She never recovered from it, and when she died, with much peace we handed her over to the Lord whom she had come to know very late in life. We felt that the short period of mental illness was nothing in comparison to an eternity of total wholeness in heaven.

I also know that some people today are combining sensitive counseling with openness to the possibility that there is a demonic force at work in a certain situation. In fact, most people who have dabbled in the demonic or have been under a clear demonic influence need some counseling after they have been delivered from these powers.

The other extreme is never to bring up the topic of demons as a possible reason for a problem. People may not be used to ministering in this sphere and, therefore, are uncomfortable with it. Another reason why some ignore the reality of the demonic in ministry is the modern scientific approach to life. Perhaps there is a greater incidence of the typical symptoms of demon possession in cultures where people are more susceptible to fear of spirits. Satan uses other methods more frequently to control people in cultures with a more rational, materialistic, and scientific orientation to life. We have found that in the Youth for Christ work in the Sinhala language (where the youth are much less westernized), there is a much higher incidence of demonic manifestations than in the English work.

We know that Satan can "fill the heart" of people who do not show the typical signs of possession, as he did with Ananias and Sapphira (Acts 5:3), in a process some are beginning to describe as demonization.[3] This term is used for situations when Satan gets people so obsessed with an idea or course of action that they get carried away and are blinded to the consequences. Such demonization is common both in the East and the West.

So we may find a person, whom we regarded as rational and responsible, carried away by love or lust for someone, completely neglecting his or her responsibilities to family and vocation. This process is vividly described in Proverbs 7. Leaders sometimes act in harsh and unreasonable ways in their attempts to hold on to power when their leadership is threatened. Perhaps the most vivid expression of where demonization may be at work is in addiction to things such as drugs, alcohol, gambling, or sex. The weaknesses of a person, such as laziness, lack of truthfulness in speaking, tendency to watch sensually stimulating images, etc., are not the same as demonization. But Satan can use our weaknesses if we let him to demonize us.

In cases of demonization, a holistic approach to healing would be needed. This would include specific confession, prayer, surrender to God, and steps to right the wrongs committed. Others in the Christian community also can help through listening, counseling, praying, offering accountability, and disciplining.

There is an increased interest in spiritual things in what is being called postmodern Western society. Accompanying this interest has come a fascination with demonic activity. Consider the large number of films released recently in the West on demonic themes. *The Exorcist* was one of the earliest indicators of this trend. Such openness to the demonic could result in a greater susceptibility of Western people to demonic possession.

Christian workers all over the world, then, need to be alert to the possibility of demonic influences upon people and open to ministering to such people.

Classic Features of This Ministry

Mark's description in 1:23-27 presents some classic features of demon possession and the Christian response to it.

1. The demon, here called "an unclean spirit," spoke through the possessed person: "What have you to do with us, Jesus of Nazareth? Have you come to destroy us? I know who you are—the Holy One of God" (Mark 1:24).

2. Though the people there may not have recognized the true nature of Jesus, the demon did, suggesting that there was a supernatural spiritual power involved.

3. What the spirit said to Jesus (1:24) demonstrates the statement of Clinton Arnold: "Demons resist leaving their host. They may plead for their own well-being."

4. Jesus spoke directly to the evil spirit: "But Jesus rebuked him, saying, 'Be silent, and come out of him!'" (1:25). Arnold says, "We can pray and ask God to deliver someone from evil, but it may be necessary to address the spirit directly as Jesus did."[4] Paul also spoke to a spirit, for example, when he told the spirit who controlled a girl in Philippi: "I command you in the name of Jesus Christ to come out of her" (Acts 16:18).

5. As often happens, the demon left the person in the synagogue in

Capernaum with some rather violent responses: "And the unclean spirit, convulsing him and crying out with a loud voice, came out of him" (1:26).

6. Usually, as here, there is clear evidence that the demon has left the person.

Other passages give us some other features worth noting. The incident involving the delivering of the man in the country of the Gerasenes (Mark 5:1-19) gives many of these features.

7. Demons can have names. When Jesus asked for the name of the demons inhabiting the man, "He replied, 'My name is Legion, for we are many'" (Mark 5:9).

8. We note from this example that a person may be possessed by many demons. A Roman legion usually had 6,000 soldiers. Mary Magdalene had seven demons who were driven out by Christ (Mark 16:9; Luke 8:2).

9. Other instances show us how "demons can inflict self-injury and injury to others," as the description of the Gerasene demoniac shows: "He lived among the tombs. And no one could bind him anymore, not even with a chain, for he had often been bound with shackles and chains, but he wrenched the chains apart, and he broke the shackles in pieces. No one had the strength to subdue him. Night and day among the tombs and on the mountains he was always crying out and bruising himself with stones" (Mark 5:3-5).

10. We see from the passage just quoted that demons can give great physical strength to their subjects. I have been in a YFC camp where several able-bodied men found it difficult to control a teenage girl under demonic influence!

In all the cases Jesus encountered, the demon left immediately. I am familiar with many instances where people prayed for a considerable period of time before the person was finally released. Of course, Jesus did speak of a person who was freed from a demon and, being empty afterward, was then inhabited by seven demons (Matt. 12:43-45). In fact, sometimes the demons seem to possess a person several times again before there is final deliverance.

My wife leads a Bible study in our church for Buddhist inquirers. A woman came for this study who felt very uneasy the moment the study started. She would look down instead of looking at the others in the group or at the Bible. The other members would hold her hands and pray for her. She felt the same way at the worship service too. Then the leaders realized that there must be a demonic influence here. Sometimes during the service she would start shouting. She would talk as if she had the spirit of her dead father. The leaders and our pastor would take her to the parsonage and pray with her, sometimes for the whole duration of the service. She would feel a release, but the symptoms would manifest again some weeks later. Then the same procedure would be followed.

Earlier when she got these attacks, she could not go to work for about a month. The family had spent large amounts of money on exorcists, but to no avail. Now she experienced immediate release after prayer and could go back to work the next day. But she kept getting attacks when she came to church!

After about two or three months of this, she finally experienced complete release. This was almost four years ago. Now she is the principal breadwinner of her family, as her husband is a recovering drug addict. Her two children are fine Christians. The most remarkable change has been how different she looks. A beaming pleasantness has come to her face instead of the fear-filled expression she earlier had, and I can only attribute this to the work of God's grace.

Why did it take so long before final release came? Perhaps the demons had a psychological hold on her so that she was susceptible to further attacks. Perhaps she was still not a real Christian so that what happened here was like what Jesus said happened to the person who was re-inhabited by seven demons after an initial deliverance (Matt. 12:43-45). Perhaps our leaders were amateurs at this ministry, and they did not do things the right way. Certainly none of us had a special gifting for this type of work, but we had to respond to this need when it appeared in our church. And I believe God blessed our blundering but earnest efforts.

There is one situation where Christ's disciples were unable to cast out an unclean spirit. A boy who displayed characteristics similar to epilepsy was brought to them while Jesus was on the Mount of Transfiguration. When the boy's father said, "But if you can do anything, have compassion on us and help us" (Mark 9:22), Jesus replied, "If you can! All things are possible for one who believes" (9:23). So the belief of people close to the possessed person seems to have a part to play in this process. But sometimes, as in the case of the Gerasene demoniac, as far as we know, there were no people around other than those looking after the pigs, and these herders had no connection with the man. In the case of the girl who told fortunes in Philippi, her employers did not even want her to be delivered.

After the incident involving the inability to heal the boy, "when he had entered the house, his disciples asked him privately, 'Why could we not cast it out?'" (9:28). Jesus' answer was, "'This kind cannot be driven out by anything but prayer'" (9:29). Some manuscripts add "and fasting" after prayer. Whether Jesus said that or not, its inclusion in some manuscripts suggests that many in the church in the first few centuries believed that prayer and fasting were keys to preparation for such ministry. Friends of mine with a gifting for this type of ministry tell me that they usually try to spend extra times of prayer before going on such assignments. I suppose the place of prayer here is similar to its place in anointing for ministry, discussed in chapter 2.

Powerful Teaching and Miracles

The people there are amazed after Jesus delivers the man with an evil spirit in the synagogue in Capernaum. Before reporting the miracle, Mark had said that the people "were astonished at his teaching, for he taught them as one who had authority, and not as the scribes" (Mark 1:22). After the miracle, again he says, "And they were all amazed, so that they questioned among themselves, saying, 'What is this? A new teaching with authority! He commands even the unclean spirits, and they obey him'" (1:27). It is interesting that the miracle elicits a comment about the teaching.

I found twelve different Greek words used in Mark with the ideas of amazement, astonishment, trembling, or fear to present the responses of the people to Jesus' ministry (some of the twelve words are closely related to each other, as they have the same root). In 1:27, as we saw, the amazement is over the teaching, but it is connected to the miracle. Three times in Mark the amazement is exclusively over the teaching (1:22; 11:18; 12:17). This reminds us of Matthew's comment after the Sermon on the Mount: "And when Jesus finished these sayings, the crowds were astonished at his teaching, for he was teaching them as one who had authority, and not as their scribes" (Matt. 7:28-29). Twelve times in Mark there is amazement or fear as a result of miracles.[6]

The book of Acts shows a similar pattern in the early church. Twice I found mention of amazement or fear because of the message preached (Acts 4:13; 24:25). Once "the Gentiles . . . began rejoicing and glorifying the word of the Lord" as a result of some of them being saved (13:48). Once, as in Mark 1:27, there was amazement about the teaching, but it was prompted by a miracle (13:12). Eight times the amazement or fear is a response to miracles,[7] and included here is the fear in response to the death of Ananias and Sapphira (5:5, 12). Three times the amazement is over the phenomenon of tongues as a result of filling with the Spirit (2:7; 2:12; 10:45). After the jailer in Philippi found out that none of the prisoners had escaped after the earthquake, "trembling with fear he fell down before Paul and Silas" (16:29). Seeing the radical impact of the gospel upon the prisoners, he himself becomes interested and asks, "Sirs, what must I do to be saved?" (16:30). The result is that his whole family is saved.

Clearly Jesus and the first Christians created a sensation wherever they went! They were so radical in their teaching and their behavior that people were amazed by what they said and did. In Thessalonica the opponents of the gospel exclaimed, "These men who have turned the world upside down have come here also" (Acts 17:6). Christians are always a radical presence because this is a world where people are comfortable with sin and unbelief, and our message attacks sin, and the God who is with us is the almighty miracle-working God. Usually when we evangelize, people are not interested in listening to what we have to say. We have to win their attention. In the Gospels and Acts this attention was often won through powerful preaching and miracles.

In 1 Thessalonians 1:5-6, Paul says that five factors combined to result in the conversion of the Thessalonians: " . . . our gospel came to you not only in word, but also in power and in the Holy Spirit and with full conviction. You know what kind of men we proved to be among you for your sake. And you became imitators of us and of the Lord, for you received the word in much affliction, with the joy of the Holy Spirit." The five factors here are the Word, power, the Holy Spirit, full conviction, and the exemplary lives of the apostles.

I think it is enormously significant that the same evangelists attracted people through both miraculous power and convincing preaching. Power and truth are the two great attractions of Christianity to outsiders, and in the New Testament, the same people dispensed both. This was one of the surprising discoveries I made when I studied the book of Acts in order to write a commentary on it.[8] Peter, Paul, and Stephen were both apologists and miracle workers. I was particularly surprised to discover the careful apologetics in Peter's messages in Acts. Of Stephen's ministry it was said that the people "could not withstand the wisdom and the Spirit with which he was speaking" (6:10). His ministry was characterized by anointing with the Spirit and intellectual persuasiveness.

How rarely we see this combination today! Often we see churches that concentrate either on "power ministry" or on "evangelistic, apologetic, or expository ministry." We also see many churches that concentrate on maintenance—churches that are usually dying! I know several instances where people with gifting in an area of ministry different from the area emphasized by the church feel out of place in that church. When leaders in a church with a strong pulpit ministry find someone who has a burden for ministering with the sick through prayer for healing, they may say, "Perhaps you should look for a church where you are more comfortable." Leaders in a church that has a strong "power ministry" may say a similar thing to one whose interest is in apologetics.

We are seeing more and more people today who are moving to churches "where they feel more comfortable." When did comfort become such a high value in ministry and church life? Was it when we left the path of biblical Christianity? The gospel is too radical and the needs of the world too urgent for us to ever be comfortable! But many Christians today have come to think that a major goal of the church is to entertain people and supply them with services that they want, such as a good youth program or music program. In such an environment, we are going to see people moving to churches where they are comfortable. The result will be that churches are going to miss out on some vital sources of enrichment through discomfort. They will become unhealthy by missing out on biblical wholeness. Biblical churches always are uncomfortable places because they are always looking for biblical wholeness.

On the one hand, biblical truth is vast and complete. On the other hand, our minds are small, and we are incomplete. Therefore, we will always face the challenge to accept some aspect of biblical truth to which we had not yet opened ourselves. Actually this is typical of the Christian life. On the one hand, we have peace that passes understanding because God has fully accepted us. On the other hand, we have no peace because we haven't fully accepted all that God has for us. We will live with this holy tension as long as we live.

Yet we often find ways to rationalize and excuse our incompleteness. Some resort to hermeneutical devises to avoid facing up to some difficult applications of certain portions of Scripture. Those not experiencing the miraculous in their churches may say that miracles ceased with the apostolic age and thus avoid facing the implications of those passages that talk of miracles. In fact, some even condemn those who pray for miraculous healing as being unbiblical. These people say that power religion is experiential and not biblical. But as Jack Deere shows in his book *Surprised by the Power of the Spirit,* these supposedly biblical persons have let experience determine their theology at the cost of biblical truth. Their experience however was the lack of miracles, which led to belief that miracles had ceased.[9]

Those who do not grow numerically may say that that is the cost of faithfulness. They say that they have faithfully taught the Word, but that people do not want to hear the unpleasant truths in the Word. They say that they have not given in to the spirit of the age that looks for miraculous experiences and that they have refused to compromise quality for quantity. While all this may be true, it also could be that the reason they have failed to grow is that they have failed to fully open themselves to ways of ministry needed for relevance and power because they were uncomfortable with these.

Those who do not give much emphasis to the content of the gospel while emphasizing power ministry could point to the power demonstrated in their ministry and the way people are coming and being blessed by it as a justification of their methods. However, often people who come primarily for power do not stay very long in a church. Once that emphasis becomes stale or when God does not immediately grant a request for a miracle, they grow restless and go elsewhere. There is a huge turnover of worshipers in many churches that emphasize power ministry.

After many years of evangelistic ministry among non-Christians, I have come to the conviction that most people initially come to Christ because they have found that he can meet a need of theirs. But for them to stick with Christ long term, they must come to the conviction that he is the truth. When many people fell away because they found Jesus' teaching too tough to accept, he asked the disciples whether they would go too. Peter's memorable reply was: "Lord, to whom shall we go? You have the words of eternal life" (John 6:68).

Whatever our specific evangelistic call may be, God wants us to demonstrate to the world the power of the gospel. May that happen through powerful preaching, powerful ministering to people's needs, and, as taught elsewhere in the Bible, through exemplary lives (Matt. 5:16; 1 Thess. 1:5-6).

HEALING THE PHYSICALLY SICK

In the rest of Mark 1, the main theme is Jesus' ministry of healing those who were physically sick. After his time in the synagogue in Capernaum, he went to the home of Simon and Andrew where he healed Simon's mother-in-law (Mark 1:29-31). In the evening many sick and demon-possessed people were brought to him and were healed (1:32-34). The next day he left Capernaum and "went throughout all Galilee, preaching in their synagogues and casting out demons" (1:39). Later there is the account of how he touched a leper and healed him (1:40-45). Clearly, healing was an important aspect of the ministry of Jesus in Mark. From this chapter we can glean some important principles about his healing ministry. We have already mentioned some pertinent points in our discussion on casting out demons.

Personal Involvement in the Healing Process

In the healing of Simon's mother-in-law, we know that Jesus first went to her home. Then "he came and took her by the hand and lifted her up" (1:31). Such personal involvement in the healing process is a pattern seen all through his ministry. When the people brought a deaf person with a speech impediment to him, "taking him aside from the crowd privately, he put his fingers into his ears, and after spitting touched his tongue." Then he uttered the words that brought healing to him (Mark 7:33-34).

When a blind man was brought to him, "he took the blind man by the hand and led him out of the village, and when he had spit on his eyes and laid his hands on him, he asked him, 'Do you see anything?'" The man said, "'I see men, but they look like trees, walking.'" Then again he touched the man's eyes, and only then was his sight fully restored (Mark 8:22-25). We do not know why he had to go through this process. But what we see is clear involvement with the person he heals. As in the previous case, he takes the person away from the crowd so that he can deal with him personally.

Several other instances of personal involvement can be given. I find his long walk to the home of Lazarus very significant. There is no unanimity about how far Jesus had to go to reach Bethany, as there is some uncertainty about where Jesus was when he got this news. It could have been a town about twenty miles away or one about ninety miles away. Whatever it was, coming to Lazarus' hometown near Jerusalem required a long walk. Of course we know that after Jesus arrived and saw the sorrow of his friends, he wept (John 11:35).

The involvement of Jesus in the leper's healing in Mark 1 was perhaps the most striking. Mark says that Jesus "stretched out his hand and touched him" (1:41). "Lepers were . . . outcasts from the rest of society, the kind of people most healthy people preferred to ignore. Touching a leper was forbidden, and most people would have been revolted by the thought of it."[10] And Jesus touched this man! He broke with custom again when he touched the coffin of the widow's son at Nain (Luke 7:13). Such touching is an aspect of identifying with those we minister to, which was the theme of the first chapter of this book.

Among the equivalents today of first-century lepers are AIDS patients, prostitutes with sexually transmitted diseases, and drug addicts whom no one wants to be close to and care for. I think it is a shame that some famous figures such as Elizabeth Taylor and Princess Diana are known for their public show of concern for AIDS patients whereas Christians are often known only for their condemnation of the lifestyle that caused such sickness. However, I am sure that there are many Christians who work with AIDS patients all the time (not just during high-profile events), who never receive much publicity. Christians must become known as people who go to hopeless and repulsive situations because of the love of Christ.

I am reminded of the decision that Martin Luther made to stay on in Wittenberg in 1527 when the plague hit that city. The elector John ordered him to leave for Jena along with the rest of those at the university. Luther does not advocate a foolhardy approach to the problem. In fact, he "mentions practical steps that should be taken to avoid its spread. Unless there were spiritual and civic duties which kept people in Wittenberg, he argued that they should leave."[11] But, as a pastor, he had to stay. He says:

> Those who are engaged in spiritual ministry such as preachers and pastors must likewise remain steadfast before the peril of death. We have a plain command from Christ: "A good shepherd lays down his life for the sheep, but the hireling sees the wolf coming and flees" (John 10:11). For when people are dying, they most need a spiritual ministry which strengthens and comforts their consciences by word and sacrament and in faith overcomes death.[12]

The German Lutheran pastor and theologian Dietrich Bonhoeffer demonstrated a similar attitude when he was in New York during the time the Nazis ruled Germany. He had come to America after the Nazis closed most opportunities for him to exercise his ministry due to his criticism of the regime. After being in America for less than a month, he had serious misgivings about his decision to go there. He wrote to Reinhold Niebuhr, who had helped arrange the American sabbatical for him, saying, "It was a mistake for me to come to America. I have to live through this difficult period in our nation's history with Christians in Germany. I will have no right to participate in the reconstruction of Christian life in Germany after the war if I do not share the tribulations of this time with my people."[13]

The ministries of Jesus, Luther, and Bonhoeffer are far removed from the style of some of the present-day celebrity healing evangelists. They come to the meeting after it has started, perform their task, and are then quickly taken away from the people, even before the meeting is over, to the safe confines of a hotel. Biblical ministers identify with the people and move with them.

Arising out of Compassion

When Jesus saw the leper and heard his request for healing, Mark says, "Moved with pity, he stretched out his hand and touched him and said to him, 'I will; be clean'" (Mark 1:41). The verb translated "pity" (*splagchnizomai*) here is a strong word used many times for Jesus' response to the physical and spiritual needs of people.[14] Some scholars prefer to render the word in this verse as "anger" instead of "pity," as a translation of another verb (*orgizomai*), which is used in some other manuscripts.[15] But even if this were right, the idea is that Jesus was deeply moved by the leper's need. The verb meaning "compassion" is used in the record of four other miracles—healing the sick in a large crowd (Matt. 14:14), feeding the four thousand (Matt. 15:32; Mark 8:2), healing two blind men (Matt. 20:34), and raising the widow's dead son at Nain (Luke 7:13).

The normal Christian response to need is compassion. Today we are warned about getting too emotionally involved with the problems of our ministries. There is wisdom here, which we should heed. We must never get our identity from ministry in such a way that the needs of people determine our personal security. Our security must always come from Christ. But out of the strength of that security in Christ, we can embrace the needs of the world and be moved to compassion. Bob Pierce, founder of the Christian humanitarian agency World Vision, said, "Let my heart be broken by the things that break the heart of God." Paul followed his Master's attitude when, contemplating the lostness of the Jews, he said, "I have great sorrow and unceasing anguish in my heart" (Rom. 9:2). Elsewhere he spoke of "the daily pressure on me of my anxiety for all the churches" (2 Cor. 11:28). We cannot be emotionally detached from the pain of people if we truly identify with them.

I believe that if we are firmly rooted in the joy and security of the Lord, we too can take on pain in this way without breaking down emotionally.[16] Did not Paul insist: "Rejoice in the Lord always; again I will say, Rejoice" (Phil. 4:4)? Jesus told his disciples, "These things I have spoken to you, that my joy may be in you, and that your joy may be full" (John 15:11). Immediately after that he told them that they should love one another enough to give their lives for each other (John 15:12-13). First we pursue the joy of the Lord; then we open ourselves to the pain of this hurting world. I believe that the preoccupation with finding solutions to ministerial stress today could be a symptom of the fact that ministers have lost the security of being rooted in a joyous relationship with the Lord. They don't have the strength to embrace the pain that is a given factor in Christian ministry. Some in their insecurity have worked themselves into an unhealthy frenzy when faced with human need. This pattern often results in burnout. Others have avoided getting involved personally with these needs.

Discouraging Publicity

After the healing of the leper, "Jesus sternly charged him and sent him away at once, and said to him, 'See that you say nothing to anyone, but go, show yourself to the priest and offer for your cleansing what Moses commanded, for a proof to them'" (Mark 1:43-44). The words "sternly charged" are the translation of a single word that usually means "speak harshly to; criticize harshly"[17] (*embrimaomai*). Apparently there is some urgency to this request.

Similar strong words silencing those who have been healed are found elsewhere too. After Jairus's daughter was raised from the dead, "he strictly charged them that no one should know this" (Mark 5:43). Here the word used (*diastellomai*) means to "order or command."[18] After the deaf man with a speech impediment was healed, "Jesus charged [*diastellomai*] them to tell no one" (Mark 7:36). After opening the eyes of two blind men, "Jesus sternly warned [*embrimaomai*] them, 'See that no one knows about it'" (Matt. 9:30). After the Transfiguration, "as they were coming down the mountain, Jesus commanded [*entellomai*, "to command, order"] them, 'Tell no one the vision, until the Son of Man is raised from the dead'" (Matt. 17:9).

What accounts for these urgent commands to keep silent after a miracle (most of which were not followed by the beneficiaries of Christ's healing)? Perhaps we should mention here the "Messianic secret" theory put forward by the German New Testament scholar William Wrede (1859-1906). At the turn of the last century Wrede argued that Jesus himself did not claim to be the Messiah and that the disciples became convinced that he was the Messiah only after his resurrection. Wrede said that the secrecy motif expressed in the commands to silence was Mark's invention, created to explain how Jesus could be proclaimed as the Messiah when he never claimed to be and was not recognized as such during his earthly ministry.[19] Wrede's book played a major role in developing an approach to the Gospels that viewed them as theological documents and discounted their historical accuracy. In this view some of the supposed events in the Gospels were actually fabricated to depict a theological truth the author wanted to emphasize. This approach is still popular among certain schools of biblical studies.

I believe, however, that there is ample evidence to believe that the Gospels were indeed written to represent what really happened.[20] If so, why did Jesus request the people to be silent? Several reasons have been given, and I believe there is truth in many of them. One thing is sure, unlike the healers of his day, "Jesus has no interest in taking on the role of a celebrity healer."[21] Fame "was not his desire but his fate."[22] The implication is that Jesus did not go after a healing ministry and that he did not publicize it. Earlier we saw that he took some of the people he was going to heal away from the crowd.

However, many of those who have a healing ministry today extensively publicize their ministries. Though the Christians are a small minority in Sri Lanka, it is common to find posters on our roads advertising healing meetings. Some have pictures of people who have been healed and short summaries of how it happened. D. A. Carson says, "There is no record of Jesus going somewhere in order to hold a healing meeting, or of Jesus issuing a general invitation to be healed, or of Jesus offering generalized prayers for healing."[23] I believe that Jesus' charge to secrecy is a warning to us about the dangers of organizing healing meetings and using the prospect of healing as a major attraction in our evangelistic ministry.

One of the great dangers of an overemphasis on healing is that it can eclipse the gospel in evangelism. This danger also could have influenced Jesus' call for secrecy. As Stephen Short put it, "Jesus did not wish for people to come to him merely to receive physical benefits."[24] Many non-Christians come to Christian meetings primarily in order to have some physical or material need met. Once they come, we share the gospel with them. But I have found that it is very difficult for them to make the transition from felt needs to the gospel in their thinking. They listen to our explanation of the gospel and perhaps even accept it, but deep down, when they think of Christianity and the Christians, what they think is, *This is a place where I can have my physical and material needs met.* So it is difficult for them to really hear the gospel even though it is told to them clearly.

For this reason the gospel must always be uppermost in our program. Compassion is an aspect of the gospel. Therefore, it will always be an aspect of our ministry in the world. But if the acts of compassion are done primarily to "win people to our side" and to grow as a church, we can end up with a lot of problems. People could go through the motions of committing their lives to Christ and joining the church while their primary focus is still, "What material and physical benefits can I get from this church?" When we see this happening, we may need to take some definite steps to correct the misunderstanding.

After the feeding of the five thousand, the people wanted to take Jesus by force and make him king. When Jesus realized this, he immediately "withdrew again to the mountain by himself" (John 6:15). When the people caught up with him, they asked him, "Rabbi, when did you come here?" (6:25). "Jesus answered them, 'Truly, truly, I say to you, you are seeking me, not because you saw signs, but because you ate your fill of the loaves. Do not labor for the food that perishes, but for the food that endures to eternal life, which the Son of Man will give to you. For on him God the Father has set his seal'" (6:26-27). Jesus was pushing to turn their focus away from free food to the truth of the gospel. In this narrative Jesus' difficult teaching on the bread of life came next (6:28-59). "When many of his disciples heard it, they said, 'This is a hard saying; who can listen to it?'" (6:60). The result was that "After this many of his disciples turned back and no longer walked with him" (6:66). Jesus would rather have a few real believers than many followers who came along for the wrong reason.

The life and ministry of the Indian preacher Sadhu Sundar Singh was often accompanied by miracles, and he would talk about these when he was preaching. But when he found that it was causing misunderstanding and detracting from the gospel message, he avoided mentioning them.[25]

Some ministries separate their social action divisions quite markedly from their evangelistic division. We have to do this in war-torn northern Sri Lanka where those permitted to do social action are not permitted to do evangelism. So we have two different organizations with two different offices in the towns where we do both these ministries. I do not think there is a single solution to this problem. Each ministry must grapple to see how best to combine meeting needs and preaching the gospel in the particular context in which they are operating.

John Wesley thought that one reason why Jesus asked that his miracles not be publicized is "that he might not enrage the chief priests, scribes, and Pharisees, who were the most bitter against him, any more than was unavoidable."[26] As they saw their power over the people being lost through the power of miracles, it would have left them even more angry because they could not perform miracles.

I think this is an appropriate issue to think about today too. We find people from other religions in Sri Lanka complaining angrily that Christians are "stealing their people" by bribing them through the promise of money and miracles. I have often wondered what prompts such an angry response. I have come to believe that the power that is manifested in the healing ministries reminds them of the defeat that they experienced in the hands of the powerful colonial powers, who unfortunately happened to be from so-called Christian nations. They think that the Christians are coming to defeat them again—this time through the power of miracles. Old wounds resurface, and the result is an angry opposition to the gospel. In this environment, I believe we would be wise not to give too much publicity to the miracles that occur in the church. We could let the message go out by word of mouth rather than through a large-scale publicity campaign.

Paul said that he became weak in order to win the weak (1 Cor. 9:22). So when people feel weak and are angry about that, our call may be to identify with them in their weakness rather than to assert our strength. I believe the same thing applies to ministry among people who were once ruled or overpowered by the group the minister/missionary belongs to. Though the events may have taken place long ago, bitter memories of such overpowering usually remain for several generations. So Christian workers from the once-powerful group will need to do all they can to identify with the weakness of the group they are ministering to.

I believe that this principle applies to ministry by Caucasians among the Native Americans and African-Americans in North America. I believe that in a day when extremist Muslims are proclaiming a holy war or jihad against "Christian" nations, it is essential that Muslims see Christians as humble servants rather than as people with superpower backing. I suppose governments may sometimes need to go to war against Muslim groups, but victory in such wars does not usually bring people closer to the gospel. In this environment Christians will have to powerfully demonstrate servanthood if they are going to win a hearing among hostile Muslims.

Let us always act with compassion when we see human need, and let us seek to bring that need under the influence of God's power. But let us beware about publicizing this power in such a way that it will detract from the gospel message.

WHAT IF YOU DON'T HAVE THESE GIFTS?

We have talked a lot about the ministries of casting out demons and healing, but the listing of gifts in 1 Corinthians 12 shows that "gifts of healing" and the gift of "working of miracles" are not given to all Christians. Yet we all encounter people who are sick, and some encounter those who are demon-possessed. So something needs to be said that applies to those who do not have these gifts—and I think I belong to this category.

1. It seems to me that *those who have these gifts would pray believing that God would miraculously heal.* At the tomb of Lazarus, Jesus "cried out with a loud voice, 'Lazarus, come out'" (John 11:43). Peter told the lame

man, "I have no silver and gold, but what I do have I give to you. In the name of Jesus Christ of Nazareth, rise up and walk!" (Acts 3:6). God seems to give faith to some to believe that there will be this instantaneous healing. Perhaps when those without these gifts pray for the sick, they may not make such confident pronouncements of instant healing.

2. However, when we encounter someone who clearly seems to be demon-possessed, there can be no doubt that God wants to completely heal this person. So even if we think we do not have a special gifting in this area, *we should command the demon to leave,* saying something like the words of Jesus: "Be silent, and come out of him" (Mark 1:25).

3. We must all *pray for the healing of people.* And we must pray with faith. James says that when one is sick, the elders of the church should be called to "pray over him" (James 5:14). Then he says, "the prayer of faith will save the one who is sick, and the Lord will raise him up" (James 5:15). These verses apply to all elders, implying that those who do not have the special gift of healing also need faith when praying. But perhaps those with the gift will have faith that a certain prayer is going to be answered in a miraculous way, and they could make a proclamation with that in view.

Praying with the sick among us is one of the key responsibilities of a Christian worker. Occasionally people have testified to a change for the better after I have prayed for them, though I do not know whether my prayers had something to do with that! I often pray for non-Christians who are sick. Even if there is no healing at once, these prayers bring these people in touch with a God to whom they can talk about their problems. This can be very impressive to those who do not know the sweetness of a love relationship with a personal God.

There was a Buddhist family in Sri Lanka where one daughter was stricken with cancer. Some Christians came and prayed for her, and she initially got better after the prayers. But she died after some time. However, the sickness brought the family in touch with God. Though their family member died, some of them subsequently became Christians, and two of them are now in full-time ministry. One of them seems to have a gift of miraculous healing.

I have never had a non-Christian refuse an offer to pray for him or her. Usually I do not talk much before I pray, though my prayer is such that one who knows very little about God and the gospel would understand what I am saying and get to know something about the God to whom I am praying. In reading up for writing this chapter, I have come to realize that I should talk more about God and the gospel, for it is in Christ's name that we pray. Putting one's faith in Christ is the most important healing that we seek.[27]

4. We must remember that not all sickness is healed instantaneously by God in answer to prayer. Sometimes people are healed gradually, and sometimes people are not healed physically. But *whether they are healed or not, the church must care pastorally for its members who are sick*. Therefore, visiting the sick is a duty of every minister of the gospel. The only time I have stayed for over a day in a hospital was when I had my appendix removed when I was about fourteen years old. The two most vivid memories I have of that time were the almost daily visits and prayers by my pastor, Rev. George Good, and the kindness of a Roman Catholic missionary nun who worked in that hospital. Sickness, then, makes people vulnerable and receptive to the care of the church.

5. Sometimes we may *direct people among us to those who have the gift of healing*. Those who minister healing may belong to another denomination, but because we are all part of the same body of Christ, this does not need to be a problem. Many ministers fear that if they send people to someone else, they may permanently lose those people to the church that offers the healing. I believe that if you show so much concern for the welfare of a person as to direct that person to another group that can help him or her, most people will sense your commitment and not leave you but will be grateful for the concern. But sometimes people may leave us.

I once directed a person whom I loved dearly and in whom I had invested a lot of time and prayer to another ministry that was specialized in helping with his special need. I felt later that he believed that it was this group that really helped him and that we had failed him. This hurt me a lot. But I can thank God that this person was helped immensely. In his immaturity he seemed to have forgotten what I did for him. I suppose if I am more mature than he is, I should be able to forgive him for that! There was a cooling off in our relationship for about five years before it returned to its original warmth. Yet this is one of the pains of ministry. We invest in people and then lose them. Sometimes they are lost to the kingdom. Other times they remain Christians but are lost to our ministries. If we want to remain happy in the ministry, we will need to prepare for such losses and learn how to keep the anger over them from spoiling our lives!

6. Often *there are psychological causes for physical sickness that we could address when ministering to the sick*. Opinions vary as to what percentage of physical sicknesses have emotional causes. Jim Glennon says that once after he had said in a talk that the figure was 60-70 percent, a medical specialist in the audience told him that in his opinion the figure was 90 percent.[28] Glennon gives instances of remarkable healing that took place after

the patients were able to deal with some painful areas of their memories and forgive those who hurt them. Again our role here may be sensing that there is a problem that needs the help of a specialist and directing the person to the specialist. It may, on the other hand, be to lead the people to emotional healing through sensitive listening, counsel, and prayer.

7. *We can direct someone with the gift of helping (1 Cor. 12:28) or serving (Rom. 12:7; 1 Peter 4:11) to minister more regularly to a sick person.* One of the delights of leadership is using our influence to match the needs of people with those who can meet those needs. Some sick people need a lot of practical help that we ministers of the Word may not be able to give. But there may be people in our ministries who are gifted in serving others, people who have a gift of visiting needy people and seeing what their needs are and doing something practical to meet those needs.

The Christian in ministry will always encounter people who are needy in the areas given prominence in the ministry of Jesus. Whether we like it or not, we need to develop some skills in dealing with these needs. Remembering that all are not specially gifted in these areas, we need to ensure that our ministry will nevertheless biblically deal with such needy people. I trust that this chapter has given some keys to such ministry.

13

VISITING HOMES

IN THE LAST CHAPTER we saw that after ministering in the synagogue on a Sabbath day, Jesus went into "the house of Simon and Andrew with James and John" (Mark 1:29). There he healed Simon's mother-in-law, who after she was healed "began to serve them" (1:31). Probably she prepared the evening meal.[1] After dinner "the whole city was gathered together at the door" (1:33) of this house. "And he healed many who were sick with various diseases, and cast out many demons" (1:34). It is significant that the gospel writers record many key events in the life of Jesus that took place in homes. He performed some important miracles in homes, and he used what happened in homes to teach important truths.

JESUS' MINISTRY IN HOMES

Consider the following evidence:

• Right at the start of his ministry, Jesus took Andrew and another disciple of John to the house where he was staying and spent so long chatting with them that they probably stayed the whole night with him (John 1:37-39).[2]

• His first miracle was at a wedding banquet, which was probably held at the home of the groom.[3] John comments that at this "first of his signs Jesus . . . manifested his glory," and the result was that "his disciples believed in him" (John 1:11).

• Mark tells us that the healing of the paralytic in Capernaum took place when "he was at home" (Mark 2:1). This was probably the home of Simon and Andrew.[4] And this time it was so crowded that the man had to be brought in through the roof. On this occasion Jesus claims to have the authority to forgive sins (Mark 2:5-11).

• Jesus went for a meal to the house of Levi where tax collectors and sinners reclined with him (Mark 2:15-16). This occasion could be classed as a "follow-up" visit to the home of a "new convert." But it was also an example of Jesus being where people out of touch with the synagogue were. In response to the queries of the Jewish leaders about the company he kept, Jesus said: "Those who are well have no need of a physician, but those who are sick. I came not to call the righteous, but sinners" (Mark 2:17).

• When he went for a meal to the home of a Pharisee, a sinful, weeping woman anointed his feet, and the ensuing conversation resulted in some important teaching on gratitude and salvation (Luke 7:36-50).

• Jesus visited the home of Jairus, a ruler of a synagogue, and healed his daughter (Matt. 9:18-26; Mark 5:35-43; Luke 8:49-56).

• Matthew 13 records several parables of Jesus. Jesus explained the meaning of the first one, the Parable of the Sower, to the disciples (Matt. 13:18-23). After that he spoke to the crowd again[5] and related three more parables—about the weeds, the mustard seed, and the leaven (Matt. 13:24-33). "Then he left the crowds and went into the house. And his disciples came to him, saying, 'Explain to us the parable of the weeds of the field'" (13:36). Here the house is a place where Jesus and the disciples are engaged in theological discussion.

• When he was at the home of Mary and Martha for a meal, a complaint from Martha about her sister opened the door for the important teaching that devotion is more important than service (Luke 10:28-42).

• He paid an evangelistic visit to the home of the hated tax collector Zacchaeus. The conversion of Zacchaeus provided an opportunity for a vivid demonstration of the fruit of repentance, and the murmuring of the people elicited from Jesus an important statement about his mission being "to seek and to save the lost" (Luke 19:10).

• He made the long walk to the house of Lazarus. It was when speaking to the grieving Martha that he made his great statement about being "the resurrection and the life" (John 11:25-26). There, seeing his friends weeping, he also wept (11:35).

• Toward the end of Jesus' public ministry, we see two times when, during meals in the homes of Simon the leper (Matt. 26:6-13; Mark 14:3-9) and Lazarus (John 12:1-8), Jesus is anointed with costly ointment. From the former incident arose Jesus' statement about the woman anointing him for burial and from the latter incident the comment about having the poor always with us.

Clearly the home is an important place of ministry. Jesus ministered in the homes of strangers (Zacchaeus), of friends (Lazarus, Mary, and Martha), of colleagues (Simon and Andrew), of public figures (the Pharisee and Jairus), of new converts (Levi), and of friends (or relatives) who were having a wedding celebration (in Cana). He went to the homes of believers (Simon, Lazarus, and Levi), of sinners (Zacchaeus), and of those not so positively inclined toward him (the Pharisee). In homes he ministered to strangers, sinners, friends, and to his own disciples and their family members.

The disciples of Jesus carried on his tradition of giving the home a high place as an arena of ministry. Jesus got them started during his lifetime when he sent them out to minister. On that occasion he said to them, "As you enter the house, greet it" (Matt. 10:12). Elsewhere I have commented on the importance that homes and hospitality have in the book of Acts.[6] In the early church evangelism took place in homes, as when Cornelius and his friends were converted (Acts 10). The traveling preachers would stay in homes as Peter did in the home of Simon in Joppa (Acts 9:42) and Paul did in the home of Lydia (Acts 16:14-15). In homes the Christians enjoyed fellowship and food together (Acts 2:46). Paul was in the habit of visiting homes regularly as part of his pastoral work (Acts 20:20).

BEING WHERE THE LOST ARE

Jesus' visits to the homes of Zacchaeus (Luke 19:5-10) and Levi, where he ate with tax collectors and sinners (Mark 2:15-17), are examples of his going to be with the lost. In Levi's home he reclined at the table. This was not the normal posture for meals among the Jews. It was done at special meals—feasts, celebrations, and times of entertainment.[7] Seeing Jesus in this relaxed mood among people regarded as sinners, the Jewish leaders asked his disciples, "Why does he eat with tax collectors and sinners?" (Mark 2:16).

Jesus' behavior was such that he earned the criticism, "Look at him! A glutton and a drunkard, a friend of tax collectors and sinners!" (Luke 7:34). Perhaps it was because he was in touch with such people that "the tax collectors and sinners were all drawing near to hear him" (Luke 15:1). Paul did the same thing when he went to Athens—the city of Socrates (Acts 17:16). The apostle would discuss his philosophical ideas with the people at the marketplace.

How easy it is for us, with all our activity with Christians, to lose touch with people who have no contact with the church! And how important it is for Christian workers to be proactive in going to places where they can interact with the unconverted.

I have learned many valuable lessons about ministry from Calvin Waugh, who recently retired after serving almost thirty years as pastor of the United Methodist Church in Alger, Ohio. Alger is a small town with a population of less than 900 people, and the church has an average attendance of about 100. This church is well known for its vital missionary program that supports many mission ventures in the United States and abroad, including our work.

But Pastor Calvin's interest in mission is not confined to projects outside Alger. He has taken me for breakfast to the local restaurant where the local townspeople and farmers gather. He visited that restaurant almost every day. The result is that Pastor Cal is a friend of many of the local people who have no contact with any church. When they have a crisis such as a death in the family, he is the one they call on for help. These occasions provide valuable evangelistic opportunities.

Some of our Youth for Christ drug rehab workers go to the places where young people taking drugs hang out—certain street corners. They make friends with these youth and are able to bring some of them within the scope of our ministry.

Christian leaders often go into social clubs and other community organizations with the same goal. Usually this involvement seems to be a waste of time, but it helps us make valuable contacts for the gospel and also helps us to understand the people we are called to reach. I find it very helpful to go to parties and receptions hosted by my non-Christian friends and relatives because I learn so much about the world at these functions.

I work primarily with the poor, and the poor in Sri Lanka travel almost exclusively by bus. Therefore, I take a few long journeys by bus each year. As I grow older, this is getting harder to do, as bus journeys in Sri Lanka are very uncomfortable. But I find that these trips are extremely helpful for my ministry, especially in helping me understand the context of the people I minister to. That understanding has a marked impact upon my preaching, teaching, and counseling.

When I was a student in the United States, I saw a board outside a church with words something to the effect: "A man's character is gauged by the company he keeps." The first thought that came to me was that Jesus kept the company of tax collectors and sinners!

The reason many Christians are reluctant to hang around with sinful people is that they can become vulnerable and succumb to the temptations that often come in subtle but powerful forms in such company. Three days before writing this, I returned from a retreat of the leaders of our ministry. We discussed the plans of one of our divisions whose volunteers and staff are hoping to go to places usually regarded as too sinful and dangerous for

Christians. We talked about the dangers of such work and discussed the examples of some Christian workers who went into such places and succumbed to the temptations there.

We concluded that those who are going into such ministry would need to have a strong accountability group where they can share their experiences and temptations and always discuss the wisdom of what they are doing. We also decided that people should go to such places out of a burning passion to reach the lost, even though they may have little opportunity to talk about the Lord while there.

EVANGELISTIC HOME VISITS

The evangelistic visits to homes recorded in the Gospels and Acts were, I believe, planned visits to specific homes, such as the home of Zacchaeus. This is different from the practice of visiting all the houses in an area, as practiced by the Jehovah's Witnesses and Christian groups such as Every Home Crusade. However, there is nothing in Scripture to indicate that visiting specific homes is not a legitimate and effective way of doing evangelism.

In our Youth for Christ ministry our volunteers and staff make a lot of evangelistic visits to homes of people we have contacted through our various outreach programs. Usually before an important evangelistic meeting, our volunteers will try to visit all their contacts in their homes to invite them to the meeting. These visits have proved to be a very effective means of reaping an evangelistic harvest of youth contacted through our sports, music, drama, and educational programs. I am also familiar with effective evangelistic visitation programs where church members visit contacts using materials produced by the Evangelism Explosion ministry.

Perhaps one of the most famous evangelistic visits in history is that of Edward Kimball to his eighteen-year-old Sunday school student, Dwight Lyman Moody. The youth had been in his class for almost a year. He had joined the Sunday school as part of an agreement with an uncle who had employed him to work in his shoe shop. The uncle felt that going to church would keep the young Moody out of trouble. At that time Moody had no intention of committing his life to Christ until he had had his "fun" and was much older.

The church was having a mission ("revival meetings"), and Kimball felt a burden to visit young Moody and talk to him about his relationship with the Lord. He went to the shoe shop and found him at the back of the shop, wrapping up shoes and stacking them on the shelves. He challenged him about his relationship with the Lord. As Kimball puts it, "It seemed that the young man was just ready for the light that broke upon him, for there, at once, in the back of that shoe store in Boston," Moody "gave himself and his life to Christ."[8] Though this visit did not take place in a home, it took place on Moody's "home turf," and thus I include it.

My most memorable experience of evangelistic visitation was when I visited the home of a young Youth for Christ staff worker. His father was dying, and the son wanted me to come and talk to the man about Christ. This man had been a pioneer in the Communist movement in Sri Lanka and was of an intellectual bent. I started by talking about his sickness and his various vocational experiences and was going on for some time with friendly conversation. But the young YFC worker was getting impatient. Soon he butted into the conversation and told me, "Ajith, you wanted to tell something to my father." That provided an introduction for me to start talking about the gospel.

After I had explained the gospel, I asked him if he would like to commit his life to Christ. To my surprise he immediately answered yes. I explained once again what it means to give one's life to Christ, and I asked him to repeat a prayer of confession and commitment after me, which he did. What a change came over that dying man! He lived for another week, and he seemed to be so full of joy. When Christians came to see him, he would ask them to pray and to sing hymns. Later I had the joy of speaking at a thanksgiving service for him. I talked not only of his earthly achievements, which were many, but also of his relationship with the Lord and of how he was ready to die.

Just as Jesus went to the homes of Zacchaeus and Levi, we too can visit the homes of people shunned by the rest of society. The very fact that we go into these homes can become a huge opening for the gospel.

The Maltose people are a mountain tribe in India with such a high mortality rate that they were expected to become extinct by 2025. They almost never bathe because they have no access to water. Consequently, the rest of society shuns them. People will not go near them because of the odor. Missionaries from the Friends Missionary Prayer Band began a work among this tribe. They not only visited their villages, but they stayed in their homes, even sleeping beside them.

By 1996 about 34,000 of the 85,000 people in this tribe had become Christians, and with the consequent change in lifestyle there has been a marked drop in the mortality rate. The missionaries have paid a great price to reap this harvest. Four missionaries have died of the diseases that have been killing the Maltose—malaria, tuberculosis, and kala-arzar. One of those who died was the young son of Patrick Joshua, the national leader of the Prayer Band. He had received his M.A. in social work and went to live among these people to help with their social reconstruction. After his death three other young people went to fill his place—a costly but precious sacrifice indeed that included identification with the people through receiving their hospitality.

Visiting the homes of non-Christians, then, can open many doors to evangelism.

PASTORAL HOME VISITS

The practice of visiting homes fits in with the metaphor of the Shepherd who does not wait for lost sheep to come to him, but leaves the ninety-nine and goes out in search of a single lost sheep. Christian leaders are always going where people are, and, as the home is the most important place in a person's life, they should often be found in people's homes. Most of Jesus' visits to homes mentioned above were in response to a need or a crisis. Similarly Christian workers are there with their people when they face a crisis. I believe that one aspect of the ministry of prayer to which the apostles devoted themselves (Acts 6:4) was praying with people in their times of need.

I have found that sometimes we don't have to do much when we go to these homes. Just being there to listen and to chip in when there is a need is all that is required. At an appropriate time we could pray with the family. Such involvement gives the family a sense that the Christian leader has "been there" with them in their troubles.

The *Constitutions of the Holy Apostles,* a collection of church canons compiled between 350-400 but probably of second- and third-century origin, says: "Like a compassionate shepherd, be a diligent feeder of the flock. Search out and keep an account of the flock. Seek out one that has need, just as the Lord God our gracious Father has sent his own Son, the good Shepherd and Savior, to seek us."[9] After this the parable of the lost sheep is quoted verbatim.

If we are to follow the analogy of the Parable of the Lost Sheep in a thoroughgoing manner, then the lost sheep is a member of the fold but has gone astray. Matthew's version of this parable clearly implies that when Jesus talked of the lost sheep, he was referring to believers who have strayed away from God (Matt. 18:12-14). The paragraphs before and after this parable are about how believers can stray from God's ways. So the Christian leader goes after Christians who have strayed from the fold.

Usually those who have strayed are angry with the leaders, and their behavior is an affront to these leaders. Perhaps they are talking against the leaders. When people act in this way, the leaders are usually very hurt and angry. In such situations I have heard leaders say that they will not go to these people but that these people should come to them. But we are devoted to the welfare of the flock. The fact that we have been insulted or hurt is secondary. The primary concern is bringing the straying sheep back into the fold.

This may not be the world's pattern for the behavior of leaders. But when it comes to the Christian principle of love, we always go beyond what the world considers appropriate. The father discarded cultural restraints and probably lifted his cloak and ran toward his returning prodigal son (Luke 15:20). Kenneth Bailey, an expert on Middle Eastern culture, explains, "An oriental nobleman with flowing robes never runs anywhere. To do so is humiliating." He quotes Aristotle who said, "Great men never run in public."[10] The prodigal son had brought great disgrace to the family, but all of that was set aside at the prospect of welcoming him back home.

Similarly we go after those who, having strayed away, have brought dishonor to our name by the way they behaved and talked. That is secondary; the primary concern is to woo them back home. We can deal with the other issues later. They would not have the strength to deal with those issues unless they saw a love that conquers their insecurities and guilt. The hardness of their hearts would melt at the sight of such love, and a door would be open for repentance, confession, and restitution.

We should never forget that Jesus took the initiative in loving us and dying for us. It is because we saw such love and such provision for our sins that we had the courage to turn from our sins and hope for God's mercy. If he had waited for us to repent before he showed us his love, we would have never repented. Just as God took the initiative in saving us, we take the initiative in working for the restoration of those who have gone astray. And a key to that is visiting them.

So when an angry letter comes from a disgruntled member, or we hear that angry words have been said about us, our first thought may be to consult a lawyer and to draft a letter that protects us from legal action. But let me encourage you instead to go and meet such people, talk to them, and do all you can to restore them. It may take two hours before they tell you what is on their minds. The first hour may be spent on superficial talk or denial of the situation. And most of us would be tempted to just give up and leave. But if we persevere, we could have a chance to restore a fallen person and to help transform an enemy into a friend.

VISITING AS AN EXPRESSION OF SERVANTHOOD

What we have been saying fits in with our understanding of Christian ministry as servanthood. The idea of the Christian worker visiting people simply because he or she loves them and wants to help them is a revolutionary one in cultures where people often have to pay for the services of a religious worker. A Hindu journalist writing in an Indian newspaper about the conversion to Christianity of large numbers of tribal people who live up in the mountains gave three reasons for the success of Christian evangelism. He said, first, that the Christian evangelists go to remote places where outsiders are not willing to go. Even the government census workers usually give a rough estimate of how many people live in these tribal villages without making the tough journey up the mountains. Second, he said that the Christian missionaries give leadership to the locals in a relatively short time, thus giving them a sense of identity and self worth. Third, he said Christianity is a "cheap religion." By that he meant that you do not have to pay to receive the services of a Christian clergyman.

Several times, when visiting homes of Buddhists or converts from Buddhism, people have told me that to get a Buddhist monk to come to their home, they have to provide transportation, give him a gift—usually a saffron robe—and offer him with a meal of his choice. The fact that we come without asking for anything in return and often without even being asked to come is a powerful witness to the Christian gospel.

As youth workers we visit the homes of our youth when their family members are sick. We go to pray with them at special times, such as before a family member goes to the hospital for an operation. We go to pray for students just before an exam. Sometimes non-Christian parents call for our workers to come when there is a family crisis because they have come to view our workers as people who are there for them when they have a need.

Because the English Puritan Richard Baxter (1615-1691) was pastor of a large congregation (in Kidderminster), he could not visit all of them. So he had the members of his congregation come to the church to meet him. In his classic book *The Reformed Pastor*, he explains how he met with fifteen to sixteen families a week, usually giving "Monday and Tuesday from morning almost to night" for this. He would meet up to 800 families in a year. He was so convinced of the effectiveness of meeting members personally in this way that he said, "I find more outward signs of success with most that do come, than from all my public preaching to them."[11]

Of course, when we visit people in this way, we come to know those we minister among. Gilbert Burnet (1643-1715), a Scottish-born Anglican bishop of Salisbury in England, published an influential book on pastoral care in 1692. He writes, "As the foundation upon which all other parts of the pastoral care may be well managed, he ought frequently to visit the whole parish from house to house, that he may know them and be known by them."[12]

The early Methodist movement had both the rich and the poor among its members. The rich Christians began to move closely with and be in the same small group as the poorer Christians. The poorer ones would talk about all the hardships that they faced in their places of work. The rich Christians were filled with outrage over the injustices in their society, and they began to speak out against social injustice. The result was that the Methodist Revival had a profound impact in establishing social justice in Britain.[13]

The greatest and most influential theologians in history, whose writings had such penetrative insight that they markedly influenced the history of the church, were those who had intimate contact with people through pastoral ministry. St. Augustine (354-430) is widely regarded as the most influential theologian in church history after the apostle Paul. His original dream had been to live in a monastery where he could meditate, pray, study, and write. He had a little monastic community in a place called Tagaste. But he was a good preacher, and so he would often be invited to preach in churches. He accepted some of these invitations but avoided going to churches that did not have a pastor for fear that he would be asked to be the pastor.

Once when he was visiting Hippo, he went to the worship service there. The pastor, Bishop Valerius, seeing him in the congregation, told the people that he needed another pastor to help him in the work. The congregation got the message and dragged Augustine to the front and ordained him as a deacon on the spot. He began to weep, and the people thought that he was weeping because he had been ordained a deacon rather than an elder. But the real reason was that he realized that his dream of a tranquil life was now gone forever! Augustine stayed in Hippo and served there until his death almost forty years later. Pastoral challenges made writing difficult at times. His book on the Trinity took him seventeen years to finish because he had to drop this project each time a challenge came his way that needed to be addressed. But what an impact he had! That impact was surely connected with the fact that he was always close to the people of the church![14]

We sometimes think of John Calvin as a dour academic, more at home in the study than in the parish. The truth is that he was a busy pastor while being a prolific theological writer. One writer says of him, "He robbed himself of sleep. His home was always open to anyone seeking advice. He was constantly in touch with all the affairs of church and state. He visited the sick and lackadaisical, and knew almost every citizen."[15] Calvin once wrote, "Since my arrival here I can only remember having been granted two hours in which no one had come and disturbed me."[16]

In the previous chapter we mentioned that Luther risked his life during the plague by his decision to stay on in Wittenberg and minister to the dying and the bereaved. John Wesley traveled as much as 20,000 miles a year on horseback and delivered about 800 sermons a year. The edition that I have of his literary works includes fourteen volumes each of over 500 pages. But his *Journals* record many instances of his going from house to house visiting people or having people come to where he was staying so that he could talk personally to them.

The church in the West, because of its affluence, can afford to have its ministers specialize in their areas of expertise and giftedness. But there has been an unhealthy trend in larger churches where those who preach do not do much visiting or offer other pastoral care. People are hired primarily to attend to such tasks. This would surely result in the preachers having less contact with the people, and that in turn will affect their ability to communicate penetrating insights to their hearers. They may preach technically brilliant messages but lack the insight that comes only through close contact with people.

Indeed a pastor of a large congregation may not be able to visit every single member. There has to be delegation of some of these responsibilities. Even in smaller churches the preacher should train lay members to attend to some of the pastoral care of the church. But every preacher, whether of a small or a large congregation, must do some visiting and give some pastoral care. It is the responsibility of the pastor and the leaders of the congregation to ensure that the pastor does not get so snowed under by the load of pastoral visitation that other aspects of his life and ministry are adversely affected.

PRONOUNCING BLESSING ON PEOPLE

While the idea of giving specific blessing to people is not something closely connected with home visits in the life of Jesus, it is something that we in Sri Lanka do often during home visits. I was prompted to write this section two days after I had "completed" writing this chapter. It was Christmas day, and when I chatted with a member after our church service, she told me that her newly married son was sick with chicken pox and was really suffering! She said that he had wanted me to pray over some water and send it home with her to anoint him. I told her that I do not do that type of thing, but I went to his home that morning and prayed for him.

As I was returning home after this visit, I was reflecting on what had happened. This youth is a convert from Buddhism, but unfortunately he was now not very close to the church or, I believe, to the Lord. In his time of sickness he sensed that he needed a blessing from God, and he asked for blessed water. I had been praying for a few years that this boy would fully return to the Lord, and I pounced on the opportunity to have an influence for Christ in his life.

Writer Mary Evans explains that "to bless somebody is to express a hope or prayer that good, desirable things will happen to that person."[17] The practice of leaders pronouncing blessings on people appears often in the Old Testament. Sometimes it was a blessing pronounced to a whole people who were gathered together. The most famous of these was the Aaronic blessing, which we still use: "The LORD bless you and keep you; the LORD make his face to shine upon you and be gracious to you; the LORD lift up his countenance upon you and give you peace" (Num. 6:24-26). The Bible records blessings that leaders such as Moses, Aaron, Joshua, and David gave to God's people (Exod. 39:43; Lev. 9:22-23; Josh. 22:62; 2 Sam. 6:18). The benedictions (invocations of blessing) we use, usually at the close of Christian gatherings, are today's equivalents of this Old Testament practice.

At other times these blessings are given specifically to individuals. The blessing that Isaac wanted to give to Esau, but which Jacob stole, is an example (Gen. 27—28). When Jacob arrived in Egypt and met Pharaoh, the patriarch blessed Pharaoh before leaving his presence (Gen. 47:10). Before his death Jacob blessed Joseph while laying his hand on his two sons, Ephraim and Manasseh (Gen. 48:14). Joshua blessed Caleb when he gave him his inheritance (Josh. 14:13).

Sometimes along with the blessing came a word of prophecy or prediction of what God would do for the person being blessed. Jacob gave such a word when blessing Joseph (Gen. 48:15-16). Eli did this when blessing Elkanah and Hannah, the parents of Samuel: "May the Lord give you children by this woman for the petition she asked of the Lord" (1 Sam. 2:20). The next verse says that she bore three more sons and two daughters.

I found three examples in the Gospels that are significant to our study of leaders pronouncing a blessing. When Joseph and Mary brought the baby Jesus to the temple and encountered Simeon, the old man immediately uttered words of praise over seeing the salvation that God had prepared for the world. Then he blessed Mary and Joseph and prophesied to Mary about what would happen to and through Jesus (Luke 2:25-32). The other two examples are from the ministry of Jesus. The first is when the children were brought to him: " . . . he took them in his arms and blessed them, laying his hands on them" (Mark 10:16). The second is just before his ascension: " . . . lifting up his hands he blessed them. While he blessed them, he parted from them and was carried up into heaven" (Luke 24:50-51).

We note that in both instances of Jesus blessing the people, he used his hands. He laid his hands on the children when he blessed them. Later the church practiced the laying on of hands in various situations such as commissioning individuals to some service (Acts 6:6; 13:3). People seeking healing asked Jesus to lay hands on the sick (Mark 5:23; 7:32). Jesus and the early church leaders did this on other occasions of healing too (Mark 8:23; Luke 4:40; 13:13; Acts 9:12, 17; 28:8). When Jesus raised his hands to bless the apostles before his ascension (Luke 24:50), he was acting like Aaron, the high priest, who "lifted up his hands toward the people and blessed them" (Lev. 9:22).

All the evidence above shows that when we bless people, we are acting in a priestly role. The hand laid on people or stretched toward them indicates that a blessing is being passed on from the "priest" to the people. The blessing, of course, is not inherent to the priest. It is from God, with the priest acting as a mediator. This is something that all believers can now do—"to act as mediators of God's power and as facilitators of God's purposes."[18]

This calling to mediate God's blessing is something that we must take very seriously. We should ensure that we are in tune with God so that the things we say or pray in the blessing are in line with God's desires for the person being blessed. Usually when I have to pray for someone in this way, I ask God to guide me to say the right thing, and I try to be in as receptive a mood as possible to God's voice. A day or two after typing this, I will visit the home of a Youth for Christ staff worker whose wife has given birth to a son. For some days I have been praying and thinking about what I should say when I pray for that baby and his parents.

NOT A POPULAR MINISTRY

The ministry of visitation has never been too popular among Christian ministers. Toward the end of the seventeenth century, Gilbert Burnet wrote, "I know this way of parochial visitation is so worn out, that perhaps neither priest nor people will be very desirous to see it taken up." He says, therefore, that the bishops should preach a sermon to the clergy explaining "the reasons and ends of doing it that would remove the prejudices which might arise against it."[19]

Because of the negative attitudes of ministers to this practice, we may need to stress afresh its vital importance. Besides, this is part of God's work, and all work done for God in keeping with God's wishes is great and supremely important. George Herbert (1593-1633), in his classic seventeenth-century manual of pastoral care, *The Country Parson,* addressed the issue of the relative unimportance that ministers give to pastoral visitation. He said that the minister "holds the rule that nothing is little in God's service; if it once have the honor of that name, it grows great instantly. Therefore neither does he disdain to enter into the poorest cottage, though he even creep into it, and though it smell ever so loathsomely. For both God is there, and also those for whom God died."[20]

Some of us may feel that we are not gifted in ministering to the sick, visiting homes, and such pastoral duties. Yet that is our call. In our ministry we do many things that we may not like to do and for which we are not particularly gifted. However, tackling these tasks really enriches our ministries. We saw above that visitation gets us close to people and to their needs, and we get to know them better. This contact in turn enables us to minister to them much more effectively. These experiences will influence our preaching and improve our skills in applying the Word to our hearers. So whether we like it or not, we do it; for we are servants of the people, and we must be close to them and their needs.

I have found the words of the great British New Testament scholar F. F. Bruce very helpful. When asked about the principles he followed in determining God's will for his life, he replied: "Very simply: First I do what I am paid to do; then I do what I have to do; and then I do what I would like to do."[21] I think we are not very skilled at doing many of the things we have to do in ministry. But if we have adequate opportunity to use our gifts, then we could handle having to do things that we don't like and are not gifted for.

As a Bible teacher I have found that having to do things I don't enjoy has really helped me to apply biblical truth to my hearers, even though I often complain about those things. So ultraspecialization can be a dangerous thing. We in poorer nations cannot afford it. But those who study in the West and come back to minister in poorer countries often feel unfulfilled because they are doing a lot of things deemed unnecessary according to the value system they absorbed in the West. But I think overspecialization is a luxury we don't need in either richer or poorer countries. This practice can produce specialists who are out of touch with their context of ministry.

Christian ministers specialize out of a generalist background. That is, while they do many different types of ministries, they also take time to exercise their special gifts. I have come to believe that if we really like about 20 percent of the work we do and generally find about 40 percent acceptable, then we can handle the 40 percent that we do not like.[22] But as we saw above, the 40 percent that we don't like may be vital in giving relevance and depth to our ministry. If, however, we find that in the exercise of our responsibilities, there is almost nothing that we like and feel competent at doing, then perhaps we are in the wrong work.

14

PRAYING

IN 2001 I CELEBRATED twenty-five years at my job as Director of Youth for Christ (YFC) in Sri Lanka. I needed to write a short article in connection with that in our YFC prayer bulletin. I decided to write on what I considered to be the most important work I have done during these twenty-five years. I confessed that I have not done enough of that work, but I consider the little that I did to be the most important work I have done. I am talking about prayer.

Prayer has already been discussed several times in this book. In chapters 2 and 12 we discussed the connection between prayer and anointing for ministry. Chapters 3 and 7 talked about grappling with God in prayer in connection with our personal challenges. Chapter 4 was about retreats, of which prayer is a very important ingredient. In chapter 10 we discussed the need to pray for those we lead. In several other chapters different aspects of prayer have been brought up. As prayer is such an important part of the Christian minister's life and ministry, it should not surprise us that a book on ministry includes so much about it. Here we will look at the practice of prayer as a key ingredient of the ministerial lifestyle.

In a helpful article on prayer in the Synoptic Gospels, Howard Marshall points out that Jesus would have followed the usual Jewish practices of prayer and that the writers of the Gospels would not have mentioned that, as it was something quite normal. It was something less ordinary that would merit mention in the Gospels. Therefore, Marshall says, "When prayer is mentioned by the Synoptic evangelists, it must be for special reasons, and we are entitled to ask in each case why."[1] James Dunn says, "Although his praying covered the usual times of prayer, morning and evening, his need of prayer, at least on these occasions [mentioned in the Gospels], went far beyond the formal saying of prayers."[2]

THE SECRET PLACE OF PRAYER

Mark 1 has such a reference to the praying of Jesus. Verse 35 says, "And rising very early in the morning, while it was still dark, he departed and went out to a desolate place, and there he prayed." The mention of "a desolate place" suggests that he went there to be away from people. The parallel reference in Luke does not mention that Jesus prayed (Luke 4:42), suggesting that getting away from the people was a major reason for going to the desolate place for his prayer time. Later in Mark 1 we are told that Jesus spent time in desolate places because people were coming after him (1:45).

Luke says that Jesus "would withdraw to desolate places and pray" (Luke 5:16). The wording here suggests that this was a regular practice. Among these desolate places he went to were the mountains. It was when he was praying on the mountain that he was transfigured (Luke 9:28). When describing Jesus' going to the Garden of Gethsemane to pray after the Last Supper, Luke says it "was his custom" to go to the Mount of Olives (Luke 29:39). There, though he was with his disciples, "he withdrew from them about a stone's throw, and knelt down and prayed" (Luke 22:41). Sometimes he would spend the whole night in prayer on the mountain: "In these days he went out to the mountain to pray, and all night he continued in prayer to God" (Luke 6:12).

Elsewhere Jesus said, "But when you pray, go into your room and shut the door and pray to your Father who is in secret" (Matt. 6:6). Many, however, like Jesus who had "nowhere to lay his head" (Luke 9:58), do not have the luxury of a secret place in their homes. Therefore, they need to improvise. As I do a lot of my study and writing late into the night, I do not get up very early in the morning. I usually have my prayer time after others are up. Sometimes I find that the phone rings so much that I either have to take it off the hook or go to a nearby church to have my prayer time. It is comforting to us to know that Jesus had similar problems and worked at ways to overcome them. What we can learn from his example is that we must all have our secret places when we can be away from people so that we can spend time in uninterrupted prayer.

All ministers will be called upon often to pray in public. But public prayer can never be a substitute for private prayer. Private prayer is a basic feature of the Christian life and thus a key aspect of preparation for public ministry. Methodist preacher E. M. Bounds once wrote, "Some Methodist preachers pray too short in private and too long in public. As a rule, private prayers ought to be long and public ones short." He goes on to say, "It is absolute crucifixion to stay on the knees during these long, lifeless prayers."[3] His point is that not only do the public prayers of those who spend little time in private prayer drag on, but they drag on lifelessly. One who is not in intimate personal contact with God cannot lead God's people into his presence.

A BASIC FEATURE OF THE MINISTERIAL LIFESTYLE

In the narrative in Mark 1, while Jesus was praying in the early morning on the mountain, the disciples, who must have awakened after Jesus left the house, searched for him (1:36). When they found him, they said, "Everyone is looking for you" (1:37). Scholars say that the word translated "looking" (*zëteö*) "seems to imply an unwelcome following."[4] That this was the case is implied in Jesus' response: "Let us go on to the next towns, that I may preach there also, for that is why I came out" (1:38). What seemed to be a great opportunity for ministry was not to be taken up, as this was not God's will for him.

Two interesting factors in this narrative point to the priority of prayer in Jesus' life. First, Jesus must have been very tired after such a hectic Sabbath day. If he was anything like me, he would not have had a natural inclination to get up "very early in the morning" to pray after such a busy day. Second, there was a large ministry awaiting him, which he was disregarding at that time. For Jesus, spending quality, undisturbed time with God after a hectic day of ministry was a priority. After the feeding of the five thousand, he did a similar thing. He sent his disciples by boat to the other side of the lake, "to Bethsaida, while he dismissed the crowd. And after he had taken leave of them, he went up on the mountain to pray" (Mark 6:45-46).

We all have times like this when the pressures of ministry are so intense that we could easily forego our time with the Lord. A week before writing this, I was at the National Youth Leaders' Training Conference organized by YFC. All our staff workers were extremely busy and really pushing themselves to the limit in order to run it smoothly. I was there as a speaker. I got up fairly early each morning to have my time with the Lord. But I almost felt guilty about this as my colleagues were working so hard while I seemed to be relaxing in the presence of God! But actually I was working! For a leader, an important aspect of work is praying. That is why the early church decided to release the apostles from some duties in order that these men could concentrate on prayer and the ministry of the Word (Acts 6:4).

Paul demonstrated that prayer is work in his description of Epaphras, the founder of the church in Colossae. Epaphras was now with Paul far away from Colossae. Paul says, "Epaphras . . . greets you, always *struggling* on your behalf in his prayers, that you may stand mature and fully assured in all the will of God. For I bear him witness that he has *worked hard* for you and for those in Laodicea and in Hierapolis" (Col. 4:12-13, italics mine). The two words used for work here are very strong words. The verb translated "struggling" is *agōnizomai*, which takes meanings such as to "struggle, fight; do one's best; compete (of athletic contests)."[5] "Worked" comes from a noun, *ponos,* which means "work that involves much exertion or trouble."[6] And that idea is strengthened by the addition of the adjective *polus,* which means "much." These three words together suggest that Epaphras, though far away, was really working hard for them. But the work he was doing was praying.

I have heard people say that wives on their knees keep their husbands on their feet. This may be true. With firm scriptural backing, I can say that the prayers of leaders often keep those they lead growing and thriving in their work. The most vivid example is Moses, with his arms propped up by Aaron and Hur, praying on the mountain while Joshua and his army battled the Amalekites below (Exod. 17:8-13). The fortunes of the army fluctuated according to the intensity of Moses' praying on that occasion.

There is no alternative to prayer in a Christian worker's life. The great Scottish preacher Robert Murray McCheyne (1813-1843) said, "What a man is on his knees before God, that he is—and nothing more."[7] One cannot take shortcuts in the life of prayer. All Christian ministry is ministry in the Spirit, and for that we must linger with the Spirit. We simply cannot have a ministry that has spiritual depth, and therefore lasting effects, unless our lives are steeped in prayer.

The world with its false values and attractions will keep bombarding us with relentless consistency. If we do not counteract that influence with quality time with God, we will soon find that we have become like Peter, to whom Jesus said, "You are not setting your mind on the things of God, but on the things of man" (Matt. 16:23). Jesus told his disciples in the garden, "Watch and pray that you may not enter into temptation" (Matt. 26:41). However, Jesus knew that though these disciples would like to pray, they were too sleepy to do so. So he ended that verse saying, "The spirit indeed is willing, but the flesh is weak." As in Gethsemane, that principle applies to prayer today also. It is a comfort to know that "the Spirit helps us in our weakness. For we do not know what to pray for as we ought, but the Spirit himself intercedes for us with groanings too deep for words" (Rom. 8:26).

We may not at first recognize that we have lost our spiritual vitality through neglecting prayer. We always have our abilities and our training to fill the void created by the loss of God's nearness. I think people can survive and actually thrive without God's anointing, by relying on their abilities to carry them through—for a while. If we are hardworking, gifted, well organized, and good motivators of others, our ministries may even grow numerically. Many people choose churches based on the programs offered, and many churches have attractive programs even if the leaders are not walking close to the Lord. But the spiritual power won't be there, and that means that ultimately they are failures. Usually people sensitive to the things of God can sense the emptiness of the ministry, but they may not talk about it, especially if the leader is producing in terms of achieving measurable goals.

Paul said, "I beat my body and make it my slave so that after I have preached to others, I myself will not be disqualified for the prize" (1 Cor. 9:27 NIV). Part of this beating of the body that a Christian leader does is to refuse to be distracted so that quality time may be given to prayer.

I write this as a fellow pilgrim. One would have thought that after so many years, I would have mastered the art of moving to prayer when I should. But I haven't. This is a battle that has to be waged every day. I find it much easier to do some other work, and daily I have to firmly decide to refuse that inclination so that I can pray. Often I have failed in this area, and I can therefore say that any fruit from my ministry has not been owing to my faithfulness but to God's mercy. But I have determined that, despite my workaholic tendencies, I will wage this battle for quality times of prayer as long as I live.

PRAYERS AT IMPORTANT TIMES IN JESUS' MINISTRY

It is well known that the Gospels often describe Jesus praying before an important event in his life and ministry.

- Our text from Mark 1 comes at the start of his ministry just after there was a huge response with large numbers coming on a Sabbath day. He had to make a decision as to whether he would ride on this wave of popularity or whether he should adopt a different strategy. The choice of a rather negative word to describe the crowds "looking" (*zēteō*) for him (Mark 1:37) prepared us to read of his decision to go elsewhere without pandering to this crowd. But before the decision was communicated to the disciples, Jesus had been alone in a special place in prayer.

- He was in prayer when the Holy Spirit came upon him after his baptism (Luke 3:21).

• He spent forty days fasting (and obviously praying too) before he launched out on his ministry (Matt. 4:2).

• Before choosing his disciples, "he went out to the mountain to pray, and all night he continued in prayer to God" (Luke 6:12). In the morning he went straight into the work of choosing the Twelve.

• His conversation with the disciples in Caesarea Philippi is considered a pivotal point in his ministry (Luke 9:18-27). There he asked them what the people, and then what they themselves, believed about who he was. Then he made a full disclosure for the first time on record of the nature of his work as Savior, especially the need for him to be killed and to rise again. But just prior to recording this conversation, Luke says, "Now it happened that as he was praying alone, the disciples were with him" (9:18).

• We know that the Transfiguration took place when "he took with him Peter and John and James and went up on the mountain to pray. And as he was praying, the appearance of his face was altered, and his clothing became dazzling white" (Luke 9:28-29). He was probably praying alone on this occasion because Luke reports that while he was transfigured, "Peter and those who were with him were heavy with sleep" (9:32).

• Luke described the situation that prompted the giving of the very important Lord's Prayer to the disciples as follows: "Now Jesus was praying in a certain place, and when he finished, one of his disciples said to him, 'Lord, teach us to pray, as John taught his disciples'" (11:1). This was to become the standard prayer of a majority of Christians for the rest of Christian history.

• We know how Jesus took his disciples to the Garden of Gethsemane before his death. He told most of them, "Sit here while I pray" (Mark 14:32). But he took Peter, James, and John a little further and told them how sorrowful he was. Then "going a little farther, he fell on the ground and prayed" (14:35). Matthew says "he fell on his face" and prayed (Matt. 26:39). From the Old Testament we see that the Jews used numerous postures when praying.[8] But the posture used by Christ here indicates that there was a special earnestness and urgency to this prayer.

After surveying some of the above texts, James Dunn says, "Jesus was a man of prayer whose natural response particularly to situations of crisis and decision was to seek God alone in prayer."[9]

When discussing prayer as a condition for anointing in chapter 2, fasting in chapter 4, and praying for the sick and possessed in chapter 12, I mentioned the need for special times of prayer before special events. The above list of times Jesus prayed before key events tells us that special seasons of prayer before important occasions is a standard Christian practice. We need to be in tune with God when we make major decisions or lead God's people through significant experiences. Prayer is the best way to do that. If we are leaders, we will usually be very busy before such an event. If so, we will need to plan our schedule carefully so that we can release ourselves for prayer. Perhaps we will need to delegate some responsibilities to ensure this time.

I have come up with the following examples of important events in a Christian worker's life when we need to especially go to a season of prayer:

A staff or committee retreat when the group will seek God's face for a vision of the work before them or when the leader will communicate his or her vision to the people.

- A staff or leaders' conference.
- Before going to pray for someone who is demon-possessed.
- Before a difficult meeting when a lot of conflict is anticipated.
- An interview for a new job or before making a decision about whether to accept a job that has been offered.
- Before preaching (I need special prayer times whenever I speak, but this is particularly needed before a big conference because I have found that such speaking appointments are very draining both spiritually and emotionally).
- Before deciding what one is going to preach on for the next few months at church (many ministers decide on their sermon topics for about three months at a time).
- Before making a final decision as to who will be one's partner in life.

PRAYERS ON THE RUN

Often Jesus spontaneously moved into prayer in the middle of a conversation.

- After denouncing some cities where the people had not repented, Jesus thanked God that even though the wise did not understand the truth, little children did (Matt. 11:25-26). Then he moved back into conversation with those who were around him.
- Once after he had talked about his impending death and about the principle that death precedes life, he expressed his apprehensions about his death to God. He said, "Now is my soul troubled. And what shall I say? 'Father, save me from this hour'? But for this purpose I have come to this hour. Father, glorify your name" (John 12:27-28).
- When he came to the tomb where Lazarus was laid, he "lifted up his eyes and said, 'Father, I thank you that you have heard me. I knew that you always hear me, but I said this on account of the people standing around, that

they may believe that you sent me'" (John 11:41-42). Immediately after that he cried, "Lazarus, come out."

• We find Jesus giving thanks when he fed the multitude (Matt. 15:36; Mark 6:41) and when he instituted the Lord's Supper (Mark 14:23; Luke 22:19).

• Three of his seven recorded words from the cross were spoken to God. He asked God to forgive those who crucified him (Luke 23:34). He cried in despair over his sense that God had forsaken him (Matt. 27:46). And just before dying he commended his spirit to God (Luke 23:46).

What I have listed are the recorded prayers of Jesus that were audibly heard by others. There must have been many more instances when Jesus silently prayed to his heavenly Father. In chapter 10 we called these prayers on the run, "flash prayers" or "arrow prayers."

Similarly we too can break into prayer when we see something about which we need to talk to God.

• When we are counseling someone, we could be pleading with God to help us.

• When we are facing opposition, we could be asking God to help us to respond properly.

• Before I go up to speak, I am usually praying to God asking for his help.

• Often while I speak, also I am praying, asking for help and also requesting God to speak to those in the audience.

• I have found it very helpful to be talking to God silently when I am having an argument with my wife. That way we will not panic and lose control and say things that we will later regret. When God has come into the equation, we can proceed with hope, knowing that God will help us not only solve this problem, but also turn it into something good. This changes our whole attitude, and that moderates the way we argue.

• Sometimes, like Jesus we could break into prayer in the middle of a conversation with others.

• When we are at a meeting and are struggling to find a solution to a problem, we could pause in the middle of the discussion to ask God's help.

I led the audience through the closing moments of the YFC training conference mentioned above. The final speaker did a good job of bringing his talk to a conclusion and leading the people in an act of dedication. I had planned to do something similar, and so I had to find some other meaningful way to close the conference. I was pleading with God for guidance. I was seated next to the person who was going to interpret into the Tamil language what I said in the Sinhala language. I told him my dilemma and prayed together with him asking for help. I went to the platform with a rough idea about what I would do, but praying hard and thinking hard and with my mind fully open to God's prompting. I think it went well!

I once spent a six-month sabbatical with my family at Gordon-Conwell Theological Seminary in the United States in 1988. I was attached to the Missions division, which was led by the late Dr. Christy Wilson. Getting to know Dr. Wilson and his wife, Betty, has been one of the highlights of my experiences in ministry. What a godly and gracious couple! Dr. Wilson could eminently adorn the designation "prayer warrior." If I ever mentioned a need or a concern to him, he would immediately take it to God. Once I met him in a department store, and in the course of the conversation I mentioned a problem about seats for the flights back to Sri Lanka. He immediately said, "Let's pray about it," and he prayed right there inside the busy department store. From him I learned the value of automatically slipping into prayer in the middle of a conversation, just as Jesus did.

Jesus moved so effortlessly into prayer because, as James G. S. S. Thomson has said, "Prayer was the atmosphere in which he lived; it was the air he breathed."[10] Similarly, if we are to be effective in flash-praying, we need to be in tune with God. Such sensitivity usually comes through unhurried time spent with him. Therefore, I am rather skeptical when I hear people say that they don't set aside a special time for prayer, that they survive on flash prayers. Usually it takes me about fifteen minutes to get into the mood of prayer during my intercessions. For the first fifteen minutes I may pray for only a few people as my mind finds it difficult to concentrate. Then, once I am in the mood for prayer, I can pray at a faster rate. When I leave, my tie with God has been renewed so that I can move into flash prayers quite naturally. Flash prayers then are never a substitute for our quiet time, for time spent alone with God.

THE CONTENT: THANKSGIVING, SUPPLICATION, AND INTERCESSION

As we look at the content of the prayers of Jesus, we see three major emphases—thanksgiving, supplication, and intercession. We are not looking at the model prayer of Jesus, the Lord's Prayer, which was given to all believers and certainly is the model for ministers also. That prayer lacks thanksgiving and intercession but has adoration. Here we will look at the prayers that have been recorded in the Gospels, which Jesus himself prayed.[11]

Thanksgiving

The thanksgiving prayers of Jesus recorded in the Gospels would fall into the category of "prayers on the run." These include his prayers giving thanks before the feeding of the five thousand (John 6:11) and the four thousand (Matt. 15:35), at the Last Supper (Matt. 26:27), and as he broke bread in the home of the disciples in Emmaus (Luke 24:30 NIV[12]).

In two other prayers Jesus responds to a situation by simply saying a word of thanks to God. The first of these comes along with a statement "to denounce the cities where most of his mighty works had been done, because they did not repent" (Matt. 11:20). However, after denouncing them for their rejection of his teaching, he acknowledges that some others did accept it. He said, "I thank you, Father, Lord of heaven and earth, that you have hidden these things from the wise and understanding and revealed them to little children; yes, Father, for such was your gracious will" (11:25-26). The other time was at the tomb of Lazarus, when he prayed something like a prayer of testimony with an evangelistic goal. John reports, "And Jesus lifted up his eyes and said, 'Father, I thank you that you have heard me. I knew that you always hear me, but I said this on account of the people standing around, that they may believe that you sent me'" (John 11:41-42).

Thanksgiving forms an important part of Paul's prayers, for giving thanks is mentioned fifteen times in the prayers in the Epistles. Once he has a general thanksgiving for God's gift (2 Cor. 9:15). Ten times he thanks God for the faith, testimony, and Christian experience of his readers.[13] He thanks God for the fellowship in the gospel that he enjoys with his readers (Phil. 1:3-5). He blesses (*eulogētos*) and thanks (*charis*) God for the grace he himself has experienced (2 Cor. 1:3-4; 2:14) and for the fact that the Lord called him to the ministry (1 Tim. 1:12-17). In view of this impressive list, it should not surprise us that Paul says, "Give thanks in all circumstances; for this is the will of God in Christ Jesus for you" (1 Thess. 5:18).

The evidence above should convince us that thanksgiving is a key aspect of the lifestyle of the Christian worker. In chapter 7 we said that we must not allow anger to control our lives. In chapter 11 we talked about the importance of joy in our experience. A key to both of these factors is having a heart of thanksgiving. We note that Jesus found something to thank God for even when he was denouncing cities that had rejected his message (Matt. 11:20-26). Paul even thanked God for the Corinthians who gave him considerable heartache (1 Cor. 1:4-9).

We can have a heart of thanksgiving if we acknowledge God in every situation in life. We believe he is sovereign; we know he will turn every situation into something good. So we can always thank him. We can forgive those who have hurt us and affirm that even their unkindness will become an opportunity for our good. This will help remove the debilitating burden of anger and bitterness and keep our joy fresh till we die.

Bernard Gilpin was an Anglican preacher of the sixteenth century who was arrested for preaching the gospel. He was being taken on horseback to London for his trial, and he kept remarking, "Everything is for the best." His captors made fun of these remarks. On the way he fell from his horse and broke his leg. This made his captors especially merry. But Gilpin quietly remarked, "I have no doubt but that even this painful accident will prove to be a blessing." He was delayed because of the injury and arrived in London some days later than had been expected.

When they reached the prison, they heard the bells ringing merrily in the city. They asked the reason and were told, "Queen Mary is dead, and there will no more be burning of Protestants!"

"Ah," said Gilpin, "you see, it is all for the best."[14]

That is the attitude with which we can face life. It is a discipline we develop of doggedly holding on to the fact that God is with us and working for us. Then we can give thanks in all circumstances, as Paul asked us to do.

Supplication

In a surprising number of the recorded prayers of Jesus, he is praying for himself. And all of them have to do with the really tough work of dying for the sins of the world. As his death drew near and he contemplated its implications, he prayed, "Now is my soul troubled. And what shall I say? 'Father, save me from this hour'? But for this purpose I have come to this hour. Father, glorify your name" (John 12:27-28). Then at the Last Supper, he prayed, "Father, the hour has come; glorify your Son that the Son may glorify you, since you have given him authority over all flesh, to give eternal life to all whom you have given him" (John 17:1-2). Later in the Garden he was in agony as he contemplated his death, and he prayed, "Abba, Father, all things are possible for you. Remove this cup from me. Yet not what I will, but what you will" (Mark 14:36). Hebrews 5:7 describes this battling with God in prayer quite vividly: "In the days of his flesh, Jesus offered up prayers and supplications, with loud cries and tears, to him who was able to save him from death, and he was heard because of his reverence."

The remaining two prayers are uttered from the cross itself when he asked God why he had forsaken him (Mark 15:34) and when he commended his spirit to God (Luke 23:46).

I suppose avoiding death on the cross was the greatest temptation that Jesus encountered, and it was about this that he prayed most when he prayed for himself. In the same way we too pray for ourselves especially regarding our areas of vulnerability—areas where we are tempted to do things that are not according to God's will.

I have used a prayer list for my personal devotions for at least thirty-eight years. Some years ago I realized that I was not praying much for myself. I spent most of my prayer time praying for others. Yet there were many, many areas of my life where I was failing and areas where I was vulnerable to temptation. I decided to write down these areas at the top of my prayer list. I believe it would be good for all leaders to give a prominent place in their prayers to their own weaknesses and challenges.

Intercession

As we have discussed intercessory prayer in our study of discipling in chapter 10, we will not discuss it at length here. Let me just mention the occasions of intercessory prayer recorded in the Gospels. The first is Jesus' prayer for Simon that, though he would deny Christ, his faith would not fail and that after his repentance he would strengthen his brothers (Luke 22:31-32). The next prayer is the Great High-Priestly Prayer where he prays for his disciples (John 17:6-19, 24-26) and for those who would believe later (17:20-23). The other recorded prayer is from the cross when he asked God to forgive those who killed him because they did not know what they were doing (Luke 23:34).

In chapter 10 we saw something about Paul's intercessory prayer life. We pointed out that in ten of his thirteen letters, he mentioned praying for the recipients of the letters.

It is interesting to note that Jesus is still praying for us and that the fullness of our salvation depends on his prayers on our behalf. Hebrews 7:25 says, "Consequently, he is able to save to the uttermost those who draw near to God through him, since he always lives to make intercession for them." Just as intercession is a vital work that he does, it is also a vital work that we do.

Several years ago I expressed to a colleague that I was very concerned about the loss of prayer momentum in Youth for Christ. He replied that perhaps we have gotten careless here because we are not facing a crisis. I thought about that and came to realize that we were indeed facing a huge crisis. We faced the crisis of millions of people in our nation heading into a Christless eternity. We faced the crisis of hundreds of young people who had met Christ through our ministry who were living defeated Christian lives. And we faced the crisis of a church in desperate need of revival.

When we come close to the heart of God and see how far the church and we ourselves are falling short of his standards, then our hearts will be inflamed with the desire to see all of God's purposes fulfilled, and earnest intercessory prayer will result. The eminent church historian Earle E. Cairns in his historical study of revival says, "Prayer ranks first in the coming of revival . . . . There cannot be revival unless Christians pray for it."[15] God knows we need revival, and if we were near to God's heart, we too would know that. Then we would commit ourselves to the ministry of intercession and encourage others to become intercessors too.

THE DISCIPLES SAW HIM PRAYING

Several times in the Gospels we find that, though Jesus was with the disciples, he was often actually alone in prayer. We have already mentioned the instances at the Mount of Transfiguration and in the Garden of Gethsemane. Before his conversation with the disciples in Caesarea Philippi, when Jesus asked the question, "Who do the crowds say that I am?" Luke says that "he was praying alone, [and that] the disciples were with him" (Luke 9:18).

Watching him at prayer seems to have created a thirst in the disciples for a vibrant prayer life. Luke says, "Now Jesus was praying in a certain place, and when he finished, one of his disciples said to him, 'Lord, teach us to pray, as John taught his disciples'" (Luke 11:1). Jesus' response was to teach them the Lord's Prayer (11:2-4). So Jesus gave his disciples ample opportunity to observe his prayer life. Paul also talked often about his prayer life in his Epistles.

In the same way, it would be helpful for those we lead to know something about our own prayer life. We must not, of course, fall into the trap of parading our prayer life in a boastful manner for others to see, as Jesus warned in the Sermon on the Mount (Matt. 6:5-6). If we remain close to those we lead, they will observe us at prayer. We can also chat with them about our experiences in prayer.

Paul told Timothy, "You, however, have followed my teaching, my conduct, my aim in life, my faith, my patience, my love, my steadfastness, my persecutions and sufferings . . ." (2 Tim. 3:10-11). The word translated "followed" here (*parakolutheö*) has the idea of "to conform to someone's belief or practice by paying special attention, follow faithfully, follow as a rule."[16] As we saw in chapter 10, leaders provide an example to others of how Christians behave. One of the things that Timothy would have observed from Paul's example would have been his prayer life.

In my own life, I have been greatly helped by the examples of praying by several elders whom I had the privilege of observing. As a boy I knew how much time my mother spent in prayer. When I stayed over at my maternal grandmother's house, if I got up to go to the bathroom in the early morning while it was still dark, I had to go through her room. I would see her kneeling behind her bed praying with her head covered. Later I found out that my grandmother had prayed for me every day since my birth.

Early in my ministry I traveled to some villages in Sri Lanka with an aging evangelist, Samuel Mendis, from whom I learned a lot about evangelizing the poor. On one of our trips, we spent the night in a classroom in a school. We put two or three wooden benches side by side and slept on those. When I got up fairly early in the morning, I saw that this old man was already awake and kneeling in prayer. This left a lasting impression on my mind.

For us who are parents, our children will get several important messages about God and how he is to be followed simply by observing our prayer habits. When I was a child, I went to a Bible camp with my family where the main speaker was Theodore H. Epp, the founder of *Back to the Bible Broadcast*. I remember only one thing he said: that when his children were small, they knew that there was one time in the day when they could not go into their father's room. That was the time he spent alone with God. Such a prohibition certainly inculcated a respect for God in the lives of his children.

PRAYER AS A PREVENTATIVE TO BURNOUT

We note again that this time of prayer that Jesus spent early in the morning in Mark 1:35 was after a very busy Sabbath day. He had healed many people in addition to preaching. Such work can be emotionally and spiritually exhausting. I believe that it would have given him much refreshment to get away from the crowds to be alone with God in prayer after such a hectic day.

To be sure, prayer is seldom what we naturally do after a heavy day of work. I find that most often I have trouble giving myself to prayer on my day off each week. My tendency is to want to "goof off." I do think we need some refreshing, relaxing "goofing-off" time after high-pressure activities. In fact, we need to plan for relaxation, for otherwise with all the impure entertainment around, we could be lured into something sinful.

I have to plan particularly for recreation when I am traveling. I try to avoid hotels. I find that staying in homes is much more wholesome and a better aid to identifying with people. Indeed, our hosts may talk too long when we are tired, but that is a great way to get to know people. If I am staying in a hotel, when I come to my room after a busy day, my mind is usually too active for me to go to sleep at once. I could be tempted to watch unedifying television. So I have to make plans prior to this about what I will do. Recreation and fun help to relieve stress. But if we indulge in something impure, we encounter a new category of pressure, the pressure of an uneasy conscience.

Unhurried times with God are also a great way to release pressure. Indeed, we may not feel like spending time this way the morning after a busy day, but if we do it anyway, we will find great refreshment. I think the life of Jesus speaks specifically to the busy, activist Christian workers of today. Jesus was also a really hard worker. Mark highlights this fact. Twice he says that Jesus did not even have time to eat because of the crowds clamoring for his attention (3:20; 6:31). But Mark also gives attention to the times that he spent alone with God.

Jesus was a contemplative activist, and that is what we all should aim at being. Archbishop Donald Coggan, commenting on Mark's portrayal of Christ working and praying, says, "Thus there would seem to have been a kind of rhythm about the life of Jesus—withdrawal and work; withdrawal and work."[17] I often tell our Youth for Christ staff that our lives follow a similar pattern. We receive strength from being with the Lord, and then we go into a hostile world and get bashed there. Then we come back to God in order to recover from the battle and get back our strength. Thus strengthened, we go back into the world to get bashed again! But the strength we get from God enables us to go on battling for the kingdom of God.

Work, of course, must never keep us from prayer. Actually when we have an extra load of work to do, we should be praying more than usual, in order that we have the strength to do that work "in the Spirit." Usually the opposite happens. When we have extra work to do, one of the first things we drop is our prayer time. Martin Luther wrote, "I am so busy that I find that I cannot do with less than four hours a day in the presence of God."[18] Unlike in the West, we do not have petrol (gas) stations everywhere in Sri Lanka. So if we are going on a long trip, we need to fill up the tank of the vehicle before we embark. Similarly, for Luther an extra load of work required extra strength, and this caused him to spend extra time with the Lord. I know of no one who has remained fresh in ministry over a long period of time who did not daily spend unhurried moments with the Lord in prayer and Bible reading.

In recent times I have been reflecting much on the idea that prayer is one of the surest means of preventing burnout in the ministry. This is a vital topic today because ministry burnout has reached epidemic proportions. Many have told me recently that the schedule I keep makes me a prime candidate for burnout. I suppose the jury is not in on this yet, as I am fifty-three years old now, and I hope I have a few more years of ministry left. Perhaps fifteen years from now I will be able to speak with more confidence on this issue. But I do believe that time spent daily lingering in the presence of God is a great preventative to burnout and other ill effects of stress and hard work. Here are some reasons for that belief. Some of these have been mentioned in earlier chapters, but it is helpful to bring them together here under this discussion.[19]

First, *if spending a good time with God each day is a nonnegotiable factor in our daily calendar, then this time could really help slow us down* and heal that unhealthy restlessness and rushed attitude that often causes burnout. There are few things that help heal our restlessness as much as time spent in the presence of God. If a fixed time has been set apart each day for prayer, then there is no point rushing through the exercise, as we are going to spend that blocked-out amount of time whether we rush or not. So we are forced to change gears from stressful hurry to restful waiting in God's presence.

Your quiet time is like traveling by train to the office when you are really under pressure with a lot of work to do. You run from home to the station, and after arriving at your destination, you run from the train station to the office. But when you are on the train, no amount of running or fretting will help you. You might as well relax and enjoy the ride. It's the same with prayer. However stressed you may be with the load of work, if spending an hour with God is a nonnegotiable part of your daily schedule, then you can do it in a relaxed manner while all around you there may be reasons for stress and hurry!

Secondly, *an hour or more spent each day in the presence of the almighty and sovereign Lord of the universe does wonders to our sense of security* (Ps. 46:1-11), the lack of which is another common cause of burnout. We reckon that the one who is with us and from whom we derive our strength is the Lord of all. The Word says, "The eternal God is your dwelling place, and underneath are the everlasting arms" (Deut. 33:27). There is great security here!

With this security comes "the peace of God, which surpasses all under-standing" (Phil. 4:7)—surely a wonderful treasure to take through life. When we do not have security in our relationship with God, we will be restlessly running from activity to activity, subconsciously hoping that our activity will fill the void in our lives. We are afraid to stop and be silent before God lest it cause us to face up honestly to what is happening in our lives. So we go on with our busy activity till we drive ourselves into the ground!

The peace we just described is the result of presenting our requests to God (Phil. 4:6). *When we spend time with God, we are able to cast all our anxiety on him because he cares for us* (1 Peter 5:7). It was during a time of deep crisis in our ministry that I discovered the great release that comes from con-sciously handing over my burdens to God. I had difficulty going to sleep because I was overwhelmed by worry over the situation. I learned to confess my inability to bear these burdens alone, and I placed them upon God by a conscious act of release. And release was what I felt as a result.

When we pray, we open up our hearts to God's healing comfort. And if someone has hurt us, then we are going to grapple with God over that. This grappling gives God an opportunity to break through into our lives with his comfort. And that comfort enables us to overcome bitterness over what peo-ple have done to us. What a heavy burden bitterness is for a person to bear! It will drag us down in our spiritual lives and make us prime candidates for burnout.

Actually, just as burnout is a problem, so is depression among older Christians who have been kind and considerate people most of their lives even though they have been treated badly by many people. But underneath this kind-looking exterior hides great emotional pain. Once these people get older, they do not have the strength to hold back their pain. Then like children they express what is in the heart. What comes out is bitter depression. It is so important that we seek healing for these wounds before we grow old. Others will help us here. But ultimately what gives us permanent healing is the com-fort of the Lord. God can heal us if we open ourselves to him in prayer instead of hiding our pain.

If, during our time with God, we do a lot of intercession, we have become conduits of love. When we pray for others, love is flowing out of our lives. But this is not a love that drains us of our emotional strength. We are praying, which means that we are in touch with him who is the inex-haustible source of love. As love goes out through prayer, God's love comes in, and the regular flow of love in and out of our lives makes us glow with the joy that love alone can produce. Paul says, "God's love has been poured into our hearts through the Holy Spirit who has been given to us" (Rom. 5:5). The word translated "poured" (*ekcheo*) "denotes both abundance and diffusion. . . . The idea of spiritual refreshment and encouragement is conveyed through the metaphor of watering."[20] When we are in vital touch with God, we have access to sufficient quantities of love so that we will come out glowing after our times of intercession.

If we work hard, but do not receive our strength from God, we will indeed burn out. To get God's strength, we need to be in touch with God, and the best way to stay close to him is to pray. Someone has said, "Seven prayerless days makes one *weak*." Isaiah 40:31 says, "They who wait for the Lord shall renew their strength; they shall mount up with wings like eagles; they shall run and not be weary; they shall walk and not faint."

So our time spent with God each day becomes the most refreshing thing that we do. Such freshness attacks those triggers of burnout that often accompany the stresses and strains of ministry.

I will bring this book to a close by expressing my hope that the reader will always remain fresh in the Lord's work and thus will not be hindered from seeing the glory of God in the ministry. It is indeed a glorious work, and if our ministries are going to be healthy, we must always have before us this vision of its glory.

NOTES

Acknowledgments

1 Robert E. Coleman, *The Mind of the Master* (Wheaton, Ill.: Harold Shaw Publishers, repr. 2000).

2 Robert E. Coleman, *The Master Plan of Evangelism,* 30th Anniversary Edition (Grand Rapids: Fleming H. Revell, 1993).

Chapter 1 Identifying with People

1 Larry W. Hurtado, *Mark: The New International Biblical Commentary* (Peabody, Mass.: Hendrickson Publishers, 1989), 1.

2 Nathaniel was from Cana in Galilee (John 21:2).

3 Craig L. Blomberg, *The New American Commentary: Matthew* (Nashville: Broadman Press, 1992), 81.

4 Donald English, *The Message of Mark: The Mystery of Faith,* The Bible Speaks Today (Downers Grove, Ill., and Leicester, England: InterVarsity Press, 1992), 39.

5 See Jonathan Edwards, *A History of the Work of Redemption,* in *The Works of Jonathan Edwards,* vol. 1 (Edinburgh: Banner of Truth, 1834, repr. 1974), 272-80, 572.

6 For an exposition of this concept, see Daniel P. Fuller, *The Unity of the Bible* (Grand Rapids: Zondervan Publishing House, 1992), 209, and my *The Supremacy of Christ* (Wheaton, Ill.: Crossway Books, 1995), 162-63.

7 See Murray J. Harris, *Slave of Christ: A New Testament Metaphor for Total Devotion to Christ* (Leicester: InterVarsity Press, 1999).

8 Laurence W. Wood, "Telling the Old, Old Story in the Postmodern Age," *The Asbury Herald,* Autumn 1996, 3.

9 Matt. 5:10-12; Luke 6:23; John 16:20-24; Acts 5:41; Rom. 5:3-11; 12:12; 2 Cor. 6:10; 7:4; 8:2; 12:10; Phil. 1:18; 2:17; Col. 1:24; Heb. 12:2; James 1:2; 1 Peter 1:6-9; 4:12-13; Rev. 12:11-12.

10 For this interpretation of the expression, "I fill up in my flesh what is still lacking in regard to Christ's afflictions," see David E. Garland, *The NIV Application Commentary: Colossians* (Grand Rapids: Zondervan Publishing House, 1998), 118-23.

11 Dennis F. Kinlaw, *Preaching in the Spirit* (Grand Rapids: Francis Asbury Press, Zondervan Publishing House, 1985), 87.

12 From W. T. Purkiser, *The New Testament Image of the Ministry* (Grand Rapids: Baker Book House, repr. 1974), 64.

Chapter 2 Empowered by the Spirit

1 Barclay M. Newman, Jr., *A Concise Greek-English Dictionary of the New Testament* (United Bible Societies, 1971; Deutsche Bibelgesellschaft Stuttgart, 1993). Taken from the electronic version by iExalt, Inc., 1998.

2 See Morna D. Hooker, *The Gospel According to St. Mark, Black's New Testament Commentary* (Peabody, Mass.: Hendrickson Publishers, repr. 1991), 46.

3 Frederick Danker, *A Greek-English Lexicon of the New Testament and Other Early Christian Literature,* 3rd ed., based on Walter Bauer's Lexicon in German and other previous editions by William F. Arndt, F. Wilbur Gingrich, and F. W. Danker (Chicago, London: University of Chicago Press, 2000), 164. See this article for a classification of the various uses of *baptizō.*

4   Robert E. Coleman, *The Mind of the Master* (Wheaton, Ill.: Harold Shaw Publishers, 2000), 35-36.

5   Some of the fruit of this study is recorded in my article "The Holy Spirit: The Divine Implementer of Mission," in *Global Missiology for the 21ˢᵗ Century: The Iguassu Dialogue,* ed. William D. Taylor (Grand Rapids: Baker Book House, 2000), 232-36.

6   Cited in J. Christy Wilson, Jr., *More to Be Desired Than Gold* (privately published, 1992), 78.

7   *George Mueller: Man of Faith,* ed. A. Sims (privately published in Singapore by Warren Myers), 51; taken from *An Hour with George Mueller* (Grand Rapids: Zondervan Publishing House).

8   Danker, *A Greek-English Lexicon,* 143.

9   Robert E. Coleman, *"Nothing to Do but to Save Souls": John Wesley's Charge to His Preachers* (Grand Rapids: Zondervan Publishing House, 1990), 28.

10 A. J. Appasamy, *Sundar Singh: A Biography* (Madras: The Christian Literature Society, 1966), 26-27.

11 W. E. Sangster, *Power in Preaching* (Grand Rapids: Baker Book House, repr. 1976), 106.

12 Ibid., 107.

13 I copied this quote down from a *Decision* magazine several years ago.

Chapter 3 Affirmed by God

1   Willem A. Van Gemeren, "Psalms," *Expositor's Bible Commentary* (Grand Rapids: Zondervan Publishing House, 1998). I have used the software version.

2   Donald English, *The Message of Mark: The Mystery of Faith,* The Bible Speaks Today (Downers Grove, Ill., and Leicester, England: InterVarsity Press, 1992), 40.

3   Van Gemeren, "Psalms," *Expositor's Bible Commentary.*

Chapter 4 Retreating from Activity

1   Craig L. Blomberg, *The New American Commentary: Matthew* (Nashville: Broadman Press, 1992), 83.

2   Henri Nouwen, *The Way of the Heart: Desert Spirituality and Contemporary Ministry* (San Francisco: Harper & Row, 1981), 63.

3   J. C. Pollock, *Hudson Taylor and Maria* (Eastbourne: Kingsway Publications, repr. 1983), 215.

4   Eugene H. Merrill, "Fast, Fasting," *Evangelical Dictionary of Biblical Theology,* ed. Walter A. Elwell (Grand Rapids: Baker Book House, 1996), 246. See this article for examples of these three types of fasting.

5   Craig S. Keener, *A Commentary on the Gospel of Matthew* (Grand Rapids: Wm. B. Eerdmans Publishing, 1999), 227.

6   John Wesley, *The Works of John Wesley,* Vol. 5 (Grand Rapids: Baker Book House, repr. 1984), 346.

7   Merrill, "Fast, Fasting," *Evangelical Dictionary,* 246.

8   Wesley, *Works,* Vol. 7, 288-89.

9   Ibid., Vol. 8, 316-17.

Chapter 5 Affirming the Will of God

1   Leon Morris, *The Gospel According to Matthew* (Grand Rapids: Wm. B. Eerdmans Publishing; Leicester, England: InterVarsity Press, 1992), 71.

2   Craig Keener, *A Commentary on the Gospel of Matthew* (Grand Rapids: Wm. B. Eerdmans Publishing, 1999), 138.

3   Ibid., 139.

4   J. A. Broadus, *Commentary on the Gospel of Matthew* (Valley Forge, Pa.: Judson Press, reprint of 1886 edition), 64.

5   John Wesley, *The Works of John Wesley,* Vol. 3, *Journals* (Grand Rapids: Baker Book House, repr. 1984), 225.

6   *Spiritual Secrets of George Mueller,* selected by Roger Steer (Wheaton, Ill.: Harold Shaw Publishers; Robesonia, Pa.: OMF Books, 1985), 72.

7   Jean Cadier, *The Man God Mastered,* trans. O. R. Johnstone (London: Inter-Varsity Fellowship, 1960), 105.

8   Roger Steer, *J. Hudson Taylor: A Man in Christ* (Singapore: OMF Books, 1990), 299.

Chapter 6 Saturated in the Word

1   Leon Morris, *The Tyndale New Testament Commentaries: Luke: An Introduction and Commentary,* rev. ed. (Grand Rapids: Wm. B. Eerdmans Publishing; Leicester: InterVarsity Press, 1988), 83.

2   Earle E. Ellis, *The New Century Bible: The Gospel of Luke* (Greenwood, S.C.: The Attic Press, 1974), 77.

3   Robert E. Coleman, *The Mind of the Master* (Wheaton, Ill.: Harold Shaw Publishers, 2000), 54.

4   Robert E. Coleman, *The Master Plan of Discipleship* (Old Tappan, N.J.: Fleming H. Revell, 1987), 105.

5   F. F. Bruce, *The New International Commentary on the New Testament: The Book of Acts,* rev. ed. (Grand Rapids: Wm. B. Eerdmans Publishing, 1988), 335.

6   From A. Skevington Wood, *Captive to the Word: Martin Luther, Doctor of Sacred Scripture* (Grand Rapids: Wm. B. Eerdmans Publishing, 1969), 72.

7   John Wesley, *The Works of John Wesley,* Vol. 5 (Grand Rapids: Baker Book House, 1872, repr. 1984), 3.

8   A. Skevington Wood, *The Burning Heart: John Wesley, Evangelist* (Grand Rapids: Wm. B. Eerdmans Publishing, 1967), 212.

9   Ibid., 213.

10 E. W. Bacon, *Spurgeon: Heir to the Puritans* (Grand Rapids: Baker Book House, 1967), 109.

11 Willem A. Van Gemeren, "Psalms," *Expositor's Bible Commentary,* vol. 5 (Grand Rapids: Zondervan Publishing House; taken from the electronic version).

12 *George Mueller: Man of Faith,* ed. A. Sims (privately published in Singapore by Warren Myers), 52; taken from *An Hour with George Mueller* (Grand Rapids: Zondervan Publishing House), 51.

13 From Wood, *Burning Heart,* 211.

14 For a critique of this approach see David F. Wells, *No Place for Truth* (Grand Rapids: Wm. B. Eerdmans Publishing Co., 1993).

15 C. S. Lewis, *Reflections on the Psalms* (New York: Harcourt, Brace and World, 1958), 62.

16 Carl F. H. Henry, *Confessions of a Theologian* (Waco, Texas: Word Books, 1986), 67 (italics his).

17 Dietrich Bonhoeffer, *Meditating on the Word,* trans. and ed. David McI. Gracie (Boston: Cowley Publications, 2000), 22-23 (italics mine).

18 From Sherwood Eliot Wirt and Kersten Beckstrom, *Living Quotations for Christians* (New York: Harper & Row, 1974), 216.

19 *The Table Talk of Martin Luther,* ed. Thomas S. Kepler (New York: The World Publishing Company, 1952), 7.

20 Quoted in W. T. Purkiser, *The New Testament Image of the Ministry* (Grand Rapids: Baker Book House, 1970), 55.

21 Quoted in ibid., 56.

22 John Stott, *I Believe in Preaching* (London: Hodder & Stoughton, 1982), 125. The American edition is entitled *Between Two Worlds* (Grand Rapids: Wm. B. Eerdmans Publishing Co., 1981).

23 For a recent appeal for expository preaching, see R. Kent Hughes, "Restoring Biblical Exposition to Its Rightful Place," in John H. Armstrong, ed., *Reforming Pastoral Ministry: Challenges for Ministry in Postmodern Times* (Wheaton, Ill.: Crossway Books, 2001), 83-95.

Chapter 7 Facing Wild Animals

1   I am indebted to J. A. Brooks, *The New American Commentary: Mark* (Nashville: Broadman Press, 1991) and Robert A. Guelich, *The Word Biblical Commentary: Mark 1—8:26* (Dallas: Word Publishing, 1989) for some of the material in this section.

2   John Wesley, "Hebrews," in *Classic Bible Commentary*, ed. Owen Collins (Wheaton, Ill.: Crossway Books, 1999), 1445.
3   See Billy Graham, *Angels: God's Secret Agents* (Dallas: Word Publishing, 1986).
4   Barclay M. Newman, Jr., *A Concise Greek-English Dictionary of the New Testament* (United Bible Societies, 1971; Deutsche Bibelgesellschaft Stuttgart, 1993). Taken from the electronic version by iExalt, Inc., 1998.

Chapter 8 Bearing Good News

1   Larry W. Hurtado, *Mark: The New International Biblical Commentary* (Peabody, Mass.: Hendrickson Publishers, 1989), 1.
2   Ibid., 22.
3   I have presented this in contemporary English, from Robert Mounce, "Gospel," *Evangelical Dictionary of Theology*, ed. Walter Elwell (Grand Rapids: Baker Book House, 1984), 472.
4   Cited in David L. Larsen, *The Company of the Preachers: A History of Biblical Preaching from the Old Testament to the Modern Era* (Grand Rapids: Kregel Publications, 1998), 282.
5   Cited in Stanley N. Gundry, *Love Them In: The Life and Theology of D. L. Moody* (Grand Rapids: Baker Book House, 1976), 97-98.
6   Quoted in Sherwood E. Wirt, *Billy: A Personal Look at the World's Best-Loved Evangelist* (Wheaton, Ill.: Crossway Books, 1997), 47.
7   From *The Best of Vance Havner* (Grand Rapids: Baker Book House, 1988), 91.
8   Larry Hurtado, *Mark*, 22.
9   George Eldon Ladd, *The Presence of the Future: The Eschatology of Biblical Realism* (Grand Rapids: Wm. B. Eerdmans Publishing Co., 1974).
10 George Eldon Ladd, *The Gospel of the Kingdom: Scriptural Studies in the Kingdom of God* (Grand Rapids: Wm. B. Eerdmans Publishing Co., 1959), 123.
11 Donald English, *The Message of Mark: The Mystery of Faith*, The Bible Speaks Today (Downers Grove, Ill., and Leicester: InterVarsity Press, 1992), 50.
12 See Murray J. Harris, *Slave of Christ: A New Testament Metaphor for Total Devotion to Christ* (Leicester: InterVarsity Press, 1999).
13 See Charles Templeton, *Farewell to God* (Toronto: McCelland and Stewart, 1996).
14 See Billy Graham, *Just as I Am: The Autobiography of Billy Graham* (HarperCollins Worldwide, 1997), 137-39 and William Martin, *A Prophet with Honor: The Billy Graham Story* (New York: William Morrow and Co., 1991), 110-13.
15 Martin, *Prophet with Honor*, 112.
16 Jill Morgan, *A Man of the Word: Life of G. Campbell Morgan* (Grand Rapids: Baker Book House, 1972 reprint), 39-40.
17 J. I. Packer, *"Fundamentalism" and the Word of God* (Grand Rapids: Wm. B. Eerdmans Publishing Co., 1958).
18 On the issue of doubt, see Os Guinness, *God in the Dark: The Assurance of Faith Beyond a Shadow of Doubt* (Wheaton, Ill.: Crossway Books, 1996).
19 Dennis F. Kinlaw, *Preaching in the Spirit* (Grand Rapids: Zondervan Publishing House, 1985), 30.

Chapter 9 Growing in a Team

1   Much of the material in the last two paragraphs is from my book *The NIV Application Commentary: Acts* (Grand Rapids: Zondervan Publishing House, 1998), 141-42.
2   *Crucial Questions About Hell* (Eastbourne, UK: Kingsway Publications, 1991; Wheaton, Ill.: Crossway Books, 1994).
3   *Reclaiming Friendship* (Leicester: InterVarsity Press, 1991; Scottdale, Pa. and Waterloo, Ont.: Herald Press, 1993).
4   Barclay M. Newman, Jr., *A Concise Greek-English Dictionary of the New Testament* (United Bible Societies, 1971; Deutsche Bibelgesellschaft Stuttgart, 1993). Taken from the electronic version by iExalt, Inc., 1998.
5   "Twelve Rules of a Helper," cited in D. Michael Henderson, *John Wesley's Class Meeting: A Model for Making Disciples* (Nappance, Ind.: Evangel Publishing House, 1997), 168.

6   J. C. Pollock, *Hudson Taylor and Maria* (Eastbourne, UK: Kingsway Publications, 1983 reprint), 60.

7   Ibid., 61.

8   Chris Wright, "Personal Struggle and the Word of Lament," *Truth on Fire: Keswick Ministry 1998,* ed. David Porter (Carlisle, Cumbria: OM Publishing, 1998), 29.

9   See my *The Supremacy of Christ* (Wheaton, Ill.: Crossway Books, 1995), chaps. 2-4.

10 The book I was studying was Jeff VanVonderen, *Good News for the Chemically Dependent and Those Who Love Them* (Minneapolis: Bethany House Publishers, 1991), chap. 3.

11 Henderson, *John Wesley's Class Meetings,* 117-18. This book provides a helpful introduction to Wesley's small groups.

12 www.menofintegrity.org

Chapter 10 Discipling Younger Leaders

1   Robert E. Coleman, *The Master Plan of Evangelism,* 30th Anniversary Edition (Grand Rapids: Fleming H. Revell, 1993).

2   1 Cor. 4:17; Phil. 2:22; 1 Tim. 1:2, 18; 2 Tim. 1:2; 2:1; Tit. 1:4; Philem. 10.

3   Cleon L. Rogers, Jr., and Cleon L. Rogers III, *The New Linguistic and Exegetical Key to the Greek New Testament* (Grand Rapids: Zondervan Publishing House, 1998), 500.

4   From *Daily Readings from F. W. Boreham,* selected by Frank Cumbers (London: Hodder and Stoughton, 1976), 297.

5   This is demonstrated in a book on Sathya Sai Baba, possibly the world's most popular guru, by Tal Brooke, *Avatar of Night* (Berkeley, Calif.: End Run Publishing, 1999).

6   Richard K. Curtis, *They Called Him Mister Moody* (New York: Doubleday, 1962), 150. Cited in Warren W. Wiersbe and Lloyd M. Perry, *The Wycliffe Handbook of Preaching and Preachers* (Chicago: Moody Press, 1984), 204.

7   R. T. France, *Jesus the Radical: A Portrait of the Man They Crucified* (Leicester: InterVarsity Press, 1989), 68.

8   Donald Guthrie, *A Shorter Life of Christ* (Grand Rapids: Zondervan Publishing House, 1970), 136.

9   On this see my *Spiritual Living in a Secular World* (London: Monarch, 2002).

10 "Occupations and Professions, Steward," *NIV Bible Dictionary,* ed. J. D. Douglas and Merrill C. Tenney, 1989 (from Zondervan Reference Software, 1999).

11 I owe this insight to my friend and former colleague Richard Brohier.

12 Barclay M. Newman, Jr., *A Concise Greek-English Dictionary of the New Testament* (United Bible Societies, 1971; Deutsche Bibelgesellschaft Stuttgart, 1993). Taken from the electronic version by iExalt, Inc., 1998.

13 Clement of Alexandria, *Who Is the Rich Man Being Saved?* #42. Cited in J. Ramsey Michaels, "Finding Yourself an Intercessor: New Testament Prayer from Hebrews to Jude," in *Into God's Presence: Prayer in the New Testament,* ed. Richard N. Longenecker (Grand Rapids and Cambridge: Wm. B. Eerdmans Publishing Co., 2001).

14 On this see Chuck Lowe, *Territorial Spirits and World Evangelization* (Ross-Shire: Christian Focus Publications; Sevenoaks, Kent: OMF, 1998).

15 See Ruth Bell Graham, *Prodigals and Those Who Love Them* (Colorado Springs: Focus on the Family Publishing, 1991).

16 Roger Steer, *George Mueller: Delighted in God* (Wheaton, Ill.: Harold Shaw Publishers, 1975), 267.

Chapter 11 Launching Disciples into Ministry

1   The definitions here are from Barclay M. Newman, Jr., *A Concise Greek-English Dictionary of the New Testament* (United Bible Societies, 1971; Deutsche Bibelgesellschaft Stuttgart, 1993). Taken from the electronic version by iExalt, Inc., 1998.

2   Peter T. O'Brien, *The Letter to the Ephesians* (Grand Rapids: Wm. B. Eerdmans Publishing Co.; Leicester: Apollos, 1999), 279.

3   *Spiritual Secrets of George Mueller,* selected by Roger Steer (Wheaton, Ill.: Harold Shaw Publishers; Robesonia, Pa: OMF Books, 1985), 111-12.

4   From Sherwood Eliot Wirt and Kersten Beckstrom, *Living Quotations for Christians* (New York: Harper & Row, 1974), 266.

5   James Moffatt, *The New Testament: A New Translation* (London: Hodder and Stoughton; New York: George H. Doran Co., 1913), 191.

6   Cleon L. Rogers, Jr., and Cleon L. Rogers III, *The New Linguistic and Exegetical Key to the Greek New Testament* (Grand Rapids: Zondervan Publishing House, 1998), 325.

7   Cited in C. E. B. Cranfield, *A Critical and Exegetical Commentary on the Epistle to the Romans*, vol. 1 (Edinburgh: T. & T. Clark Ltd., 1975), 263.

8   Rogers and Rogers, *New Linguistic and Exegetical Key*, 332.

9   Robert E. Coleman, *The Master Plan of Evangelism*, 30th Anniversary Edition (Grand Rapids: Fleming H. Revell, 1993).

10 D. A. Carson, *The Gospel According to John* (Leicester: InterVarsity Press; Grand Rapids: Wm. B. Eerdmans Publishing Co., 1991), 567.

Chapter 12 Ministering to the Sick and Demon-Possessed

1   See Chuck Lowe, *Territorial Spirits and World Evangelization* (Ross-Shire: Christian Focus Publications; Sevenoaks, Kent: OMF, 1998).

2   See Timothy Warner, "Power Encounter with the Demonic," in *Evangelism on the Cutting Edge*, ed. Robert Coleman (Old Tappan, N.J.: Fleming H. Revell, 1986), 89-101; Timothy Warner, *Spiritual Warfare: Victory over the Powers of This Dark World* (Wheaton, Ill.: Crossway Books, 1991).

3   Peter H. Davids, "A Biblical View of the Fruits of Sin," *The Kingdom and the Power*, ed. Gary S. Greig and Kevin N. Springer (Ventura, Calif.: Regal, 1993), 118-20.

4   See the helpful little article by Clinton E. Arnold, "Exorcism 101," *Christianity Today*, September 3, 2001, 58.

5   Ibid.

6   Mark 2:12; 4:41; 5:15, 20, 33, 42, 61; 6:50, 51; 9:6, 15; 16:8.

7   Acts 2:43; 3:11, 12; 5:5, 11, 24; 8:13; 12:17.

8   Ajith Fernando, *NIV Application Commentary: Acts* (Grand Rapids: Zondervan Publishing House, 1998).

9   Jack Deere, *Surprised by the Power of the Spirit* (Grand Rapids: Zondervan Publishing House, 1993).

10 Craig S. Keener, *The IVP Bible Background Commentary: New Testament* (Downers Grove, Ill.: InterVarsity Press, 1993), 139.

11 Derek J. Tidball, *Skillful Shepherds: An Introduction to Pastoral Theology* (Grand Rapids: Zondervan Publishing House, 1986), 181.

12 Quoted in ibid., 181-82.

13 Quoted in Eberhard Bethge, *Bonhoeffer* (London: HarperCollins Publishers, 1979), 62.

14 Matt. 9:36; 14:14; 15:32; 20:34; Mark 1:41; 6:34; 8:2; Luke 7:13.

15 Morna D. Hooker, *The Gospel According to St. Mark, Black's New Testament Commentary* (Peabody, Mass.: Hendrickson Publishers, repr. 1991), 79; C. E. B. Cranfield, *The Gospel According to St. Mark, The Cambridge Greek Testament Commentary* (Cambridge: Cambridge University Press, 1959), 92.

16 See my "Joy and Sacrifice in the Lord," in *Doing Member Care Well*, ed. Kelly O'Donnell (Pasadena: William Carey Library, 2002), chapter 22.

17 Barclay M. Newman, Jr., *A Concise Greek-English Dictionary of the New Testament* (United Bible Societies, 1971; Deutsche Bibelgesellschaft Stuttgart, 1993). Taken from the electronic version by iExalt, Inc., 1998.

18 Ibid.

19 William Wrede, *The Messianic Secret* (London: James Clark, 1971).

20 Of the several books written recently defending this view, my favorites are Craig Blomberg, *The Historical Reliability of the Gospels* (Leicester and Downers Grove, Ill.: InterVarsity Press, 1987) and F. F. Bruce, *The New Testament Documents: Are They Reliable?* (Leicester and Downers Grove, Ill.: InterVarsity Press, 1960). See also my *The Supremacy of Christ* (Wheaton, Ill.: Crossway Books, 1995), chapter 6: "Are the Gospels Historically Accurate Accounts?"

21 David E. Garland, *The NIV Application Commentary: Mark* (Grand Rapids: Zondervan Publishing House, 1996), 77.

22 Mary Ann Tolbert, *Sowing the Word: Mark's World in Literary-Historical Perspective* (Minneapolis: Fortress Press, 1989), 228, quoted in David Garland, *NIV Application Commentary*, 76.

23 D. A. Carson, "The Purpose of Signs and Wonders in the New Testament" in *Power Religion: The Selling Out of the Evangelical Church?* ed. Michael Scott Horton (Chicago: Moody Press, 1992), 99.

24 Stephen S. Short, "Mark," *The International Bible Commentary,* rev. ed., ed. F. F. Bruce et al. (Grand Rapids: Zondervan Publishing House, 1986), 1159.

25 John T. Seamands, *Pioneers of the Younger Churches* (Nashville: Abingdon Press, 1967), 197.

26 John Wesley, "Matthew," in *The Classic Bible Commentary,* ed. Owen Collins (Wheaton, Ill.: Crossway Books, 1999), 922.

27 This insight came to me when I was reading Jim Glennon, *Your Healing Is Within You: An Introduction to Christian Healing* (London: Hodder & Stoughton, 1978, 1996).

28 Ibid., 83.

Chapter 13 Visiting Homes

1 William L. Lane, *The New International Commentary on the New Testament: The Gospel According to Mark* (Grand Rapids: William B. Eerdmans Publishing Co., 1974), 78.

2 See Leon Morris, *The New International Commentary on the New Testament: The Gospel According to John,* rev. ed. (Grand Rapids: William B. Eerdmans Publishing Co., 1995), 139.

3 See ibid., 157.

4 Lane, *Mark,* 93.

5 Leon Morris, *The Gospel According to Matthew* (Grand Rapids: William B. Eerdmans Publishing Co.; Leicester: InterVarsity Press, 1992), 348.

6 Ajith Fernando, *NIV Application Commentary: Acts* (Grand Rapids: Zondervan Publishing House, 1998), 123, 127, 134-35, 314-15, 321, 324-25, 330-31, 492.

7 C. E. B. Cranfield, *The Gospel According to St. Mark, The Cambridge Greek Testament Commentary* (Cambridge: Cambridge University Press, 1959), 103.

8 From John C. Pollock, *Moody: A Biographical Portrait* (Grand Rapids: Zondervan Publishing House, 1963), 13.

9 *Constitutions of the Holy Apostles,* Book II, Section III, chap. 20; quoted in Thomas C. Oden, *Classical Pastoral Care,* vol. 4, *Crisis Ministries* (Grand Rapids: Baker Book House, 1994), 27.

10 Kenneth E. Bailey, *Poet and Peasant* (Grand Rapids: Wm. B. Eerdmans Publishing Co., 1976), 181.

11 Richard Baxter, *The Reformed Pastor* (Carlyle, Pa., and Edinburgh: Banner of Truth, 1979 reprint), 43; quoted in Oden, *Classical Pastoral Care,* vol. 4, 28.

12 Gilbert Burnet, *Of the Pastoral Care,* chap. 8; quoted in Oden, *Classical Pastoral Care,* vol. 4, 27.

13 This point was made by Dr. Allan Coppedge in a seminar on John Wesley's theology held at the ministers' conference at Asbury Theological Seminary in February 1989.

14 Taken from David Bentley-Taylor, *Augustine: Wayward Genius* (Grand Rapids: Baker Book House, 1981), 58.

15 J. van Zyl, "John Calvin: the Pastor," in *The Way Ahead,* quoted in Derek J. Tidball, *Skillful Shepherds: An Introduction to Pastoral Theology* (Grand Rapids: Zondervan Publishing House, 1986), 190.

16 van Zyl, in *Skillful Shepherds,* 190.

17 M. J. Evans, "Blessing and Cursing," *The New Dictionary of Christian Ethics and Pastoral Theology,* ed. David J. Atkinson and David H. Field (Leicester and Downers Grove, Ill.: InterVarsity Press, 1995), 197.

18 Ibid., 73.

19 Gilbert Burnet, *Of the Pastoral Care,* chap. 8; quoted in Oden, *Classical Pastoral Care,* vol. 4, 28.

20 George Herbert, *The Country Parson,* chap. 14; quoted in Oden, *Classical Pastoral Care,* vol. 4, 29.

21   Murray J. Harris, "Frederick Fyvie Bruce," *Bible Interpreters of the Twentieth Century,* ed. Walter A. Elwell and J. D. Weaver (Grand Rapids: Baker Book House, 1999), 221.

22   I received this insight over twenty years ago at a seminar conducted by Christian human resource consultant Dick Hagstrom. However, the figures he used may be different from what I have used here.

Chapter 14 Praying

1   I. Howard Marshall, "Jesus—Example and Teacher of Prayer in the Synoptic Gospels," *Into God's Presence: Prayer in the New Testament,* ed. Richard N. Longenecker (Grand Rapids and Cambridge: Wm. B. Eerdmans Publishing Co., 2001), 116.

2   J. D. G. Dunn, "Prayer," *Dictionary of Jesus and the Gospels,* ed. Joel B. Green and Scot McKnight (Leicester and Downers Grove, Ill.: InterVarsity Press, 1992), taken from the electronic version.

3   Lyle Wesley Dorsett, *E. M. Bounds: Man of Prayer* (Grand Rapids: Zondervan Publishing House, 1991), 133-34.

4   Morna D. Hooker, *The Gospel According to St. Mark, Black's New Testament Commentary* (Peabody, Mass.: Hendrickson Publishers, repr. 1991), 76.

5   Barclay M. Newman, Jr., *A Concise Greek-English Dictionary of the New Testament* (United Bible Societies, 1971; Deutsche Bibelgesellschaft Stuttgart, 1993). Taken from the electronic version by iExalt, Inc., 1998.

6   Frederick Danker, *A Greek-English Lexicon of the New Testament and Other Early Christian Literature,* 3rd ed., based on Walter Bauer's Lexicon in German and other previous editions by William F. Arndt, F. Wilbur Gingrich, and F. W. Danker (Chicago and London: University of Chicago Press, 2000), 852.

7   From Sherwood Eliot Wirt and Kersten Beckstrom, *Living Quotations for Christians* (New York: Harper & Row, 1974), 177.

8   See Howard Peskett, "Prayer in the Old Testament Outside the Psalms," *Teach Us to Pray,* ed. D. A. Carson (Grand Rapids: Baker Book House, 1990), 25.

9   Dunn, "Prayer," *Dictionary,* taken from the electronic version.

10   James G. S. S. Thomson, *The Praying Christ* (Grand Rapids: Wm. B. Eerdmans Publishing Co., 1959), 37. Quoted in Robert E. Coleman, *The Mind of the Master* (Wheaton, Ill.: Harold Shaw Publishers, 2000), 39.

11   For the lists of prayers mentioned in this section I am indebted to Donald Coggan, *The Prayers of the New Testament* (New York: Harper & Row, 1967).

12   While several Bible versions use "blessed" here, the NIV uses "gave thanks," which correctly communicates the meaning of *eulogeö* here.

13   Rom. 1:8; 1 Cor. 1:4-9; Eph. 1:16; Col. 1-4; 1 Thess. 1:2-4; 2:13; 2 Thess. 1:3-4; 2:13-14; 2 Tim. 1:2-3; Philem. 4.

14   Taken from Tom Carter, comp., *Spurgeon at His Best* (Grand Rapids: Baker Book House, 1988), 323-34.

15   Earle E. Cairns, *An Endless Line of Splendor* (Wheaton, Ill.: Tyndale House Publishers, 1986), 340-41.

16   Danker, *A Greek-English Lexicon,* 767.

17   Coggan, *Prayers of the New Testament,* 16.

18   Quoted in Coggan, *Prayers of the New Testament,* 16.

19   Some of the following material appears in my "Joy and Sacrifice in the Lord," in *Doing Member Care Well: Perspectives and Practices from Around the World,* ed. Kelly O'Donnell (Pasadena: William Carey Library, 2002), chap. 22.

20   Cleon L. Rogers, Jr., and Cleon L. Rogers III, *The New Linguistic and Exegetical Key to the Greek New Testament* (Grand Rapids: Zondervan Publishing House, 1998), 325.

INDEX